A-Z NOTTINGHAM

CONTENTS

REFERENCE

Motorway	M1
A Road	A609
Proposed	
B Road	B684
Dual Carriageway	
One-way Street	
Traffic flow on A Roads is indicated by a heavy line on the driver's left.	
All one way streets are shown on Large Scale Pages 4-5	
Restricted Access	
Pedestrianized Road	
Residential Walkway	
Track & Footpath	
Local Authority Boundary	
Postcode Boundary	
Railway	Tunnel / Station / Level Crossing
Nottingham Express Transit	Stops / One-Way / Two-Way
Built-up Area	DEAN AV

Map Continuation	32
Large Scale City Centre	4
Car Park (selected)	P
Church or Chapel	†
Fire Station	■
House Numbers A & B Roads only	20 / 8
Hospital	H
Information Centre	i
National Grid Reference	450
Police Station	▲
Post Office	★
Toilet	▽
with facilities for the Disabled	♿
Educational Establishment	
Hospital or Hospice	
Industrial Building	
Leisure or Recreational Facility	
Place of Interest	
Public Building	
Shopping Centre or Market	
Other Selected Buildings	

SCALE

Map Pages 6-81	Map Pages 4-5
1:15840 (4 inches to 1 mile) 6.31cm to 1km	1:7920 (8 inches to 1 mile) 12.63cm to 1km
0 ¼ ½ Mile	0 ⅛ ¼ Mile
0 250 500 750 Metres	0 100 200 300 400 Metres

Geographers' A-Z Map Company Ltd.

Head Office:
Fairfield Road, Borough Green, Sevenoaks, Kent, TN15 8PP
Telephone 01732 781000 (General Enquiries & Trade Sales)
Showrooms:
44 Gray's Inn Road, London, WC1X 8HX
Telephone 020 7440 9500 (Retail Sales)
www.a-zmaps.co.uk

This Map is based upon Ordnance Survey mapping with the permission of the Controller of Her Majesty's Stationery Office.

© Crown Copyright licence number 399000. All rights reserved

Edition 5 2000

Copyright © Geographers' A-Z Map Co. Ltd. 2000

D1150939

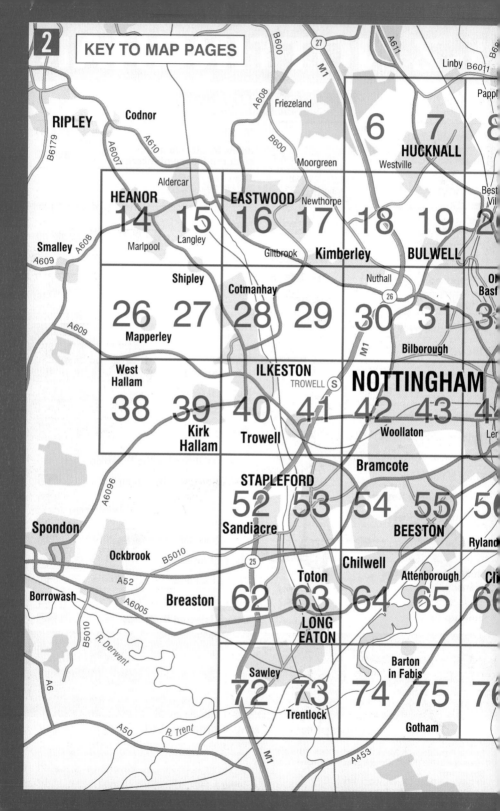

2 KEY TO MAP PAGES

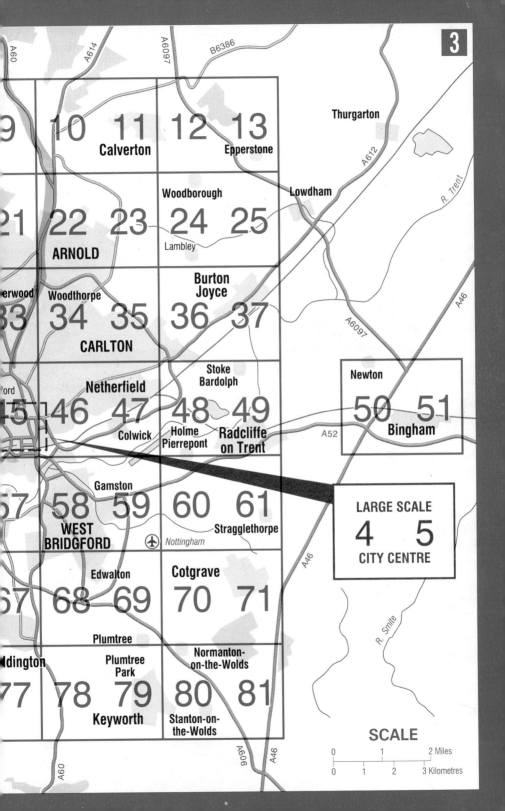

3

9 | 10 | 11 | 12 | 13

Calverton | Epperstone

Thurgarton

A60 | A614 | A6097 | B6386 | A612 | R. Trent

Woodborough

Lowdham

21 | 22 | 23 | 24 | 25

ARNOLD | Lambley

A46

erwood | Woodthorpe | Burton Joyce

33 | 34 | 35 | 36 | 37

CARLTON

A6097

ord | Netherfield | Stoke Bardolph | Newton

15 | 46 | 47 | 48 | 49 | 50 | 51

Colwick | Holme Pierrepont | Radcliffe on Trent | Bingham

A52

Gamston

57 | 58 | 59 | 60 | 61

WEST BRIDGFORD | ✈ Nottingham | Stragglethorpe

LARGE SCALE
4   5
CITY CENTRE

A46

Edwalton | Cotgrave

67 | 68 | 69 | 70 | 71

Plumtree

dington | Plumtree Park | Normanton-on-the-Wolds

R. Smite

77 | 78 | 79 | 80 | 81

Keyworth | Stanton-on-the-Wolds

A60 | A606 | A46

SCALE

0 ——— 1 ——— 2 Miles

0 — 1 — 2 — 3 Kilometres

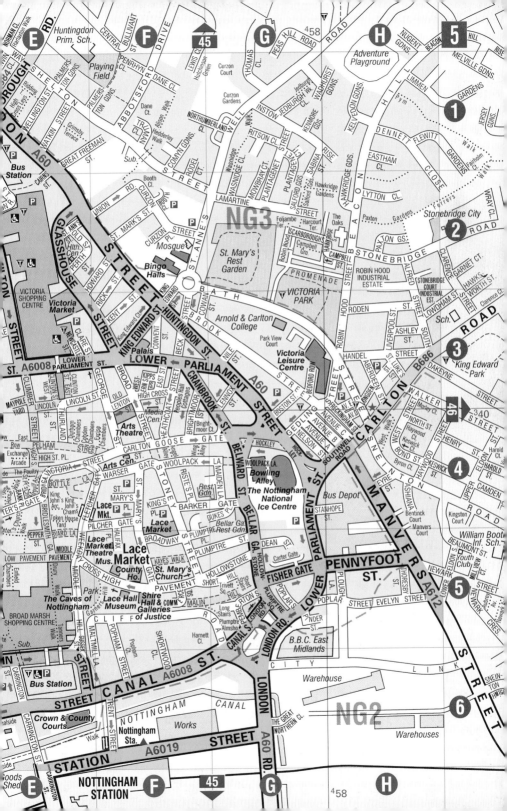

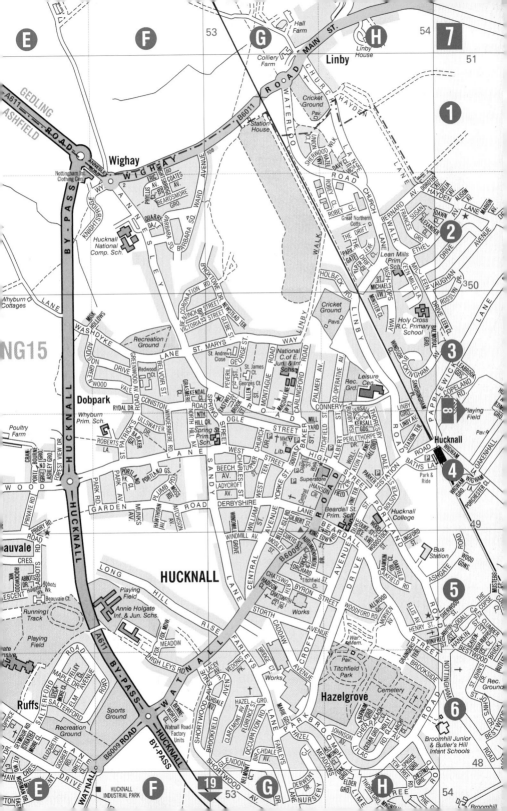

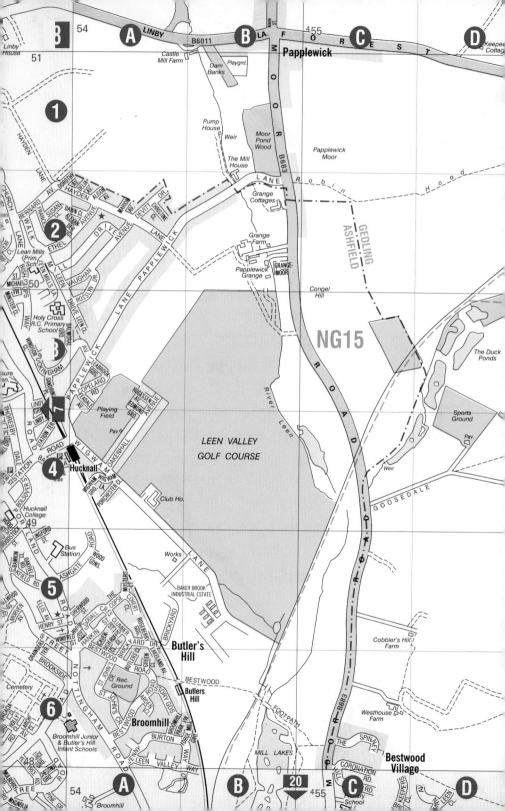

Great
Burntstump
Plantation

A Sawpit
Plantation

B Richmond's
Farm 59

C

Watchwood
Plantation

D

BURNTSTUMP

Burntstump
Plantation

1 The
Nursery Beech
Wood Spts.
Gd. Seely
Church School

urntstump
ountry Park

p Country Park
dland Walks

Cockliffe Hill
Farm

Cockliffe
House

Cockliff
Wood

Sports
Ground

Foxcovert
Plantation

GRAVELLY

HOLLOW

2 The
Warren

The
Knoll

350

Round
Plantation

Patchings Farm
Art Centre

Cottage
Wood

rnpike
antation

3

RAMSDAL
PARK GO
CENTRE

Jubilee
Plantation

6

Ramsdale
Cottages

B6386

Robin Hood
Farm

Club
House

East Hill
Plantation

The
Rowans

4

Greenwood
Bonsai Studio

NG5

Ramsdale
House

Leila's
Plantation

Ramper
Covert

49

HOLLINW

Hollin
Ho

Forest
Farm

RAMSDALE
PARK

5

MANSFIELD

North
Peacock

Ramsdale Park
Special School

Ramsdale
Hill

The
Belt

South
Peacock

6

Woodlands

Tophouse
Farm

A60

LITTLE LIME LA.

Limelane
House

LAMIN

48

ROAD

A614

OLLERTON RD

LIME

B684

LANE

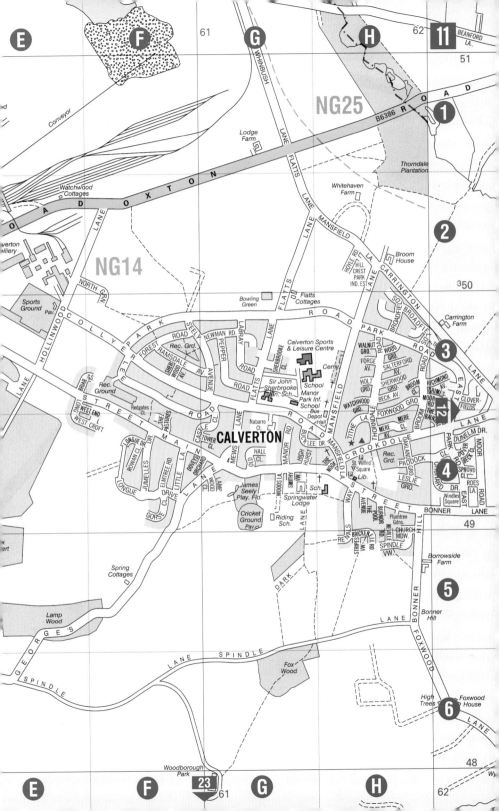

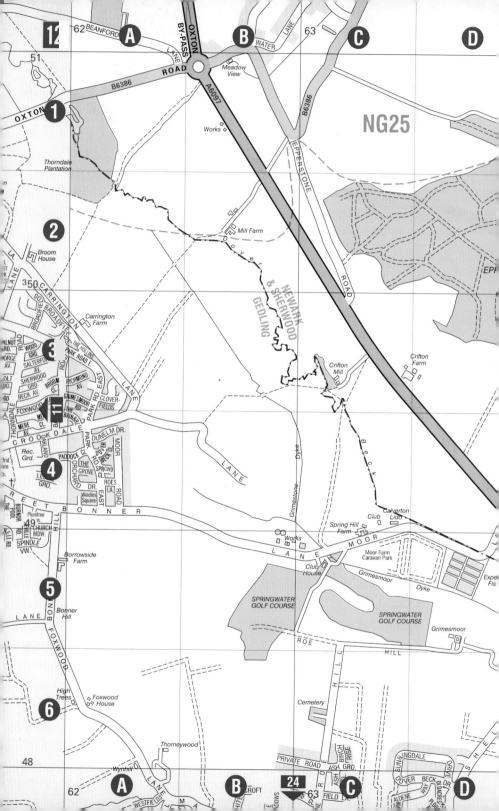

51

Rosselle Wood

Norwood Farm

Ricketwood Farm

1

Park Farm

Order

2

350

Hill Farm Cottage

3

Starling Hall

LANE

Hill Farm

HAGG

Beck

Cottage Farm

Eastwood Farm

4

Greenacres

49

NG14

Slaughter House

Kennels

Hill House

Chapel Farm

NEPPS CFT.

5

EPPERSTONE

MAIN

School

CHURCH LA.

CHAPEL

LANE

STREET

HAGG LANE

Epperstone Manor (Notts. Constabulary H.Q.)

★ PADDOCK FARM COTTS.

Pav.

Sports Ground

BLAND LA.

TOAD LA.

Shelt ill Farm

Fox Covert

A6097 BY-PASS

PARK LA.

The Old House

Beck

ROAD

GONALSTON

HAGG

Elm Park

Rifle Range

6

HILL

Epperstone

Village Hall Pav.

Epperstone Playing Field

Order

Dover

LOWDHAM

Wash Bridge

LANE

48

465

Beck

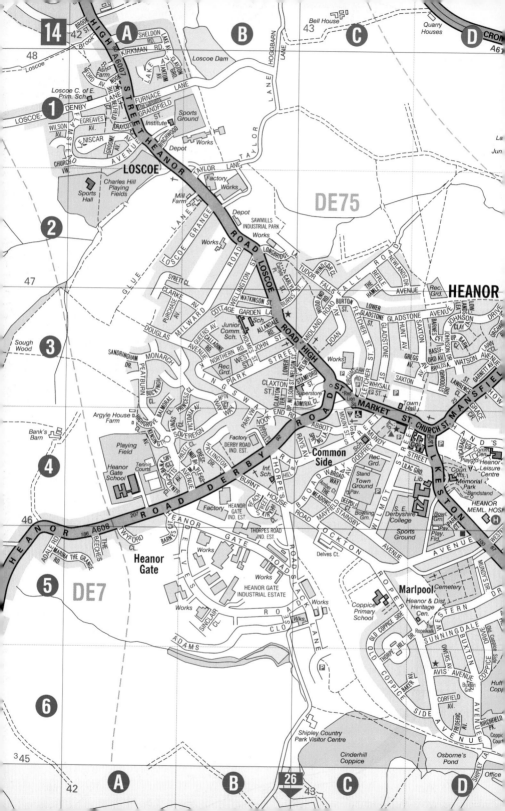

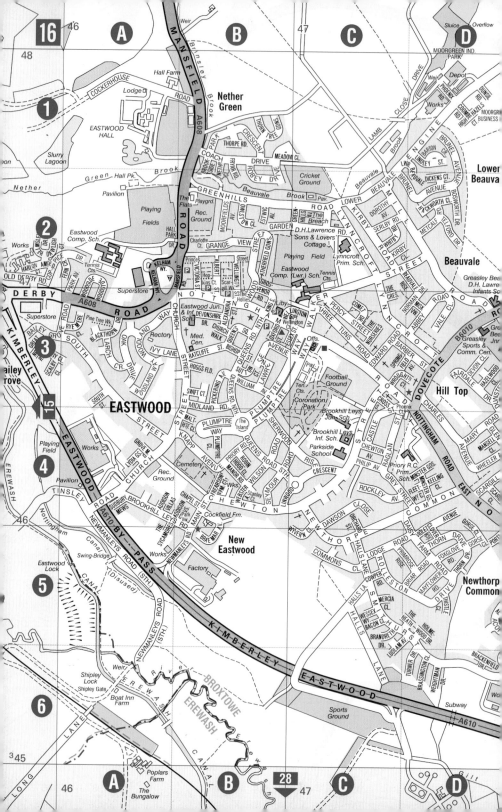

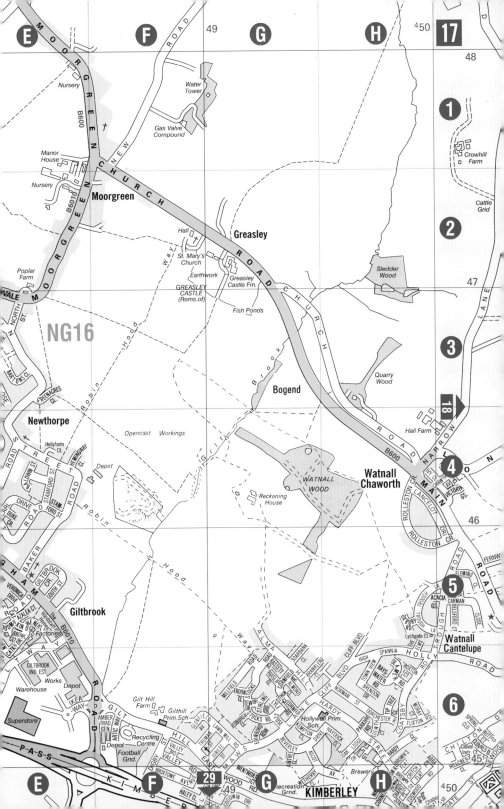

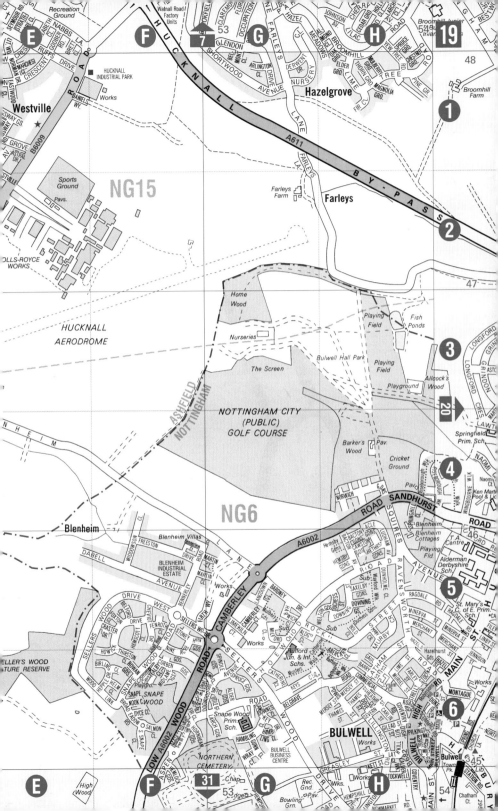

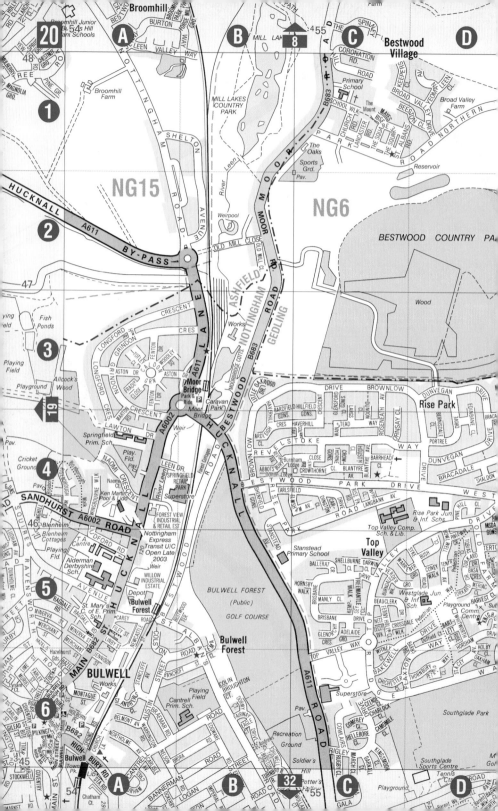

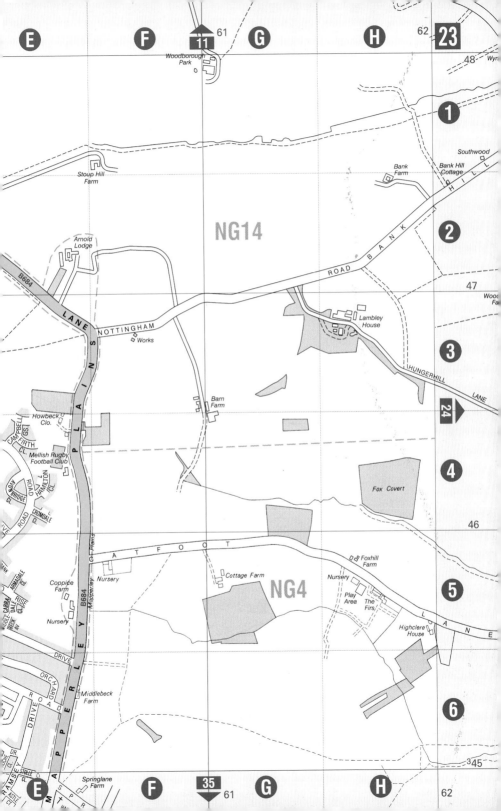

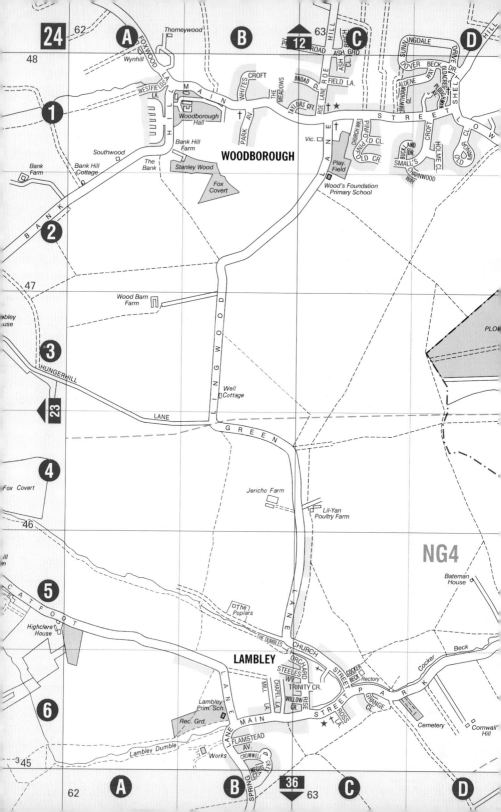

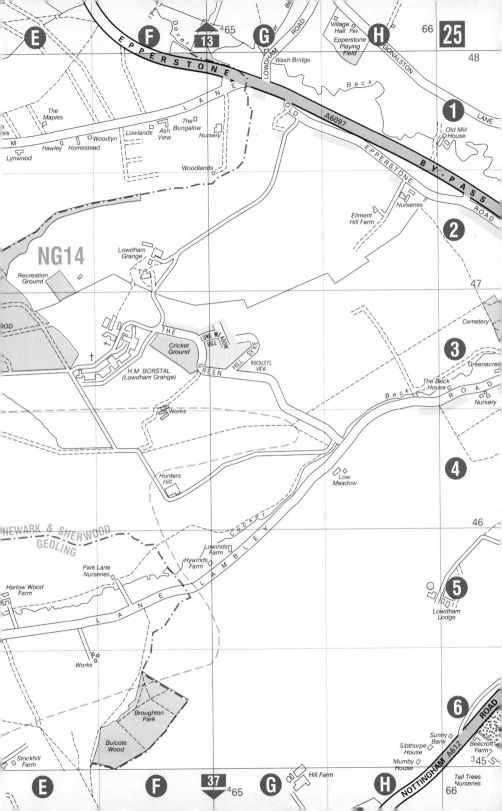

EPPERSTONE

Dover La

LANE

LOWDHAM ROAD

Village Hall
Epperstone Pav.
Epperstone
Playing Field

GONALSTON LANE

Wash Bridge

Beck

OLD

A6097

EPPERSTONE ROAD

BY-PASS

The Maples

M
Hawley Homestead

Woodlyn

Lynwood

Lowlands

Ash View

The Bungalow

Nursery

Woodlands

1

Old Mill House

NG14

Recreation Ground

Lowdham Grange

Eliment Hill Farm

Nurseries

2

47

WOOD

THE

Cricket Ground

†

H.M. BORSTAL
(Lowdham Grange)

LONG MEADOW

HILL

GREEN

HILL SYKE

ROCKLEYS VIEW

Beck

Cemetery

Greenacres

The Beck House

Nursery

ROAD

3

Works

4

Hunters Hill

Low Meadow

NEWARK & SHERWOOD
GEDLING

LANE

Cocker

LAMBLEY

46

Lowinds Farm

Hywinds Farm

Park Lane Nurseries

5

Lowdham Lodge

Harlow Wood Farm

LANE

Works

Broughton Park

Bulcote Wood

Stockhill Farm

6

ROAD

Sunny Bank

Sibthorpe House

Mumby House

NOTTINGHAM A612

Beecroft Farm

345

Tall Trees Nurseries

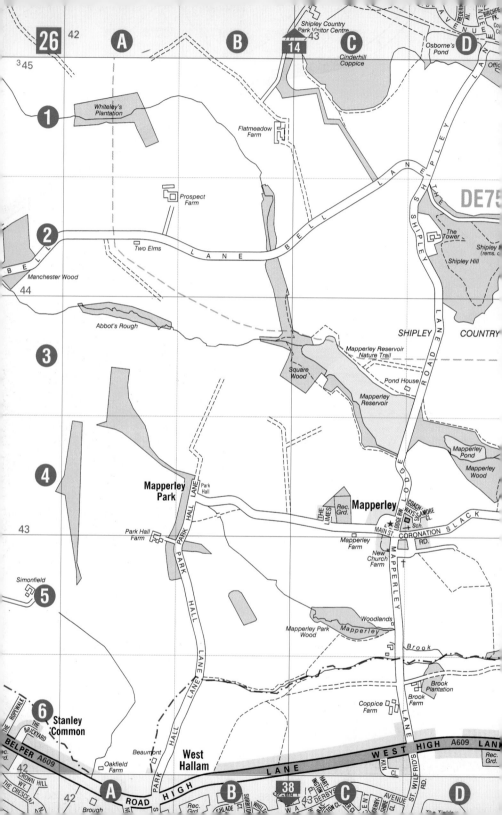

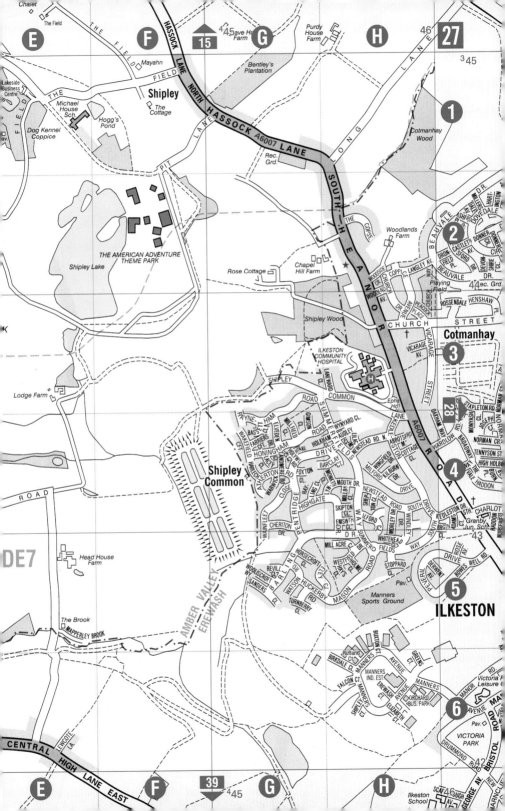

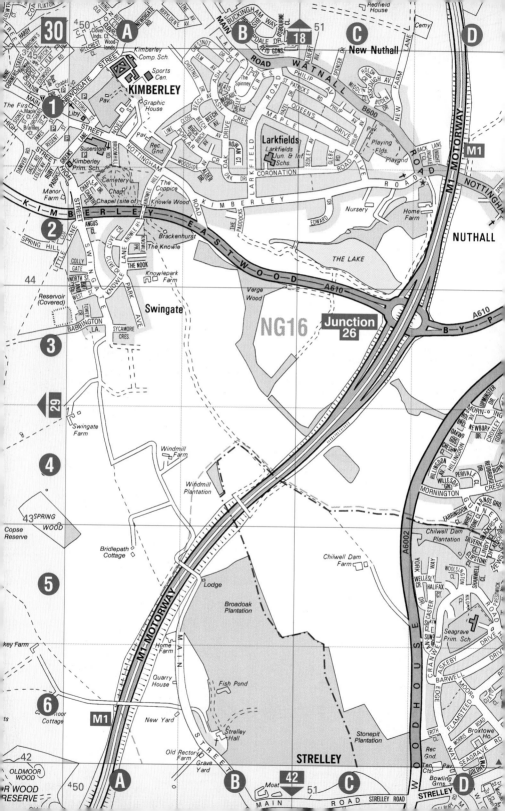

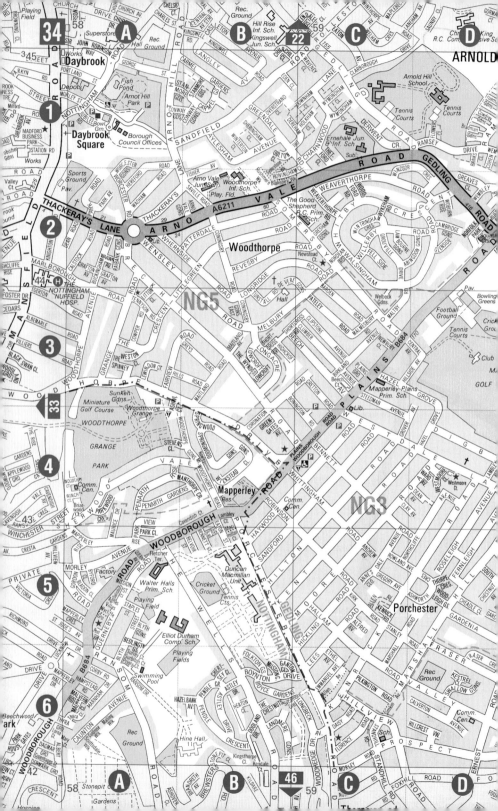

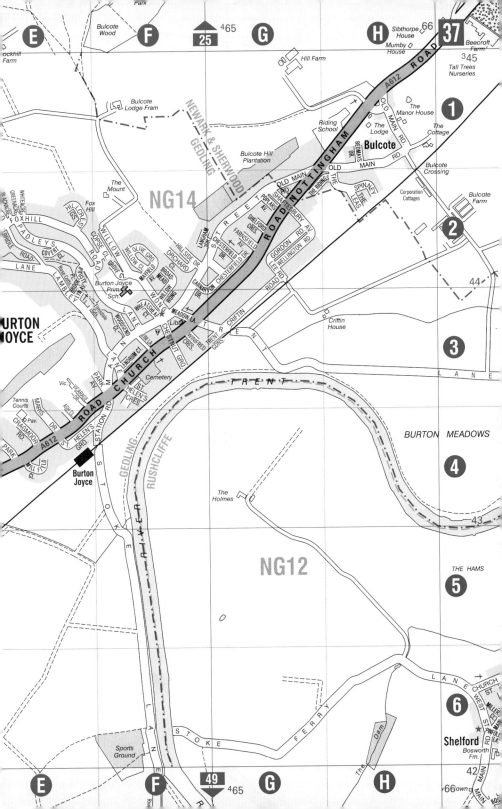

Bulcote Wood

Hill Farm

House
Mumby
House

Beecroft
Farm

Tall Trees
Nurseries

ockhill
Farm

Bulcote
Lodge Fram

The Manor House

OLD

A612

OLD MAIN RD

The Lodge

Riding
School

The Cottage

1

Bulcote Hill
Plantation

Bulcote

REDMAYS DR

OLD MAIN RD

The
Mount

NG14

THE LEAS

Bulcote
Crossing

Corporation
Cottages

Bulcote
Farm

Fox Hill

FOXHILL

HILLCRES

GREENACRES
WHITEACRES
BLACKACRES

HIGGS

COPSE CL

WILLOW ROAD

OLD MAIN ROAD

THE RIDINGS

THE SPINNEY

2

SHAFTESBURY AV

POPLARS AV

SHELFORD CRES

FARNSFIELD AV

CHESTERFIELD DR

GORDON RD

WELLINGTON RD

44

COVERT CL

BROAD MEAD

MAYFIELD

WILLOW CL

OLIVE GRO

HILLSIDE DR

LANGHAM DR

ORCHARD CL

CARNARVON DR

CHESTERFIELD DR

NOTTINGHAM ROAD

PADLEYS LANE

BRIDGE

ROAD

COVERT CL

PADGHAM CL

PECKHAM CL

Rose Cottage

Burton Joyce
Prim. Sch.

WILLOW CL

WONG

WHEATSHEAF

MEADOW LA

Lib.

CRIFTIN

TRENT GDNS

Criftin
House

3

LAMBLEY LANE

LANE

Trevglate

WOODSEND

CHESTNUT GRO

WINIFRED CRES

LANE

**URTON
OYCE**

PARK AV

CHURCH ROAD

Cemetery

ST HELEN'S
CRES

TRENT

LANE

CRAGMOOR RD

MILLFIELD CL

MARIS DR

ASH CL

VICARAGE DR

Vic.

Pav.

STATION RD

ST HELEN'S GRO

GEDLING

TRENT

BURTON MEADOWS

Tennis
Courts

A612

PARK

**Burton
Joyce**

The
Holmes

4

43

RIVER

RUSHCLIFFE

NG12

THE HAMS

5

CHURCH ST

WEST ST

MILLERS CT

PINFOLD

6

Sports
Ground

STOKE

LANE

FERRY

The Dam

Shelford
Bosworth
Fm.

42

own

MAIN ST

BOSWORTH

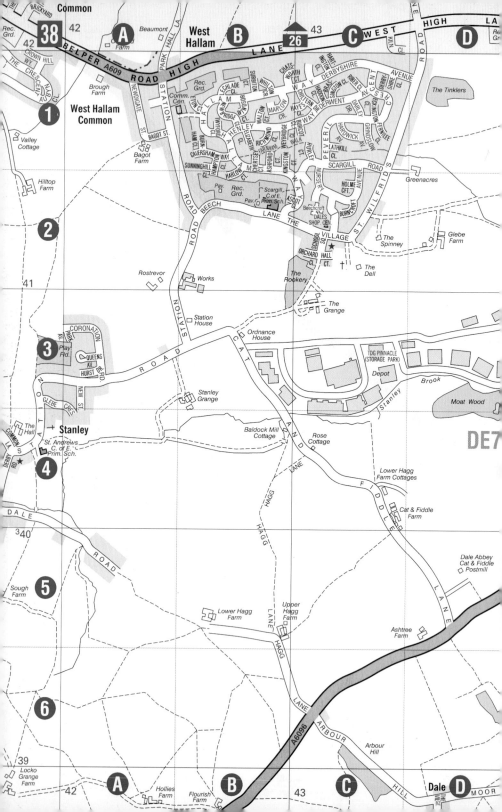

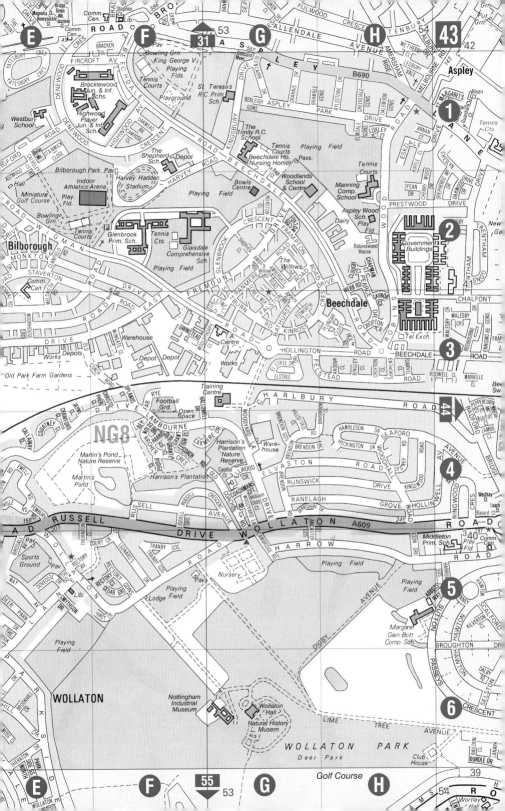

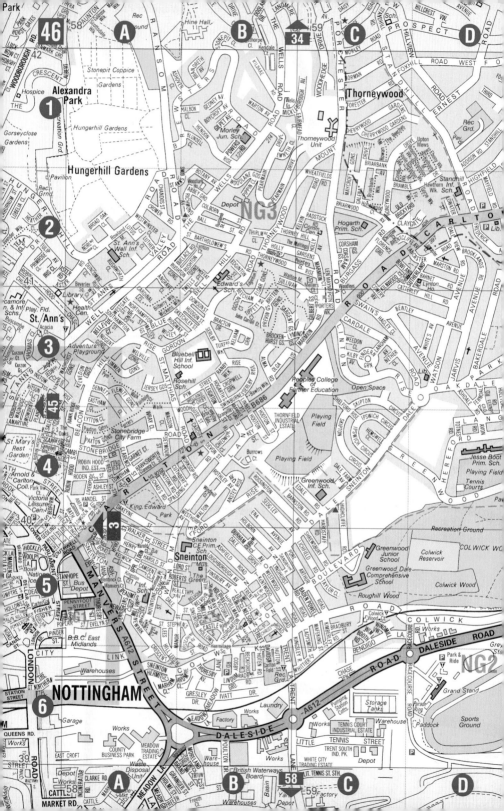

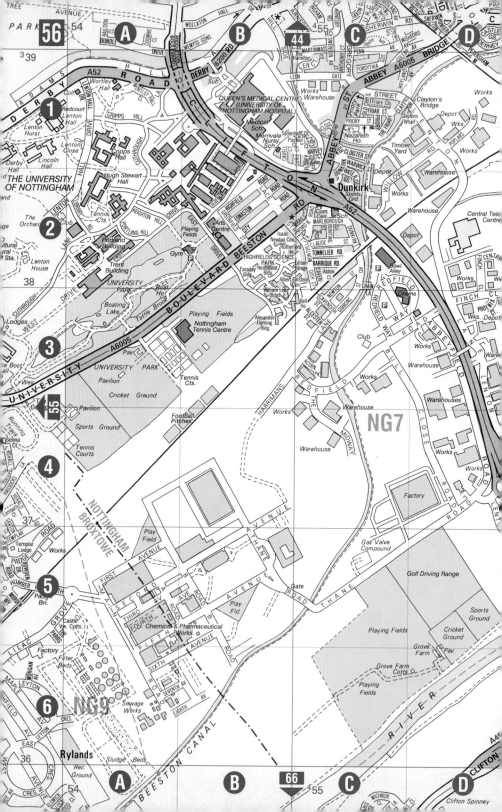

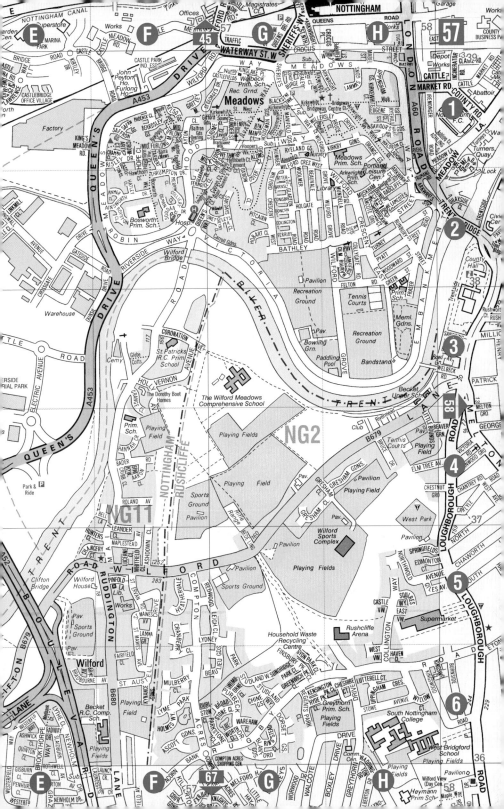

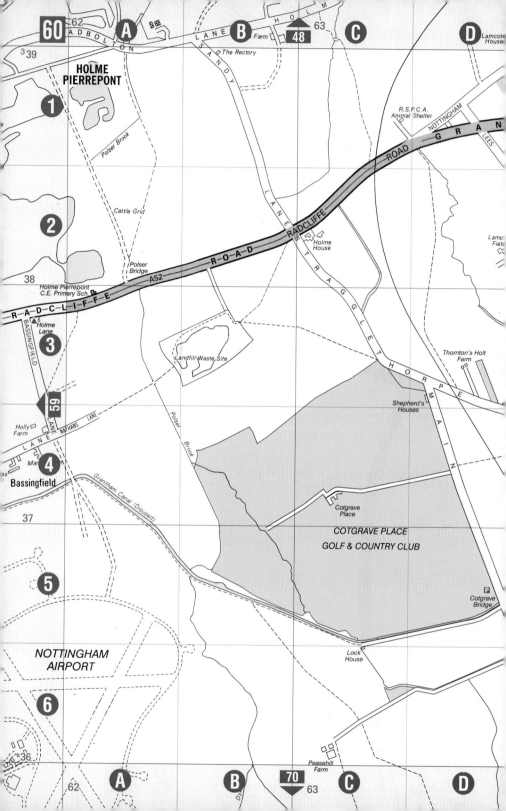

E

F

49

G

H

Radcliffe on Trent
Junior
School

Comp.
Sch.

4 65
owl.
Grn.

Cemetery

Dewberry
Hill

1

Club
House

RADCLIFFE ON TRENT
GOLF COURSE

RADCLIFFE
ON TRENT

Sunpit
Plantation

R O A D

2

Radcliffe Barn
Farm

38

Hall
Farm

3

G12

North
Farm

edhat
ation

4

Stragglethorpe

Paddock
Cottages

37

COTGRAVE COUNTRY

PARK

Brown's
Cotts.

5

L
A
N
E

Hollygate
Farm

Lock

6

Brown's
Bridge

Lock
Weirs

Homefields

Gozen
Lodge

E

Windmill
Hill

F

71

4 65

G

H
O
L
L
Y
G
A
T
E

Canal

(Disused)

36

Grantham

H

66

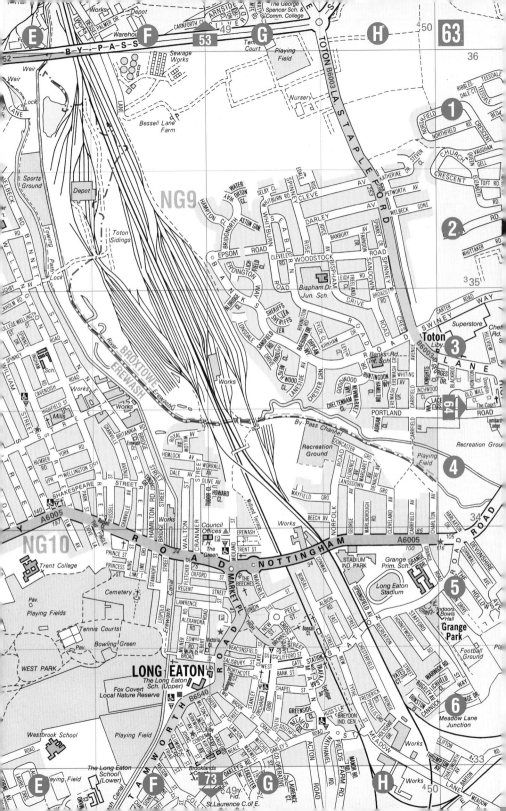

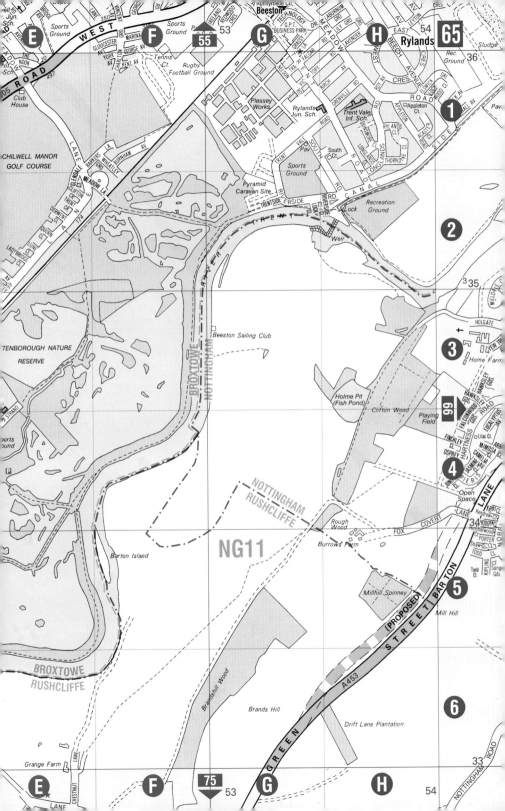

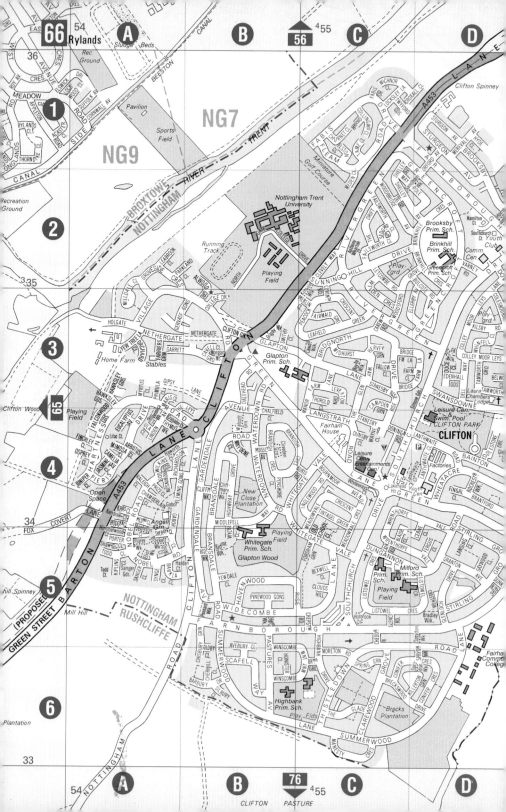

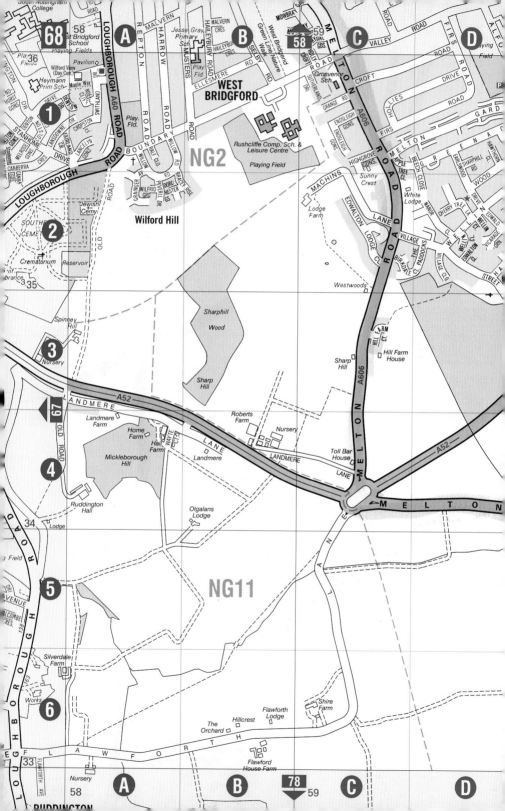

70 62 **A** **B** ▲**60** 63 **C** **D**

Peasehill
Farm

WOODGATE

NOTTINGHAM
AIRPORT

1

Thulfbeck Dyke

Chestnut
Farm

2

COTGRAVE

ngfield 3 35
se

ROAD PLUMT

NG12

Playing Field

Swimming
Pool
The
Lake

3

Tollerton
Nurseries

LANE

Boot
Pit

MILL LANE

▲**69**

Tollerton
Wood

Manor
Farm

4

OLIVER LA

Clipston

Ranch
House

34

Hoehill
Farm

GATE

Blackberry
Farm

CHURCH

Hall
Farm

Glebe
Farm

WOLDS

5

Weir

Hoe
Hill

Hoe Hill
Cottages

COTGRAVE

LANE WOLDS

CLIPSTON

THE LEYS

LAN

6

Grange
Plantation

MELTON ROAD

†

Pasture
Plantation

33

Manor
House

LANE

The
Lawns

62 **A** **Normanton-
on-the-Wolds** **B** ▼**80** 63 Wolds
Farm **C** **D**

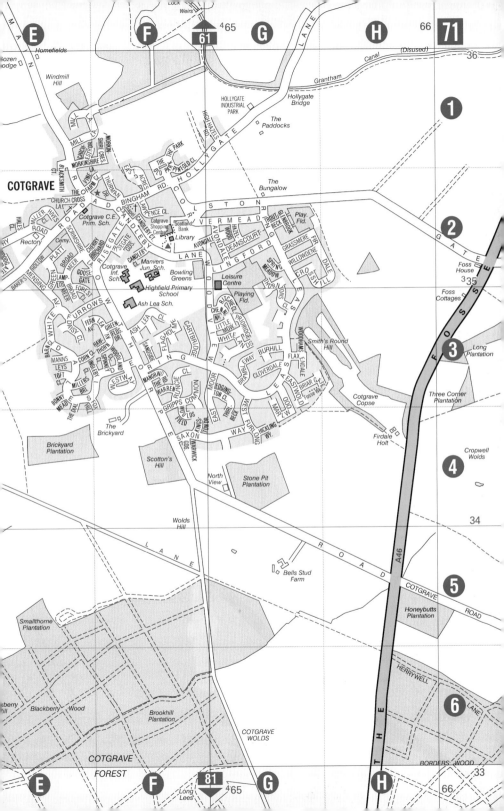

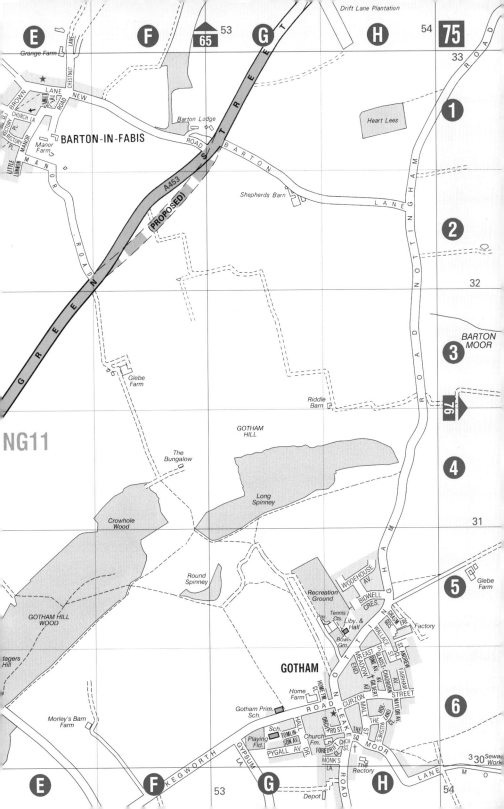

76 54

33

Plantation

eart Lees

A
B
C
D

1

CLIFTON PASTURE

▲ 55

66

SUMMERWOOD

CLAR

WAKEST

CRES

Sewage
Works

LANE

NOTTINGHAM ROAD

2

32

3 BARTON MOOR

75

4

31

NOTTINGHAM

5 Glebe
Farm

GRANE

CTRE

GDNS

Factory

WALLACE
ST
ST. ANDREW

LOST ROSE ST
CHADBURN

FAIRHAM AV.

STREET

NAYLOR AV.

6

GOTHAM

TOP RUSHES

330

MOOR

LANE

MOOR

Fairham
Brook

GOTHAM MOOR

Sewage
Works

Fairholme
Farm

A
B
C
D

LANE

54
4 55

Gotham
Moor Farm

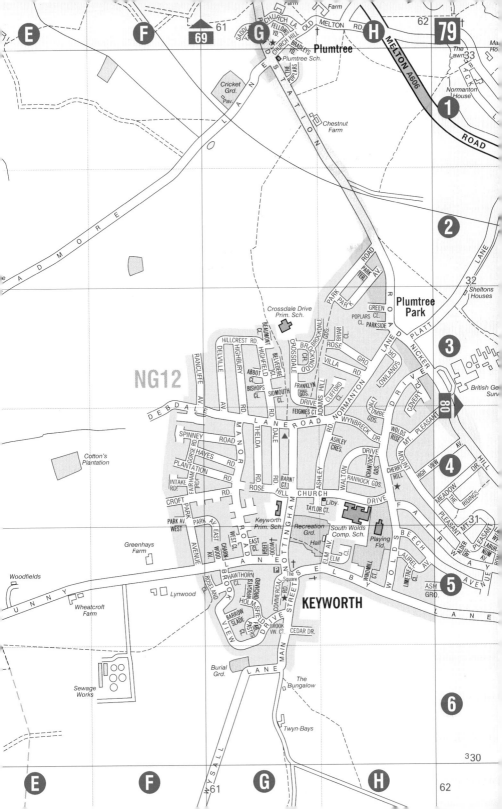

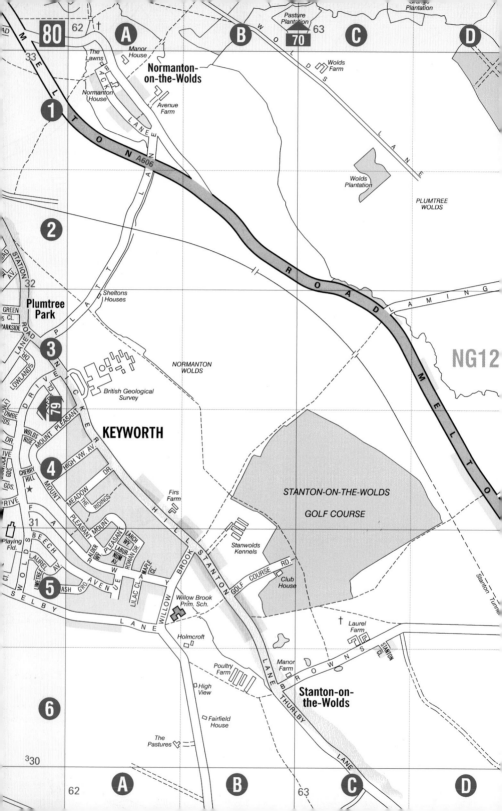

INDEX

Including Streets, Selected Subsidiary Addresses
and Selected Places of Interest.

HOW TO USE THIS INDEX

1. Each street name is followed by its Posttown or Postal Locality and then by its map reference; e.g. Aaron Clo. *Nott* —4F **57** is in the Nottingham Posttown and is to be found in square 4F on page **57**. The page number being shown in bold type. A strict alphabetical order is followed in which Av., Rd., St., etc. (though abbreviated) are read in full and as part of the street name; e.g. Abbotsbury Clo. appears after Abbot Rd. but before Abbots Clo.

2. Streets and a selection of Subsidiary names not shown on the Maps, appear in the index in *Italics* with the thoroughfare to which it is connected shown in brackets; e.g. *Albert Sq. Nott —6C **44** (off Church St.)*

3. An example of a selected place of interest is **Albion Leisure Cen.** —1B **40**

4. Map references shown in brackets; e.g. Aberdeen St. *Nott* —4A **46** (3H **5**) refer to entries that also appear on the large scale pages 4 & 5.

GENERAL ABBREVIATIONS

All : Alley	Ct : Court	Lit : Little	Rd : Road
App : Approach	Cres : Crescent	Lwr : Lower	Shop : Shopping
Arc : Arcade	Cft : Croft	Mc : Mac	S : South
Av : Avenue	Dri : Drive	Mnr : Manor	Sq : Square
Bk : Back	E : East	Mans : Mansions	Sta : Station
Boulevd : Boulevard	Embkmt : Embankment	Mkt : Market	St : Street
Bri : Bridge	Est : Estate	Mdw : Meadow	Ter : Terrace
B'way : Broadway	Fld : Field	M : Mews	Trad : Trading
Bldgs : Buildings	Gdns : Gardens	Mt : Mount	Up : Upper
Bus : Business	Gth : Garth	Mus : Museum	Va : Vale
Cvn : Caravan	Ga : Gate	N : North	Vw : View
Cen : Centre	Gt : Great	Pal : Palace	Vs : Villas
Chu : Church	Grn : Green	Pde : Parade	Vis : Visitors
Chyd : Churchyard	Gro : Grove	Pk : Park	Wlk : Walk
Circ : Circle	Ho : House	Pas : Passage	W : West
Cir : Circus	Ind : Industrial	Pl : Place	Yd : Yard
Clo : Close	Info : Information	Quad : Quadrant	
Comn : Common	Junct : Junction	Res : Residential	
Cotts : Cottages	La : Lane	Ri : Rise	

POSTTOWN AND POSTAL LOCALITY ABBREVIATIONS

Ann : Annesley	*Colw P* : Colwick Park	*L'by* : Linby	*Sand* : Sandiacre
Arn : Arnold	*Coss* : Cossall	*Locki* : Lockington	*Shard* : Shardlow
Att : Atterton	*Cotg* : Cotgrave	*Long E* : Long Eaton	*Shelf* : Shelford
Aws : Awsworth	*C But* : Cropwell Butler	*Los* : Loscoe	*Sher* : Sherwood
Bar F : Barton-in-Fabis	*Dal A* : Dale Abbey	*Low* : Lowdham	*Sher R* : Sherwood Rise
Bees : Beeston	*Day* : Daybrook	*Man I* : Manners Ind. Est.	*Ship* : Shipley
B Vil : Bestwood Village	*Den V* : Denby Village	*M'ley* : Mapperley (Ilkeston)	*Smal* : Smalley
Bilb : Bilborough	*Dray* : Draycott	*Map* : Mapperley (Nottingham)	*Snei* : Sneinton
Bing : Bingham	*Eastw* : Eastwood	*N'fld* : Netherfield	*Stan* : Stanley
Blen I : Bleneim Ind. Est.	*Edw* : Edwalton	*New B* : New Basford	*Stan C* : Stanley Common
Borr : Borrowash	*Epp* : Epperstone	*Newt* : Newthorpe	*Stan D* : Stanton-by-Dale
Bradm : Bradmore	*For F* : Forest Fields	*New* : Newton (Alfreton)	*S'fd* : Stapleford
Bramc : Bramcote	*Gam* : Gamston	*Nwtn* : Newton (Nottingham)	*Stock* : Stockhill
Breas : Breaston	*Ged* : Gedling	*Nott* : Nottingham	*Strel* : Strelley
Brins : Brinsley	*Gilt* : Giltbrook	*Nut* : Nuthall	*T'wd* : Thorneywood
Bul : Bulcote	*Got* : Gotham	*Old B* : Old Basford	*Thrum* : Thrumpton
Bulw : Bulwell	*Greas* : Greasley	*Oxt* : Oxton	*Toll* : Tollerton
Bun : Bunny	*Hean* : Heanor	*Pap* : Papplewick	*Trow* : Trowell
Bur J : Burton Joyce	*Hol P* : Holme Pierrepont	*Park T* : Park, The	*Wat* : Waterthorpe
C'tn : Calverton	*Huck* : Hucknall	*Plum* : Plumtree	*Watn* : Watnall
Cltn : Carlton	*Ilk* : Ilkeston	*Quar H* : Quarry Hill Ind. Est.	*W Bri* : West Bridgford
Carr : Carrington	*Keyw* : Keyworth	*Q Dri* : Queens Drive Ind. Est.	*W Hal* : West Hallam
Clif : Clifton	*Kimb* : Kimberley	*Rad T* : Radcliffe-on-Trent	*Wilf* : Wilford
Clip : Clipstone	*Lamb* : Lambley	*R'hd* : Ravenshead	*Woll* : Wollaton
Cols B : Colston Bassett	*Lan M* : Langley Mill	*Red* : Redhill	*Wdbgh* : Woodborough
Colw : Colwick	*Lent* : Lenton	*Ris* : Risley	*Wd'p* : Woodthorpe
Colw I : Colwick Ind. Est.	*Lent L* : Lenton Lane Ind. Est.	*Rud* : Ruddington	

INDEX

Acton Av. Long E —1G 73
Acton Av. Nott —3B 32
Acton Clo. Long E —1G 73
Acton Gro. Long E —1G 73
Acton Rd. Arn —5H 21
Acton Rd. Long E —6G 63
Acton Rd. Ind. Est. Long E —1G 73
Acton St. Long E —1G 73
Adale Rd. Smal —5A 14
Adams Clo. Hean —5B 14
Adams Ct. Ilk —4A 28
Adams Hill. Keyw —4H 79
Adams Hill. Nott —1H 55
Adam St. Ilk —3C 40
Adbolton Av. Ged —6G 35
Adbolton Gro. W Bri —1D 58
Adbolton La. W Bri & Hol P —2D 58
Adbolton Lodge. Cltn —3G 47
Adderley Clo. Nott —1E 33
Addington Ct. Rad T —5G 49
Addington Rd. Nott —3D 44
Addison Dri. Nott —3E 7
Addison Rd. Cltn —1D 46
Addison St. Nott —2F 45 (1C 4)
Addison Vs. Eastw —4A 16
  (in two parts)
Adelaide Clo. S'fd —2H 53
Adelaide Gro. Nott —5C 20
Adel Dri. Ged —5G 35
Adenburgh Clo. Bees —4D 64
Admiral Clo. Hean —3C 14
Adrian Clo. Bees —4H 63
Aeneas Ct. Nott —1F 45
Agnes Vs. Nott —5A 34
Aidan Gdns. Nott —3E 21
Ainsdale Cres. Nott —4G 31
Ainsley Rd. Nott —3B 44
Ainsworth Dri. Nott —2F 57
Aintree Clo. Kimb —6G 17
Aira Clo. Gam —5F 59
Airedale Clo. Long E —1C 72
Airedale Ct. Bees —1A 64
Airedale Wlk. Nott —6C 42
Aitchison Av. Huck —4F 7
Alandene Av. Watn —6A 18
Albany Clo. Arn —6A 22
Albany Clo. Huck —6C 6
Albany Ct. S'fd —2G 53
Albany Rd. Nott —1E 45
Albany St. Ilk —3C 40
Albemarle Rd. W'd'p —3H 33
Alberta Ter. Nott —1E 45
Albert Av. Cltn —2D 46
Albert Av. Nott —1B 44
Albert Av. Nut —6C 18
Albert Av. S'fd —4F 53
Albert Ball Clo. Nott —5D 20
Albert Einstein Cen. Nott —2B 56
Albert Gro. Nott —4D 44
Albert Hall. Nott —5F 45 (4C 4)
  (off Circus St.)
Albert Rd. Bees —3G 55
Albert Rd. Bun —6A 78
Albert Rd. Lent —6D 44
Albert Rd. Long E —5F 63
Albert Rd. Nott —6H 33
Albert Rd. Sand —5D 52
Albert Rd. W Bri —3B 58
Albert Sq. Nott —6C 44
  (off Church St.)
Albert St. Eastw —2B 16
  (in two parts)
Albert St. Ged —6H 35
Albert St. Huck —4H 7
Albert St. Ilk —1A 40
Albert St. Nott —5G 45 (4E 5)
Albert St. Rad T —6F 49
Albert St. S'fd —4F 53
Albion Cen., The. Ilk —1B 40
Albion Leisure Cen. —1B 40
Albion Ri. Arn —4B 22
Albion Rd. Long E —5H 63
Albion St. Bees —4F 55
Albion St. Ilk —6B 28
Albion St. Nott —6G 45 (6D 4)
Albury Dri. Nott —5H 31
Albury Sq. Nott —5E 45 (4A 4)
Alcester St. Nott —3C 56
Aldene Ct. Bees —6D 54

Aldene Way. Wdbgh —1C 24
Aldercar La. Lan M —1F 15
Alder Gdns. Nott —6G 19
Aldermens Clo. Nott —1G 57
Alderney St. Nott —6D 44
Alderton Rd. Nott —1G 33
Alder Way. Keyw —5A 80
Aldgate Clo. Nott —5G 19
Aldred's La. Hean & Lan M —4E 15
Aldridge Clo. Bees —3G 63
Aldrin Clo. Nott —2F 31
Aldworth Clo. Nott —1F 33
Aldwych Clo. Arn —4E 21
Aldwych Clo. Nut —5D 30
Alexander Clo. Huck —2H 7
Alexander Fleming Building. Nott —3B 56
Alexander Rd. Nott —5E 45 (5A 4)
Alexandra Cres. Bees —5G 55
Alexandra Gdns. Nott —6F 33
Alexandra M. Nott —1F 45
Alexandra Rd. Long E —5F 63
Alexandra St. Eastw —3B 16
Alexandra St. Nott —1F 45
Alexandra St. S'fd —5F 53
Alford Clo. Bees —6G 55
  (in two parts)
Alford Rd. W Bri & Edw —5D 58
Alfred Av. Nott —5C 34
Alfred Clo. Nott —3G 45
Alfred St. Central. Nott —3G 45
Alfred St. N. Nott —3G 45
Alfred St. S. Nott —4A 46 (2H 5)
Alfreton Rd. Nott —2C 44 (2A 4)
Alison Av. Huck —2A 8
Alison Wlk. Nott —3H 45 (1F 5)
Allandale Rd. Hean —3B 14
Allen Av. Nott —6C 34
  (in two parts)
Allendale. Ilk —2A 40
Allendale Av. Bees —3D 64
Allendale Av. Nott —6F 31
Allen Fld. Ct. Nott —6D 44
Allen St. Huck —3G 7
Allen's Wlk. Arn —4B 22
All Hallows Dri. Ged —5H 35
Allington Av. Nott —6D 44
Allison Gdns. Bees —1H 65
Allison Gdns. Ilk —6C 28
All Saints St. Nott —3E 45 (1A 4)
All Saints Ter. Nott —3E 45 (1A 4)
Allwood Dri. Cltn —1G 47
Allwood Gdns. Huck —5H 7
Alma Clo. Ged —5A 36
Alma Clo. Nott —3G 45 (1D 4)
Alma Hill. Kimb —5G 17
Alma Rd. Nott —3B 46
Alma St. Nott —1E 45
Almond Clo. Huck —6H 7
Almond Clo. Kimb —6G 17
Almond Ct. Nott —1G 57
Almond Wlk. Ged —5A 36
Alnwick Clo. Nott —1B 32
Alpha Ter. Nott —3F 45
Alpine Cres. Cltn —1G 47
Alpine St. Nott —5C 32
Althorpe St. Nott —4E 45
Alton Av. Nott —1F 67
Alton Clo. W Bri —2G 67
Alton Dri. Gilt —5D 16
Alum Ct. Nott —5D 20
Alvenor St. Ilk —6B 28
Alverstone Rd. Nott —6G 33
Alvey Ter. Nott —4C 44
Alwood Gro. Nott —2B 66
Alwyn Clo. Bees —6F 55
Alwyn Rd. Nott —5F 31
Alyth Ct. Nott —4D 32
Amber Ct. Hean —4C 14
Amber Dri. Lan M —3F 15
Ambergate Rd. Nott —2G 43
  (in two parts)
Amber Hill. Nott —6F 21
Amberley Clo. Ilk —4A 28
Amber Trad. Cen. Kimb —6F 17
Ambleside. Gam —4E 59
Ambleside Dri. Eastw —2H 15
Ambleside Rd. Nott —6G 31
Ambleside Way. Ged —1B 48

American Adventure Theme Pk.
  —2G 27
Amersham Ri. Nott —6H 31
Amesbury Cir. Nott —4G 31
Amilda Av. Ilk —1B 40
Ampthill Ri. Nott —3F 33
Ancaster Gdns. Nott —4G 43
Anchor Clo. Nott —5H 31
Anchor Ct. Nott —6F 21
Anchor Rd. Eastw —2G 15
Anchor Row. Ilk —1B 40
Anders Dri. Nott —2F 31
Anderson Ct. Nott —5E 21
Anderson Cres. Bees —3E 55
Andover Clo. Nott —3H 43
Andover Rd. Nott —1C 32
Andrew Av. Ilk —2D 40
Andrew Av. Nott —5C 34
Andrews Ct. Bees —5C 54
Andrews Dri. Lan M —1E 15
Anfield Clo. Bees —3A 64
Anford Clo. Nott —2H 31
Angear Vis. Cen. —2B 56
Angela Av. Arn —3A 22
Angela Ct. Bees —3A 64
Angel All. Nott —5H 45 (4F 5)
Angelica Ct. Bing —5C 50
Angel Row. Nott —5G 45 (4D 4)
Angel Row Gallery. —5G 45 (4D 4)
  (off Angel Row)
Angletarn Clo. W Bri —5E 59
Angrave Clo. Nott —2A 46
Angus Clo. Arn —4D 22
Angus Clo. Kimb —2A 30
Anmer Clo. Nott —2F 57
Annan Ct. Nott —1H 43
Anne's Clo. Nott —5C 34
Annesley Gro. Nott —3F 45 (1C 4)
Annesley Rd. Ann —1D 6
Annesley Rd. Huck —1D 6
Annesley Rd. W Bri —4B 58
Anslow Av. Bees —3G 55
Anson Ter. Nott —2D 44
Anson Wlk. Ilk —4B 28
Anstee Rd. Long E —2E 73
Anstey Ri. Nott —4B 46
Anthony Wharton Ct. Nott —2C 66
Antill St. S'fd —5F 53
Apollo Dri. Nott —2F 31
Appleby Clo. Ilk —3B 40
Appledore Av. Nott —1D 54
Appledorne Way. Arn —4A 22
Appleton Clo. Nott —5A 66
Appleton Ct. Bees —1H 65
Appleton Rd. Bees —1H 65
Apple Tree Clo. Edw —1C 68
Appletree La. Ged —5H 35
Apple Wlk. Nott —1C 46
Applewood Gro. Nott —4H 33
Arboretum St. Nott —3F 45 (1B 4)
Arbour Hill. Dal A —6C 38
Arbrook Dri. Nott —3B 44
Arbutus Clo. Nott —4A 66
Archdale Rd. Nott —1G 33
Archer Cres. Nott —4F 43
Archer Rd. S'fd —6G 53
Archer St. Ilk —4A 28
Arch Hill. Red —2A 22
Archway Ct. Nott —3D 44
  (off Limpenny St.)
Arden Clo. Bees —3G 55
Arden Clo. Huck —6A 8
Arden Gro. Bing —4C 50
Ardleigh Clo. Nott —4B 20
Ardmore Clo. Nott —6B 46
Ardsley Clo. Hean —3E 15
Argyle Ct. Nott —4D 44
Argyle St. Lan M —1F 15
Argyle St. Nott —4D 44
Ariel Clo. Nott —2D 32
Arkers Clo. Nott —4B 32
Arklow Clo. Nott —5G 31
Arkwright St. Nott —1H 57
  (in two parts)
Arkwright St. N. Nott —6G 45
Arkwright St. S. Nott —2H 57
Arkwright Wlk. Nott —1G 57
  (in two parts)
Arleston Dri. Nott —6D 42
Arlington Clo. Huck —1G 19

Arlington Dri. Nott —6G 33
Armadale Clo. Arn —5E 23
Armfield Rd. Arn —1E 35
Armitage Dri. Long E —6A 64
Armstrong Rd. Nott —2F 31
Arncliffe Clo. Nott —5C 42
Arndale Rd. Nott —2G 33
Arne Ct. Nott —2G 57
Arnesby Rd. Nott —6B 44
Arno Av. Nott —1F 45
Arnold Av. Long E —3C 72
Arnold Cres. Long E —3C 72
Arnold La. Ged & Ged —2D 34
Arnold Rd. Nott —3C 32
Arnos Gro. Nott —2F 31
Arnot Hill Rd. Arn —6A 22
Arnot House. Cltn —1G 47
  (off Foxhill Rd. E.)
Arno Va. Gdns. Wd'p —2B 34
Arno Va. Rd. Wd'p —2A 34
Arnside. S'fd —6G 53
Arnside Clo. Nott —2F 33
Arnside Rd. Nott —2E 33
A Rd. Lent —5A 56
Arran Clo. S'fd —1G 53
Arthur Av. Nott —5D 44
Arthur Av. S'fd —3H 53
Arthur Cres. Cltn —2E 47
Arthur Mee Rd. S'fd —6G 53
Arthur St. N'fld —3A 48
Arthur St. Nott —3E 45 (1A 4)
Artic Way. Kimb —6F 17
Arts Cen. —5H 45 (4F 5)
  (off Carlton St., Nottingham)
Arundel Clo. Sand —1D 62
Arundel Dri. Bees —1B 54
Arundel St. Nott —4E 45
Ascot Av. Kimb —6G 17
Ascot Clo. W Hal —2B 38
Ascot Dri. Huck —6D 6
Ascot Dri. Red —5H 21
Ascot Ind. Est. Sand —4E 53
Ascot Pl. Ilk —4G 39
Ascot Rd. Nott —2B 44
Ascott Gdns. W Bri —6F 57
Ashbourne Clo. Bees —2A 54
Ashbourne Ct. Nott —1F 31
Ashbourne St. Nott —4E 45
Ashburnham Av. Nott —5D 44
Ashchurch Dri. Nott —1D 54
Ash Clo. Bing —5G 51
Ash Clo. Bur J —3E 37
Ash Clo. Huck —6C 6
Ash Clo. Wdbgh —1C 24
Ash Ct. Cltn —2F 47
Ash Cres. Nut —1B 30
Ashdale Av. Huck —6G 7
Ashdale Rd. Arn —5C 22
Ashdale Rd. Ilk —3C 40
Ashdale Rd. Nott —3D 46
Ashdown Clo. Wilf —5F 57
Ashdown Gro. Bing —5D 50
Ashe Clo. Arn —6D 22
Asher La. Rud —1G 77
Ashfield Av. Bees —6H 55
Ashfield Rd. Nott —5B 46
Ashford Ct. W Hal —1B 38
Ashford Pl. Ilk —2A 28
Ashford Rd. Nott —1D 54
Ash Forth Av. Hean —4E 15
Ashforth St. Nott —3H 45
Ashgate Rd. Huck —5H 7
Ash Gro. Keyw —5H 79
Ash Gro. Long E —1E 73
Ash Gro. Sand —4C 52
Ash Gro. S'fd —5F 53
Ash Gro. Wdbgh —6C 12
Ashiana. Nott —5A 46 (4H 5)
Ashington Dri. Arn —3C 22
Ash Lea Clo. Cotg —3F 71
Ashley Clo. Bees —5D 54
Ashley Ct. Bees —5E 55
Ashley Cres. Keyw —4H 79
Ashley Rd. Keyw —4G 79
Ashley St. Nott —4A 46 (3H 5)
Ashling Ct. Nott —1A 58
Ashling St. Nott —1H 57
Ash Mt. Rd. Lan M —2F 15
Ashness Clo. Gam —5E 59

Ashover Clo. *Nott* —1A **46**
Ashridge Way. *Edw* —1E **69**
Ash St. *Ilk* —3A **28**
Ashton Av. *Arn* —3B **22**
Ash Tree Sq. *Bees* —3B **54**
Ash Vw. *Nott* —3D **44**
Ashview Clo. *Long E* —5D **62**
Ash Vs. *Nott* —6F **33**
Ashville Clo. *Q Dri* —2E **57**
Ashwater Dri. *Nott* —1F **35**
Ashwell Ct. *Wd'p* —3A **34**
Ashwell Gdns. *Nott* —1C **44**
Ashwell St. *N'fld* —3H **47**
Ashwick Clo. *Nott* —6E **57**
Ashworth Av. *Rud* —5G **67**
Ashworth Clo. *Nott* —4E **47**
Ashworth Cres. *Nott* —5D **34**
Askeby Dri. *Nott* —6D **30**
Aslockton Dri. *Nott* —5B **32**
Aspen Clo. *Bing* —5G **51**
Aspen Rd. *Nott* —1F **31**
Asper St. *N'fld* —2A **48**
Aspinall Ct. *Nott* —4A **44**
Aspley La. *Nott* —6F **31**
Aspley Pk. Dri. *Nott* —1G **43**
Aspley Pl. *Nott* —3D **44**
Assarts Lodge. *Nut* —3D **30**
Assarts Rd. *Nut* —3E **31**
Astcote Clo. *Hean* —4E **15**
Aster Rd. *Nott* —2H **45**
Astle Ct. *Arn* —1E **35**
Astley Dri. *Nott* —6B **34**
Aston Av. *Bees* —3G **55**
Aston Ct. *Ilk* —6B **28**
Aston Ct. *Nott* —2C **56**
Aston Dri. *Nott* —3A **20**
Aston Grn. *Bees* —2G **63**
Astral Dri. *Huck* —1E **19**
Astral Gro. *Huck* —1D **18**
  (in two parts)
Astrid Gdns. *Nott* —1D **32**
Astwood Clo. *Nott* —2E **43**
Atherfield Gdns. *Eastw* —2B **16**
Atherton Ri. *Nott* —4H **31**
Atherton Rd. *Ilk* —4G **27**
Athorpe Gro. *Nott* —4D **32**
Attenborough La. *Bees* —3D **64**
Attenborough La. N. *Bees* —2C **64**
Attenborough Nature Reserve.
  —2F **65**
Attercliffe Ter. *Nott* —2G **57**
Attewell Rd. *Aws* —2D **28**
Aubrey Av. *Nott* —5A **46** (5H **5**)
Aubrey Rd. *Nott* —5F **33**
Aubyn Clo. *Stan C* —1A **38**
Auckland Clo. *Nott* —4C **44**
Auckland Rd. *Huck* —6D **6**
Audley Clo. *Ilk* —4H **27**
Audley Dri. *Bees* —2F **55**
Augustine Gdns. *Nott* —4E **21**
Austen Av. *Long E* —2E **73**
Austen Av. *Nott* —2E **45**
Austins Dri. *Sand* —1D **62**
Austin St. *Nott* —6A **20**
Austrey Av. *Bees* —3G **55**
Autumn Ct. *Huck* —5G **7**
Avalon Clo. *Nott* —1C **32**
Avebury Clo. *Nott* —5B **66**
Avenue A. *Nott* —5H **45** (4G **5**)
Avenue B. *Nott* —5A **46** (4G **5**)
Avenue C. *Nott* —5A **46** (4G **5**)
Avenue Clo. *Nott* —5D **20**
Avenue D. *Nott* —5A **46** (4H **5**)
Avenue E. *Nott* —4A **46** (3H **5**)
Avenue, The. *C'tn* —4H **11**
Avenue, The. *Rad T* —5F **49**
Avenue, The. *Rud* —2H **77**
Averton Sq. *Nott* —6B **44**
Aviemore Clo. *Arn* —4D **22**
Avis Av. *Hean* —6D **14**
Avocet Clo. *Bing* —6G **51**
Avocet Wharf. *Nott* —1E **57**
Avon Av. *Huck* —2E **19**
Avonbridge Clo. *Arn* —4E **23**
Avondale. *Cotg* —2G **71**
Avondale Clo. *Long E* —1C **72**
Avondale Rd. *Cltn* —3F **47**
Avondale Rd. *Ilk* —4G **39**
Avon Gdns. *W Bri* —4B **58**

Avonlea Clo. *Ilk* —3D **40**
Avon Pl. *Bees* —4G **55**
Avon Rd. *Ged* —5H **35**
Avon Rd. *Nott* —4D **46**
Awsworth & Cossall By-Pass. *Aws*
  —3D **28**
Awsworth La. *Coss* —5E **29**
Awsworth La. *Kimb* —1F **29**
Awsworth Rd. *Ilk & Aws* —5B **28**
Axford Clo. *Ged* —5H **35**
Aylesham Av. *Arn* —1B **34**
Aylestone Dri. *Nott* —1H **43**
Ayr St. *Nott* —3E **45** (1A **4**)
Ayscough Av. *Nut* —1C **30**
Ayton Clo. *Nott* —1F **57**
Ayton Gdns. *Bees* —3C **64**
Azalea Ct. *Gilt* —5E **17**

B

Babbacombe Dri. *Nott* —1F **33**
Babbacombe Way. *Huck* —5D **6**
Babbington Cres. *Ged* —5G **35**
Babbington La. *Kimb* —3H **29**
Babington Ct. *Bees* —6C **54**
Back La. *C But* —1A **80**
Back La. *Hean* —4C **14**
Back La. *Ilk* —5A **28**
Back La. *Nut* —1D **30**
Bacon Clo. *Gilt* —5C **16**
Bacton Av. *Nott* —5H **19**
Bacton Gdns. *Nott* —5H **19**
Baden Powell Rd. *Nott* —5C **46**
Bader Rd. *Nott* —4F **57**
Badger Clo. *Cltn* —1G **47**
Badger Clo. *Huck* —5C **6**
Bagnall Av. *Arn* —1G **33**
Bagnall Cotts. *Nott* —2H **31**
Bagnall Rd. *Nott* —3H **31**
Bagot St. *W Hal* —1A **38**
Bagthorpe Clo. *Nott* —4E **33**
Baildon Clo. *Nott* —6A **44**
Bailey Brook Cres. *Lan M* —1E **15**
Bailey Brook Dri. *Lan M* —2E **15**
Bailey Brook Ind. Est. *Lan M*
  —3F **15**
Bailey Brook Wlk. *Lan M* —2E **15**
Bailey Clo. *Day* —6H **21**
Bailey Ct. *N'fld* —2A **48**
Bailey Gro. Rd. *Eastw* —3H **15**
Bailey La. *Rad T* —1E **61**
Bailey St. *N'fld* —2A **48**
Bailey St. *Nott* —5C **32**
Bailey St. *S'fd* —5E **53**
Bainbridge, The. *C'tn* —4A **12**
Bainton Gro. *Nott* —4D **66**
Baker Av. *Arn* —4C **22**
Baker Av. *Hean* —6D **14**
Baker Brook Ind. Est. *Huck* —5B **8**
Bakerdale Rd. *Nott* —3D **46**
Baker Rd. *Gilt & Newt* —5E **17**
Bakers Clo. *Nott* —3C **44**
Baker's Hollow. *Cotg* —2E **71**
Baker St. *Huck* —4G **7**
Baker St. *Ilk* —6B **28**
Baker St. *Nott* —2F **45**
Bakewell Av. *Cltn* —6G **35**
Bakewell Dri. *Nott* —6C **20**
Bakewell Rd. *Long E* —2G **73**
Bala Dri. *Nott* —6E **21**
Baldwin Ct. *Nott* —4D **44**
Baldwin St. *Newt* —4E **17**
Baldwin St. *Nott* —4D **44**
Balfour Rd. *Nott* —4D **44**
Balfour Rd. *S'fd* —5F **53**
Balfron Gdns. *Nott* —1F **57**
Ballantrae Clo. *Arn* —5D **22**
Ballerat Cres. *Nott* —5C **20**
Ballon Wood N. *Nott* —5C **42**
Ball St. *Nott* —2B **46**
Balmoral Av. *W Bri* —3A **58**
Balmoral Clo. *Hean* —4A **14**
Balmoral Clo. *Sand* —2D **62**
Balmoral Cres. *Nott* —4C **42**
Balmoral Dri. *Bees* —1B **54**
Balmoral Gro. *Huck* —3H **7**
Balmoral Rd. *Bing* —5C **50**
Balmoral Rd. *Colw* —3H **47**
Balmoral Rd. *Ilk* —4H **39**

Balmoral Rd. *Nott* —3F **45**
Bamkin Clo. *Huck* —5H **7**
Bampton Ct. *Gam* —4E **59**
Banbury Av. *Bees* —2H **63**
Bancroft St. *Nott* —6A **20**
Banes Rd. *Bing* —5H **51**
Bangor Wlk. *Nott* —2G **45**
Bankfield Dri. *Bees* —2C **54**
Bankfield Dri. *Ilk* —3F **39**
Bank Hill. *Wdbgh* —2H **23**
Bank Pl. *Nott* —5G **45** (4E **5**)
Banksburn Clo. *Hean* —4A **14**
Banks Clo. *Arn* —1D **34**
Banks Cres. *Bing* —5E **51**
Banks Paddock. *Bing* —5F **51**
Banks Rd. *Bees* —2G **63**
Banks, The. *Bing* —5E **51**
Bank St. *Lan M* —1G **15**
Bank St. *Long E* —6G **63**
Bankwood Clo. *Nott* —6G **31**
Bank Yd. *Bulw* —6H **19**
  (off Main St.)
Bannerman Rd. *Nott* —1A **32**
Barbara Sq. *Huck* —2F **7**
Barber Clo. *Ilk* —4A **28**
Barber St. *Eastw* —3C **16**
Barbrook Clo. *Nott* —4H **43**
Barbury Dri. *Nott* —6B **66**
Barclay Ct. *Ilk* —4H **27**
Barden Rd. *Nott* —3C **34**
Bardfield Gdns. *Nott* —3B **20**
Bardney Dri. *Nott* —5G **19**
Bardsey Gdns. *Nott* —6E **21**
Barent Clo. *Nott* —1D **32**
  (in two parts)
Barent Wlk. *Nott* —1D **32**
Barker Av. E. *Sand* —5D **52**
Barker Av. N. *Sand* —5C **52**
Barker Ga. *Huck* —4F **7**
Barker Ga. *Ilk* —5B **28**
Barker Ga. *Nott* —5H **45** (4F **5**)
Barker's La. *Bees* —1F **65**
Barkla Clo. *Nott* —5A **66**
Bar La. *Nott* —5A **32**
Bar La. Ind. Pk. *Nott* —5B **32**
Barley Cft. *W Bri* —1G **67**
Barleydale Dri. *Trow* —1F **53**
Barleylands. *Rud* —1G **77**
Barling Dri. *Ilk* —5G **27**
Barlock Rd. *Nott* —3C **32**
Barlow Dri. N. *Aws* —3D **28**
Barlow Dri. S. *Aws* —3D **28**
Barlows Cotts. *Aws* —2E **29**
Barnby Wlk. *Nott* —2G **33**
Barn Clo. *Cotg* —3E **71**
Barn Clo. *Nott* —2F **31**
Barn Cft. *Bees* —5B **54**
Barndale Clo. *W Bri* —2G **67**
Barnes Cft. *Hean* —5A **14**
  (Heanor Ga. Rd.)
Barnes Cft. *Hean* —3D **14**
  (Johnson Dri.)
Barnes Rd. *Nott* —5D **20**
Barnet Rd. *Nott* —2D **46**
Barnett Ct. *Keyw* —4G **79**
Barnfield. *Nott* —1F **67**
Barnham Clo. *Ilk* —5B **28**
Barnsley Ter. *Nott* —2C **57**
Barnston Rd. *Nott* —4B **46**
Barnum Clo. *Nott* —4E **43**
Barons Clo. *Ged* —6G **35**
Barrack La. *Nott* —5D **44**
Barra M. *Nott* —1F **57**
Barratt Clo. *Bees* —4D **64**
Barratt Cres. *Bees* —3C **64**
Barratt La. *Bees* —3C **64**
Barrhead Clo. *Nott* —4C **20**
Barrington Clo. *Rad T* —1E **61**
Barrique Rd. *Nott* —2C **56**
Barrow Slade. *Keyw* —5G **79**
Barrydale Av. *Bees* —6F **55**
Barry St. *Nott* —6H **19**
Bartlow Rd. *Nott* —2D **42**
Barton Clo. *Rud* —1F **77**
Barton Clo. *Bar F* —1G **75**
Barton La. *Bees* —4C **64**
Barton La. *Nott* —5H **65**
Barton La. *Thrum* —6C **74**
Barton Rd. *Long E* —1A **74**
Bartons Clo. *Newt* —3E **17**

Barton St. *Bees* —6G **55**
Barwell Dri. *Nott* —6D **30**
Basa Cres. *Nott* —5D **20**
Basford Rd. *Nott* —6B **32**
Baskin La. *Bees* —1C **64**
Baslow Av. *Cltn* —6F **35**
Baslow Clo. *Long E* —2C **72**
Baslow Dri. *Bees* —2G **55**
Bassett Clo. *Ilk* —4G **27**
Bassett Clo. *Kimb* —6G **17**
Bassford Av. *Hean* —3D **14**
Bassingfield La. *Gam & Rad T*
  —5F **59**
Bastion St. *Nott* —4C **44**
Bateman Gdns. *Nott* —2D **44**
Bathley St. *Nott* —2G **57**
Baths. —1D **44**
  (New Basford)
Baths La. *Huck* —4H **7**
Bath St. *Ilk* —6A **28**
Bath St. *Nott* —4H **45** (2F **5**)
Bathurst Dri. *Nott* —3G **43**
Baulk La. *S'fd* —3H **53**
Bawtry Wlk. *Nott* —3B **46**
Bayard Ct. *Nott* —4A **44**
Bayliss Rd. *Ged* —4F **35**
Bayswater Rd. *Kimb* —6H **17**
Baythorn Rd. *Nott* —3D **42**
Beacon Flatts. *Bees* —5H **55**
Beacon Hill Dri. *Huck* —6C **6**
Beacon Hill Ri. *Nott* —4A **46** (2H **5**)
Beacon Rd. *Bees* —5H **55**
Beaconsfield St. *Long E* —6G **63**
Beaconsfield St. *Nott* —1D **44**
Bean Clo. *Nott* —2F **31**
Beanford La. *Oxt* —1G **11**
Beardall St. *Huck* —4H **7**
Beardsley Gdns. *Nott* —1F **57**
  (in two parts)
Beardsmore Gro. *Huck* —2F **7**
Beastmarket Hill. *Nott* —
  5G **45** (4D **4**)
Beatty Wlk. *Ilk* —4B **28**
Beauclerk Dri. *Nott* —5C **20**
Beaufort Ct. *W Bri* —2G **67**
Beaufort Dri. *Bees* —6C **54**
Beaulieu Gdns. *W Bri* —6G **57**
Beaumaris Dri. *Bees* —1B **64**
Beaumaris Dri. *Ged* —6B **36**
Beaumont Clo. *Keyw* —3G **79**
Beaumont Clo. *S'fd* —2G **53**
Beaumont Gdns. *W Bri* —1H **67**
Beaumont St. *Nott* —5A **46** (5H **5**)
Beauvale. *Newt* —3E **17**
Beauvale Ct. *Huck* —5E **7**
Beauvale Cres. *Huck* —5D **6**
Beauvale Dri. *Ilk* —2H **27**
Beauvale Ri. *Eastw* —2D **16**
Beauvale Rd. *Huck* —5D **6**
Beauvale Rd. *Nott* —2G **57**
Beaver Grn. *W Bri* —4H **57**
Beck Av. *C'tn* —3H **11**
Beckenham Rd. *Nott* —3C **44**
Beckett Ct. *Ged* —4F **35**
Beckford Rd. *Nott* —6B **46**
Beckhampton Rd. *Nott* —5F **21**
Beckley Rd. *Nott* —5F **31**
Beckside. *Gam & Gam* —1E **69**
Beck St. *Cltn* —1F **47**
Beck St. *Nott* —4H **45** (3F **5**)
Bedale Ct. *Bees* —1A **64**
Bedale Rd. *Nott* —2G **33**
Bedarra Gro. *Lent* —5C **44**
Bede Clo. *Nott* —4E **21**
Bede Ling. *W Bri* —5G **57**
Bedford Ct. *Nott* —1D **44**
Bedford Ct. *S'fd* —2G **53**
Bedford Gro. *Nott* —2B **32**
Bedford Row. *Nott* —4H **45** (3G **5**)
Bedlington Gdns. *Nott* —5A **34**
Beecham Av. *Nott* —3B **46**
Beech Av. *Bees* —6H **55**
Beech Av. *Bing* —5G **51**
Beech Av. *Breas* —5B **62**
Beech Av. *Huck* —4G **7**
Beech Av. *Keyw* —5H **79**
Beech Av. *Long E* —4G **63**
Beech Av. *Map* —3B **34**
Beech Av. *N'fld* —3H **47**
Beech Av. *New B* —1E **45**

Beech Av. *Nut* —1B **30**
Beech Av. *Sand* —4D **52**
Beech Clo. *Edw* —1D **68**
Beech Clo. *Nott* —3A **32**
Beech Clo. *Rad T* —1F **61**
Beech Ct. *Map* —3C **34**
Beechcroft. *W Hal* —2C **38**
Beechdale Rd. *Nott* —1F **43**
Beechdale Swimming Pool.
—3A **44**
Beeches, The. *Long E* —5G **63**
Beeches, The. *Nott* —1C **46**
Beeches, The. *Smal* —5A **14**
Beech La. *W Hal* —2B **38**
Beech Lodge. *Bing* —5G **51**
Beechwood Rd. *Arn* —5C **22**
Beeston Clo. *B Vil* —1C **20**
Beeston Ct. *Nott* —6F **21**
Beeston Fields Dri. *Bees* —3C **54**
Beeston Fields Golf Course.
—4D **54**
Beeston La. *Nott* —3H **55**
Beeston Rd. *Nott* —2B **56**
Beethan Dri. *Bing* —5F **51**
Belconnen Rd. *Nott* —2D **32**
Belfield Ct. *Los* —1A **14**
Belfield Gdns. *Long E* —6G **63**
Belfield St. *Ilk* —5B **28**
Belford Clo. *Nott* —5F **19**
Belfry Way. *Edw* —1E **69**
Belgrave Av. *W Bri* —2G **67**
Belgrave Rd. *Nott* —6G **19**
Belgrave Sq. *Nott* —4F **45** (3C **4**)
Bellar Ga. *Nott* —5H **45** (4G **5**)
Belle-Isle Rd. *Huck* —5G **7**
Belleville Dri. *Nott* —6F **21**
Bellevue Ct. *Nott* —3A **46** (1H **5**)
Bell Ho. *Nott* —3C **56**
Bell La. *Smal & Ship* —2A **26**
Bell La. *Wilf* —4F **57**
Bellmore Gdns. *Nott* —4D **42**
Bells La. *Nott* —5G **31**
Bell St. *Cltn* —1F **47**
Bell Ter. *Nott* —3C **32**
Belmont Av. *Breas* —5A **62**
Belmont Av. *Nott* —6A **20**
Belmont Clo. *Bees* —1B **64**
Belmont Clo. *Huck* —1G **19**
Belper Av. *Cltn* —6F **35**
Belper Cres. *Cltn* —6F **35**
Belper Rd. *Nott* —2D **44**
Belper Rd. *Stan C & W Hal*
—6A **26**
Belper St. *Ilk* —2B **40**
Belsay Rd. *Nott* —6E **21**
Belsford Ct. *Watn* —5A **18**
Belton Clo. *Sand* —1D **62**
Belton Dri. *W Bri* —1F **67**
Belton St. *Nott* —1D **44**
Belvedere Av. *Nott* —1D **44**
Belvedere Clo. *Keyw* —3G **79**
Belvoir Clo. *Ilk* —3H **39**
Belvoir Clo. *Long E* —2G **73**
Belvoir Hill. *Nott* —5B **46**
Belvoir Lodge. *Cltn* —3G **47**
Belvoir Rd. *N'fld* —2A **48**
Belvoir Rd. *W Bri* —2C **58**
Belvoir St. *Huck* —3F **7**
Belvoir St. *Nott* —5B **34**
Belvoir Ter. *Nott* —5B **46**
Belward St. *Nott* —4H **45** (4G **5**)
Belwood Clo. *Nott* —3D **66**
Bembridge Ct. *Bees* —3A **54**
Bembridge Dri. *Nott* —1F **33**
(in two parts)
Bendigo La. *Nott* —6C **46**
Benedict Ct. *Nott* —4E **21**
Ben Mayo Ct. *Nott* —3D **44**
Benner Av. *Ilk* —4C **40**
Bennerley Av. *Ilk* —3B **28**
Bennerley Ct. *Nott* —5F **19**
Bennerley Rd. *Blen I* —5F **19**
Bennett Rd. *Nott* —4C **34**
Bennett St. *Long E* —2E **63**
Bennett St. *Nott* —5B **34**
Bennett St. *Sand* —6D **52**
Benneworth Clo. *Huck* —6F **7**
Bennington Dri. *Nott* —6C **42**
Ben St. *Nott* —3D **44**
Bentinck Av. *Toll* —4F **69**

Bentinck Ct. *Nott* —5A **46** (4H **5**)
Bentinck Rd. *Cltn* —5E **35**
Bentinck Rd. *Nott* —3D **44**
Bentinck St. *Huck* —3F **7**
Bentley Av. *Nott* —3C **46**
Bentwell Av. *Arn* —6C **22**
Beresford Dri. *Ilk* —2A **28**
Beresford Ho. *Long E* —2B **72**
Beresford Rd. *Long E* —2C **72**
Beresford St. *Nott* —4C **44**
Berkeley Av. *Long E* —1E **73**
Berkeley Av. *Nott* —1G **45**
Berkeley Ct. *Nott* —6G **33**
Berle Av. *Hean* —2C **14**
Bernard Av. *Huck* —2H **7**
Bernard St. *Nott* —6F **33**
Bernard Ter. *Carr* —6F **33**
Bernisdale Clo. *Nott* —4D **20**
Berridge Rd. Central. *Nott* —1D **44**
Berridge Rd. E. *Nott* —1E **45**
Berridge Rd. W. *Nott* —2C **44**
Berriedale Clo. *Arn* —5E **23**
Berrydown Clo. *Nott* —6A **32**
Berry Hill Gro. *Ged* —5G **35**
Berwick Clo. *Nott* —1G **33**
Berwin Clo. *Long E* —4C **62**
Beryldene Av. *Watn* —6A **18**
Besecar Av. *Ged* —5G **35**
Besecar Clo. *Ged* —5G **35**
Bessell La. *S'fd* —6E **53**
Bestwick Av. *Hean* —4F **15**
Bestwick Clo. *Ilk* —5C **40**
Bestwood Av. *Arn* —5A **22**
Bestwood Clo. *Arn* —5A **22**
Bestwood Country Pk. —2D **20**
Bestwood Footpath. *Huck & B Vil*
—6B **8**
Bestwood Lodge Dri. *Arn* —4G **21**
Bestwood Pk. Dri. *Nott* —4F **21**
Bestwood Pk. Dri. W. *Nott* —4B **20**
Bestwood Pk. Vw. *Arn* —4A **22**
Bestwood Rd. *Huck* —5A **8**
Bestwood Rd. *Nott* —5A **20**
Bestwood Swimming Pool.
—1F **33**
Bestwood Ter. *Nott* —5A **20**
Bethel Gdns. *Huck* —6C **6**
Bethnal Wlk. *Nott* —6H **19**
Betony Clo. *Bing* —6C **50**
Betula Clo. *Nott* —4A **66**
Bevel St. *Nott* —2D **44**
Beverley Clo. *Nott* —5B **42**
Beverley Gdns. *Ged* —6H **35**
Beverley Sq. *Nott* —2A **46**
Bewcastle Rd. *Nott* —4E **21**
Bewick Dri. *Nott* —4E **47**
Bexhill Ct. *Bees* —2E **55**
Bexleigh Gdns. *Nott* —1G **43**
Bexwell Rd. *Nott* —5C **66**
Biant Clo. *Nott* —4H **31**
Bible Wlk. *Nott* —4F **45** (2C **4**)
Bidford Rd. *Nott* —6F **31**
Bidwell Cres. *Got* —5H **75**
Biggart Clo. *Bees* —3C **64**
Biko Sq. *Nott* —1D **44**
Bilberry Wlk. *Nott* —3A **46**
Bilborough Rd. *Nott* —4B **42**
Bilby Gdns. *Nott* —4B **46**
Billesdon Dri. *Nott* —3D **32**
Bingham By-Pass. *Bing* —5B **50**
Bingham Ind. Pk. *Bing* —4E **51**
Bingham Leisure Cen. —5D **50**
Bingham Rd. *Cotg* —2F **71**
(in two parts)
Bingham Rd. *Nott* —5G **33**
Bingham Rd. *Rad T* —6F **49**
Bingley Clo. *Nott* —3H **43**
Birch Av. *Bees* —1H **65**
Birch Av. *Cltn* —2F **47**
Birch Av. *Ilk* —2C **40**
Birch Av. *Nut* —1B **30**
Birchdale Av. *Huck* —6G **7**
Birchfield Pk. *Hean* —6D **14**
Birchfield Rd. *Arn* —5C **22**
Birch Lea. *Red* —5H **21**
Birchover Pl. *Ilk* —2A **28**
Birchover Rd. *Nott* —4C **42**
Birch Pas. *Nott* —4E **45** (2A **4**)

Birch Ri. *Wdbgh* —6C **12**
Birchwood. *Los* —1A **14**
Birchwood Av. *Breas* —6B **62**
Birchwood Av. *Long E* —1E **73**
Birchwood Rd. *Nott* —5C **42**
Bircumshaw Rd. *Hean* —3C **14**
Birdcroft La. *Ilk* —4B **40**
Birdsall Av. *Nott* —5E **43**
Birkdale Clo. *Edw* —2C **68**
Birkdale Clo. *Man I* —6H **27**
Birkdale Way. *Nott* —5D **20**
Birkin Av. *Bees* —3A **64**
Birkin Av. *Nott* —2D **44**
Birkin Av. *Rad T* —5G **49**
Birkin Av. *Rud* —5G **67**
Birkland Av. *Map* —3C **34**
Birkland Av. *Nott* —3G **45** (1D **4**)
Birley St. *S'fd* —6F **53**
Birling Clo. *Nott* —6F **19**
Birrell Rd. *Nott* —1E **45**
Bisham Dri. *W Bri* —4D **58**
Bishopdale Clo. *Long E* —1C **72**
Bishopdale Dri. *Watn* —6B **18**
Bishops Clo. *Keyw* —3G **79**
Bishops Rd. *Bing* —4D **50**
Bishop St. *Eastw* —3B **16**
Bishops Way. *Huck* —2H **7**
Bispham Dri. *Bees* —2H **63**
Blackacre. *Bur J* —2E **37**
Blackburn Pl. *Ilk* —4A **28**
Blackcliffe Farm M. *Bradm* —4A **78**
Blackett's Wlk. *Nott* —5D **66**
Blackfriars Clo. *Nott* —5D **30**
Blackhill Dri. *Cltn* —1H **47**
Black Hills Dri. *Ilk* —3A **40**
Blackrod Clo. *Bees* —3A **64**
Blacksmith Ct. *Cotg* —1E **71**
Blackstone Wlk. *Nott* —1G **57**
Black Swan Clo. *Wd'p* —3H **33**
Blackthorn Clo. *Bing* —5G **51**
Blackthorn Dri. *Eastw* —3A **16**
Blackthorn Dri. *Nott* —3H **31**
Bladon Clo. *Nott* —5A **34**
Bladon Rd. *Rud* —6F **67**
Blair Ct. *Nott* —2G **57**
Blair Gro. *Sand* —1C **62**
Blaise Clo. *Nott* —5C **66**
Blake Clo. *Arn* —6C **22**
Blake Ct. *Long E* —2D **72**
Blakeney Rd. *Rad T* —6H **49**
Blakeney Wlk. *Arn* —2B **34**
Blake Rd. *S'fd* —5G **53**
Blake Rd. *W Bri* —4B **58**
Blake St. *Ilk* —6B **28**
Blandford Av. *Long E* —1D **72**
Blandford Rd. *Bees* —6C **54**
Bland La. *Epp* —6G **13**
Blanford Gdns. *W Bri* —6G **57**
Blankney St. *Nott* —3C **32**
Blantyre Av. *Nott* —4C **20**
Blatherwick's Yd. *Arn* —5B **22**
Bleaberry Clo. *W Bri* —6E **59**
Bleachers Yd. *Nott* —6D **32**
Bleasby St. *Nott* —5B **46**
Bleasdale Clo. *Ged* —5A **36**
Blencathra Clo. *W Bri* —6E **59**
Blenheim Av. *Nott* —5E **35**
Blenheim Clo. *Rud* —6F **67**
Blenheim Ct. *Sand* —1D **62**
Blenheim Dri. *Bees* —6C **54**
Blenheim Ind. Est. *Nott* —5F **19**
Blenheim La. *Nott* —3D **18**
Blidworth Clo. *Strel* —5E **31**
Blind La. *Breas* —5A **62**
Bloomsbury Dri. *Nut* —4E **31**
Bloomsgrove Ind. Est. *Nott*
—4D **44**
Bloomsgrove Rd. *Ilk* —5B **28**
Bloomsgrove St. *Nott* —4D **44**
Bluebell Bank. *Bing* —6D **50**
Bluebell Clo. *Huck* —5C **6**
Blue Bell Hill Rd. *Nott* —3A **46**
Bluebell Way. *Hean* —4F **15**
Bluecoat Clo. *Nott* —3G **45** (1D **4**)
Bluecoat St. *Nott* —3G **45** (1D **4**)
Blundell Clo. *Nott* —1B **46**
Blyth Gdns. *Nott* —5A **34**
Blyth St. *Nott* —6A **34**
Blyton Wlk. *Nott* —6F **21**
Boatmans Clo. *Ilk* —5B **28**

Bobbers Mill Bri. *Nott* —2B **44**
Bobbers Mill Rd. *Nott* —2C **44**
Boden Dri. *Nut* —1C **30**
Boden St. *Nott* —4D **44**
Bodmin Av. *Huck* —6C **6**
Bodmin Dri. *Nott* —5A **32**
Body Rd. *Bees* —2B **64**
Bohem Rd. *Long E* —2E **73**
Bolcote Ho. *Cltn* —1G **47**
(off Foxhill Rd. E.)
Bold Clo. *Nott* —5H **19**
Bolero Clo. *Nott* —4E **43**
Bolingey Way. *Huck* —5C **6**
Bolsover St. *Huck* —4H **7**
Bolton Av. *Bees* —1C **64**
Bolton Clo. *W Bri* —5C **58**
Bolton Ter. *Rad T* —6F **49**
Bond St. *Arn* —5A **22**
Bond St. *Nott* —5A **46** (4H **5**)
Bonetti Clo. *Arn* —2D **34**
Boniface Gdns. *Nott* —4E **21**
Bonington Dri. *Arn* —6B **22**
Bonington Gallery, The.
(off Dryden St.) —3F **45** (1C **4**)
Bonington Rd. *Nott* —3B **34**
Bonner Hill. *C'tn* —5H **11**
Bonner La. *C'tn* —4A **12**
Bonner's Rd. *Aws* —3E **29**
Bonnington Clo. *Nott* —1G **31**
(in three parts)
Bonnington Cres. *Nott* —3G **33**
Bonny Mead. *Cotg* —3E **71**
Bonsall Ct. *Long E* —5G **63**
Bonsall St. *Long E* —5G **63**
Bonser Clo. *Cltn* —2G **47**
Booth Clo. *Nott* —4H **45** (2F **5**)
Borlace Cres. *S'fd* —5G **53**
Borman Clo. *Nott* —2F **31**
Borrowdale Clo. *Gam* —5F **59**
Borrowdale Ct. *Bees* —1B **64**
Borrowdale Dri. *Long E* —1C **72**
Boscawen Ct. *Ilk* —4B **28**
Bosden Clo. *Nott* —3C **42**
Bosley Sq. *Bees* —3G **55**
Bostock's La. *Ris* —1B **62**
Bostock's La. *Sand* —2C **62**
Boston M. *Nott* —4D **32**
Boston St. *Nott* —4H **45** (3G **5**)
Bosworth Clo. *Shelf* —1H **49**
Bosworth Dri. *Newt* —2D **16**
Bosworth Wlk. *Nott* —2F **57**
Bosworth Way. *Long E* —2G **73**
Botany Av. *Nott* —2B **46**
Botany Clo. *W Bri* —2G **67**
Botany Dri. *Ilk* —2B **28**
Bothe Clo. *Long E* —1E **73**
Bottle La. *Nott* —5G **45** (4E **5**)
Boundary Cres. *Bees* —2F **55**
Boundary La. *Lan M* —2G **15**
Boundary Rd. *Bees* —2F **55**
Boundary Rd. *W Bri* —1A **68**
Bourne Clo. *Bees* —2D **54**
Bourne M. *N'fld* —3A **48**
Bourne Sq. *Breas* —3A **62**
Bourne St. *N'fld* —3A **48**
Bournmoor Av. *Nott* —4C **66**
Bovill St. *Nott* —3D **44**
Bowden Clo. *Nott* —4G **33**
Bowden Dri. *Bees* —5H **55**
Bowers Av. *Nott* —2H **45**
Bowes Well Rd. *Ilk* —5A **28**
Bowland Clo. *Nott* —2C **46**
Bowland Rd. *Bing* —5C **50**
Bowling Clo. *Stan D* —3A **52**
Bowlwell Av. *Nott* —5D **20**
Bowness Av. *Nott* —5A **32**
Bowness Clo. *Gam* —4E **59**
Bowscale Clo. *W Bri* —6E **59**
Boxley Dri. *W Bri* —1G **67**
Boyce Gdns. *Nott* —6B **34**
Boycroft Av. *Nott* —1B **46**
Boyd Clo. *Arn* —4D **22**
Boynton Dri. *Nott* —6B **34**
Bracadale Rd. *Nott* —4D **20**
Bracebridge Dri. *Nott* —3B **42**
Bracey Ri. *W Bri* —2A **68**
Bracken Clo. *Cltn* —5F **35**
Bracken Clo. *Long E* —4D **62**
Bracken Clo. *Nott* —6F **31**
Brackendale Av. *Arn* —5B **22**

Brackenfield Dri. *Gilt* —6D **16**
Bracken Rd. *Long E* —4D **62**
Bracknell Cres. *Nott* —6B **32**
Bracton Dri. *Nott* —3B **46**
Bradbourne Av. *Nott* —6E **57**
Bradbury St. *Nott* —5C **44**
Braddock Clo. *Lent* —5C **44**
Braddon Av. *S'fd* —2G **53**
Bradfield Rd. *Nott* —6F **31**
Bradford Ct. *Nott* —1G **31**
Bradgate Clo. *Sand* —1D **62**
Bradgate Rd. *Nott* —1E **45**
Bradley St. *Bees* —5G **55**
Bradley St. *Sand* —6E **53**
Bradleys Yd. *Plum* —6G **69**
Bradley Wlk. *Nott* —5D **66**
Bradman Gdns. *Arn* —1D **34**
Bradmore Av. *Rud* —5G **67**
Bradmore La. *Keyw* —3E **79**
Bradmore Ri. *Nott* —5A **32**
Bradshaw St. *Long E* —2D **72**
Bradwell Clo. *Gilt* —6D **17**
Bradwell Dri. *Nott* —5D **20**
Braefell Clo. *W Bri* —6F **59**
Braefield Clo. *Ilk* —4G **39**
Braemar Av. *Eastw* —5B **16**
Braemar Dri. *Ged* —6B **36**
Braemar Rd. *Nott* —6A **20**
Braidwood Ct. *Nott* —2D **44**
Brailsford Rd. *Nott* —2C **56**
Brailsford Way. *Bees* —4C **64**
Bramber Gro. *Nott* —6C **66**
Bramble Clo. *Bees* —3D **64**
Bramble Clo. *Long E* —4D **62**
Bramble Clo. *Nott* —4B **32**
Bramble Ct. *Ged* —6H **35**
Bramble Dri. *Nott* —2C **46**
Bramble Gdns. *Nott* —1G **43**
Brambleway. *Cotg* —3G **71**
Bramcote Av. *Bees* —5C **54**
Bramcote Dri. *Bees* —4E **55**
Bramcote Dri. *Nott* —6C **44**
Bramcote Dri. W. *Bees* —5D **54**
Bramcote La. *Bees* —5C **54**
Bramcote La. *Nott* —1D **54**
Bramcote Leisure Cen. —2B **54**
Bramcote Rd. *Bees* —4E **55**
Bramcote St. *Nott* —4C **44**
Bramcote Wlk. *Nott* —4C **44**
Bramerton Rd. *Nott* —3C **42**
Bramhall Rd. *Nott* —3C **42**
Bramley Ct. *Kimb* —1H **29**
Bramley Grn. *Nott* —6E **31**
Bramley Rd. *Nott* —6E **31**
Brampton Av. *Hean* —3E **15**
Brampton Dri. *S'fd* —6H **53**
Brancaster Clo. *Nott* —3H **31**
Brandish Cres. *Nott* —4B **66**
Brandreth Av. *Nott* —1B **46**
Brandreth Dri. *Gilt* —5C **16**
Brand St. *Nott* —1B **58**
Branklene Clo. *Kimb* —6G **17**
Branksome Wlk. *Nott* —1G **57**
Bransdale Clo. *Long E* —1D **72**
Bransdale Rd. *Nott* —4B **66**
Branston Gdns. *W Bri* —1H **67**
Branston Wlk. *Nott* —3G **33**
Brantford Av. *Nott* —4D **66**
Brassington Clo. *Gilt* —6D **16**
Brassington Clo. *W Hal* —1C **38**
Braunton Clo. *Huck* —5D **6**
Brayton Cres. *Nott* —2B **32**
Breach Rd. *Hean* —5E **15**
Breadsall Ct. *Ilk* —4B **28**
Breaston Ct. Nott —5E 21
(off Erewash Gdns.)
Breaston La. *Ris* —2A **62**
Brechin Clo. *Arn* —3D **22**
Breckhill Rd. *Wd'p & Map*
—2A **34**
Breckswood Dri. *Nott* —6C **66**
Brecon Clo. *Long E* —5C **62**
Brecon Clo. *Nott* —3G **31**
Bredon Clo. *Long E* —5C **62**
Breedon St. *Long E* —2D **62**
Brendon Ct. *Bees* —3B **54**
Brendon Dri. *Kimb* —6H **17**
Brendon Dri. *Nott* —4G **43**
Brendon Gdns. *Nott* —4G **43**
Brendon Gro. *Bing* —4C **50**

Brendon Rd. *Nott* —4G **43**
Brendon Way. *Long E* —3C **62**
Brentcliffe Av. *Nott* —2C **46**
Brentnall Ct. *Bees* —2D **64**
Bressingham Dri. *W Bri* —2G **67**
Brett Clo. *Huck* —6E **7**
Brewery St. *Kimb* —1H **29**
Brewhouse Mus. —6G 45 (6D 4)
(off Brewhouse Yd.)
Brewhouse Yd. *Nott* —6F **45** (6C **4**)
Brewsters Clo. *Bing* —5E **51**
Brewsters Rd. *Nott* —1A **46**
Breydon Ind. Cen. *Long E* —6H **63**
Briar Av. *Sand* —2D **62**
Briarbank Av. *Nott* —1C **46**
Briarbank Wlk. *Nott* —2C **46**
Briar Clo. *Bees* —2E **55**
Briar Clo. *Huck* —6D **6**
Briar Clo. *Keyw* —3H **79**
Briar Ct. *Nott* —2F **57**
Briar Gdns. *C'tn* —3E **11**
Briar Ga. *Cotg* —3G **71**
Briar Ga. *Long E* —3C **62**
Briar Rd. *Newt* —5D **16**
Briarwood Av. *Nott* —2C **46**
Briarwood Ct. *Sher* —4A **34**
Brickenell Rd. *C'tn* —5H **11**
Brickyard. *Huck* —5A **8**
Brickyard Cotts. *Nott* —2F **67**
Brickyard Dri. *Huck* —6A **8**
Brickyard La. *Rad T* —6H **49**
Brickyard Plantation Nature
Reserve. —1G **41**
Brickyard, The. *Stan C* —6A **26**
Bridge Av. *Bees* —6E **55**
Bridge Ct. *Bees* —4H **55**
Bridge Ct. *Huck* —6G **7**
Bri. Farm La. *Nott* —3C **66**
Bridge Grn. Wlk. *Nott* —6E **31**
Bridge Gro. *W Bri* —3A **58**
Bridgend Clo. *S'fd* —6F **53**
Bridge Rd. *Nott* —4D **42**
Bridge St. *Ilk* —3B **28**
Bridge St. *Lan M* —2G **15**
Bridge St. *Long E* —4F **63**
Bridge St. *Sand* —6E **53**
Bridgeway Cen. *Nott* —1G **57**
Bridgeway Ct. *Nott* —1H **57**
Bridgford Rd. *W Bri* —2A **58**
Bridgnorth Dri. *Nott* —3C **66**
Bridgnorth Way. *Bees* —2G **63**
Bridle Rd. *Bees* —2B **54**
Bridle Rd. *Bur J* —1D **36**
Bridlesmith Ga. *Nott*
—5G **45** (4E **5**)
Bridlington St. *Nott* —2C **44**
Bridport Av. *Nott* —4B **44**
Brielen Ct. *Rad T* —6G **49**
Brielen Rd. *Rad T* —6G **49**
Brierfield Av. *Nott* —1F **67**
Brierley Grn. *N'fld* —2A **68**
Brightmoor Ct. *Nott* —5H **45** (4F **5**)
Brightmoor St. *Nott* —5H **45** (4F **5**)
Bright St. *Ilk* —4A **28**
Bright St. *Nott* —4C **44**
Brindley Rd. *Nott* —4C **42**
Brinkhill Cres. *Nott* —2D **66**
Brinsley Clo. *Nott* —6G **31**
Brisbane Dri. *Nott* —5C **20**
Brisbane Dri. *S'fd* —2H **53**
Bristol Rd. *Ilk* —6A **28**
Britannia Av. *Nott* —3C **32**
Britannia Ct. *N'fld* —3A **48**
Britannia Rd. *Long E* —4F **63**
Britten Gdns. *Nott* —3B **46**
Brixham Rd. *Huck* —6D **6**
Brixton Rd. *Nott* —4C **44**
B Rd. *Lent* —5B **56**
Broad Clo. *Wdbgh* —1B **24**
Broad Eadow Rd. *Nott* —6F **19**
Broadfields. *C'tn* —3H **11**
Broadgate. *Bees* —4G **55**
Broadgate Av. *Bees* —4G **55**
Broadgate Pk. *Bees* —3G **55**
Broadholme St. *Nott* —6D **44**
Broadhurst Av. *Nott* —5B **32**
Broadlands. *Sand* —2D **62**
Broadleigh Clo. *W Bri* —2G **67**
Broad Marsh Shop. Cen. *Nott*
—5G **45** (5E **5**)

Broadmead. *Bur J* —2F **37**
Broad Meer. *Cotg* —2E **71**
Broadmere Ct. *Arn* —4D **22**
Broad Oak Clo. *Nott* —2A **46**
Broad Oak Dri. *S'fd* —5F **53**
Broadstairs Rd. *Bees* —3H **63**
Broadstone Clo. *W Bri* —6G **57**
Broad St. *Long E* —6F **63**
Broad St. *Nott* —4H **45** (3F **5**)
Broad Valley Dri. *B Vil* —1C **20**
Broad Wlk. *Nott* —4A **32**
Broadway. *Hean* —4C **14**
Broadway. *Ilk* —4A **28**
Broadway. *Nott* —5H **45** (5F **5**)
Broadway E. *Cltn* —3F **47**
Broadway Media Cen.
(off Broad St.) —4H **45** (3F **5**)
Broadwood Ct. *Bees* —3G **55**
Broadwood Rd. *Nott* —5F **21**
Brockdale Gdns. *Keyw* —3G **79**
Brockenhurst Gdns. *Nott* —3B **46**
Brockhall Ri. *Hean* —4E **15**
Brockhole Clo. *W Bri* —6F **59**
Brockley Rd. *W Bri* —4D **58**
Brockwood Cres. *Keyw* —3G **79**
Bromfield Clo. *Nott* —2E **47**
Bromley Clo. *Nott* —1H **45**
Bromley Pl. *Nott* —5F **45** (4C **4**)
Bromley Rd. *W Bri* —5A **58**
Brompton Clo. *Arn* —3E **21**
Brompton Way. *W Bri* —2G **67**
Bronte Clo. *Long E* —6C **62**
Bronte Ct. *Nott* —3E **45**
Brook Av. *Arn* —5D **22**
Brook Clo. *Long E* —2G **73**
Brook Clo. *Newt* —4D **16**
Brook Clo. *Nott* —1H **31**
Brook Cotts. *Ilk* —4B **28**
Brook Ct. *Lan M* —3F **15**
Brookdale Ct. *Nott* —2H **33**
Brooke St. *Ilk* —3D **40**
Brooke St. *Sand* —6D **52**
Brookfield Av. *Huck* —6F **7**
Brookfield Clo. *Rad T* —6F **49**
Brookfield Ct. *Arn* —6C **22**
Brookfield Ct. *Nott* —1G **57**
Brookfield Gdns. *Arn* —6C **22**
Brookfield Rd. *Arn* —6B **22**
Brookfield Way. *Hean* —4F **15**
Brook Gdns. *Arn* —5C **22**
Brookhill Cres. *Nott* —6E **43**
Brookhill Dri. *Nott* —6E **43**
Brookhill Leys Rd. *Eastw* —4A **16**
Brookhill St. *S'fd* —6E **53**
Brookland Dri. *Bees* —6D **54**
Brooklands Av. *Hean* —3D **14**
Brooklands Cres. *Ged* —6A **36**
Brooklands Dri. *Ged* —6A **36**
Brooklands Rd. *Nott* —2D **46**
Brook La. *Gam* —4E **59**
Brooklyn Av. *Bur J* —3E **37**
Brooklyn Clo. *Nott* —2B **32**
Brooklyn Rd. *Nott* —1B **32**
Brook Rd. *Bees* —3F **55**
Brooksby La. *Nott* —1D **66**
Brookside. *Eastw* —1H **15**
Brookside. *Huck* —6H **7**
Brookside Av. *Nott* —1H **54**
Brookside Clo. *Long E* —5D **62**
Brookside Gdns. *Rud* —5F **67**
Brookside Rd. *Rud* —5F **67**
Brook St. *Huck* —3G **7**
Brook St. *Los* —1A **14**
Brook St. *Nott* —4H **45** (3F **5**)
Brookthorpe Way. *Nott* —1E **67**
Brook Va. Rd. *Lan M* —3G **15**
Brook Vw. Ct. *Keyw* —5G **79**
Brook Vw. Dri. *Keyw* —5G **79**
Brookwood Cres. *Cltn* —2E **47**
Broom Clo. *C'tn* —3H **11**
Broomfield Clo. *Sand* —6C **52**
Broomhill Av. *Ilk* —3C **40**
(in two parts)
Broomhill Pk. Vw. *Huck* —6A **8**
Broomhill Rd. *Huck* —6G **7**
Broomhill Rd. *Kimb* —1A **30**
Broomhill Rd. *Nott* —1A **32**
Broom Rd. *C'tn* —4H **11**
Broom Wlk. *Nott* —1C **46**
Brora Rd. *Nott* —6B **20**

Broughton Clo. *Ilk* —4A **28**
Broughton Dri. *Nott* —5A **44**
Broughton St. *Bees* —4F **55**
Brownes Rd. *Bing* —4G **51**
Browning Clo. *Day* —6H **21**
Browning Ct. *Nott* —4F **33**
Brown La. *Bar F* —1E **75**
Brownlow Dri. *Nott* —4B **20**
Browns Cft. *Nott* —4B **32**
Brown's Flat. *Kimb* —6H **17**
Browns La. *Keyw* —6B **80**
Brown's Rd. *Long E* —5G **63**
Brown St. *Nott* —2D **44**
Broxtowe Av. *Kimb* —1F **29**
Broxtowe Av. *Nott* —5A **32**
Broxtowe Dri. *Huck* —2G **7**
Broxtowe Hall Clo. *Nott* —5G **31**
Broxtowe Ho. *Nott* —6D **30**
Broxtowe La. *Nott* —6F **31**
Broxtowe Pk. —5E **31**
Broxtowe Ri. *Nott* —4H **31**
Broxtowe St. *Nott* —5G **33**
Bruce Clo. *Nott* —1H **57**
Bruce Dri. *W Bri* —4H **57**
Brunel Av. *Newt* —1D **16**
Brunel Ter. *Nott* —4E **45**
Brunswick Dri. *S'fd* —6G **53**
Brushfield St. *Nott* —2C **44**
Brussells Ter. Ilk —6A 28
(off Bath St.)
Brusty Pl. *Bur J* —2E **37**
Bryan Ct. *Nott* —1A **44**
Buckfast Way. *W Bri* —4C **58**
Buckingham Av. *Huck* —3H **7**
Buckingham Clo. *Hean* —3A **14**
Buckingham Ct. *Sand* —2C **62**
Buckingham Rd. *Sand* —2C **62**
Buckingham Rd. *Wd'p* —2A **34**
Buckingham Way. *Watn* —6B **18**
Buckland Dri. *Wdbgh* —1C **24**
Bucklee Dri. *C'tn* —4G **11**
Bucklow Clo. *Nott* —6B **32**
Buckminster Rd. *Ilk* —5G **39**
Budby Ri. *Huck* —3H **7**
Bulcote Dri. *Bur J* —4D **36**
Bulcote Rd. *Nott* —2D **66**
Bullace Rd. *Nott* —2B **46**
Bull Clo. Rd. *Lent* —3C **56**
Buller St. *Ilk* —3C **40**
Buller Ter. *Nott* —4H **33**
Bullfinch Rd. *Nott* —3B **32**
Bullins Clo. *Nott* —4G **21**
Bullivant St. *Nott* —3H **45** (1F **5**)
Bulwell Bus. Cen. *Nott* —6G **19**
Bulwell Forest Golf Course.
—5B **20**
Bulwell High Rd. *Nott* —6H **19**
Bulwell La. *Nott* —3B **32**
Bulwer Rd. *Nott* —4D **44**
Bunbury St. *Nott* —2H **57**
Bunny La. *Keyw* —5E **79**
Bunting Clo. *Ilk* —3G **39**
Buntings La. *Cltn* —2E **47**
Bunting St. *Nott* —2C **56**
Burcot Clo. *W Hal* —1C **38**
Burford Rd. *Nott* —1D **44**
Burford St. *Arn* —5A **22**
Burgass Rd. *Nott* —2C **46**
Burge Clo. *Nott* —1G **57**
Burgh Hall Clo. *Bees* —3C **64**
Burhill. *Cotg* —3G **71**
Burke St. *Nott* —4E **45** (2A **4**)
Burleigh Clo. *Cltn* —2H **47**
Burleigh Rd. *W Bri* —5B **58**
Burleigh Sq. *Bees* —1C **64**
Burleigh St. *Ilk* —6B **28**
Burlington Av. *Nott* —4F **33**
Burlington Ct. *Nott* —4G **33**
Burlington Rd. *Cltn* —1G **47**
Burlington Rd. *Nott* —4G **33**
Burnaby St. *Nott* —3B **32**
Burnbank Clo. *W Bri* —6F **59**
Burnbreck Gdns. *Nott* —5E **43**
Burncroft. *W Hal* —2C **38**
Burndale Wlk. *Nott* —5C **20**
Burnham Av. *Bees* —1F **65**
Burnham Clo. *W Hal* —1B **38**
Burnham Lodge. *Nott* —4C **20**
Burnham St. *Nott* —5G **33**
Burnham Way. *Nott* —6G **45**

Celia Dri. *Cltn* —2F **47**
Cemetery Rd. *S'fd* —4G **53**
Central Av. *Arn* —6B **22**
Central Av. *Bees* —5D **54**
(Bramcote Av.)
Central Av. *Bees* —2E **55**
(Derby Rd.)
Central Av. *Huck* —5G **7**
Central Av. *Map* —3D **34**
Central Av. *New B* —6E **33**
Central Av. *Sand* —5D **52**
Central Av. *S'fd* —3G **53**
Central Av. *W Bri* —3B **58**
Central Av. S. *Arn* —6B **22**
Central Ct. *Nott* —2D **56**
Central St. *Nott* —3A **46**
Central Wlk. *Huck* —4G **7**
Centre Way. *Rad T* —5E **49**
Centurion Way. *Nott* —3D **56**
Cernan Ct. *Nott* —2F **31**
Cerne Clo. *Nott* —5D **66**
Chaceley Way. *Nott* —2E **67**
Chadborn Av. *Got* —6H **75**
Chaddesden, The. *Nott* —2G **45**
Chad Gdns. *Nott* —3E **21**
Chadwick Rd. *Nott* —2C **44**
Chain La. *Nott* —2C **56**
Chalfield Clo. *Nott* —4B **66**
Chalfont Dri. *Nott* —3A **44**
Challond Ct. *Nott* —5F **21**
Chalons Clo. *Ilk* —6B **28**
Chalons Way. *Ilk* —6B **28**
Chamberlain Clo. *Nott* —4A **66**
Chambers Av. *Ilk* —2D **40**
Champion Av. *Ilk* —4G **27**
Chancery Ct. *Wilf* —5E **57**
Chancery, The. *Bees* —4C **54**
Chandos Av. *N'fld* —1A **48**
Chandos St. *N'fld* —2A **48**
Chandos St. *Nott* —2A **46**
Chantrey Rd. *W Bri* —4A **58**
Chantry Clo. *Bees* —1D **64**
Chantry Clo. *Kimb* —2A **30**
Chantry Clo. *Long E* —3C **72**
Chapel Bar. *Nott* —5F **45** (4C **4**)
Chapel Ct. *Ilk* —3B **28**
Chapel La. *Arn* —5A **22**
Chapel La. *Bing* —2D **50**
Chapel La. *Cotg* —2F **71**
Chapel La. *Epp* —5G **13**
Chapel La. *Lamb* —6B **24**
Chapel M. Ct. *Bramc* —3B **54**
Chapel Pl. *Kimb* —1H **29**
Chapel St. *Bees* —3B **54**
Chapel St. *Eastw* —4B **16**
Chapel St. *Hean* —5E **15**
Chapel St. *Huck* —4G **7**
Chapel St. *Ilk* —6B **28**
(in two parts)
Chapel St. *Kimb* —1H **29**
(in two parts)
Chapel St. *Long E* —6G **63**
Chapel St. *Nott* —4E **45**
Chapel St. *Rud* —1G **77**
Chapel St. Pl. *Ilk* —6B **28**
Chapman Ct. *Nott* —2H **43**
Chapmans Wlk. *B Vil* —5F **9**
Chapter Dri. *Kimb* —2A **30**
Chard St. *Nott* —5D **32**
Chard Ter. *Nott* —5D **32**
Charlbury Ct. *Bees* —5B **42**
Charlbury Rd. *Nott* —3G **43**
Charlecote Dri. *Nott* —6C **42**
Charlecote Pk. Dri. *W Bri* —1G **67**
Charles Av. *Bees* —2G **55**
(Derby Rd.)
Charles Av. *Bees* —2C **64**
(High Rd.)
Charles Av. *Eastw* —3D **16**
Charles Av. *Sand* —5D **52**
Charles Av. *S'fd* —3H **53**
Charles Clo. *Ged* —5H **35**
Charles Clo. *Ilk* —4D **28**
Charles St. *Arn* —6A **22**
Charles St. *Huck* —4G **7**
Charles St. *Long E* —1F **73**
Charles St. *Rud* —6G **67**
Charles Way. *Bulw* —2H **31**
Charles Way Bus. Pk. *Bulw* —2A **32**
Charlesworth Av. *Nott* —1C **44**

Charlock Clo. *Nott* —6C **20**
Charlock Gdns. *Bing* —6D **50**
Charlotte Clo. *Arn* —3A **22**
Charlotte Ct. *Eastw* —2B **16**
Charlotte Gro. *Bees* —2D **54**
Charlotte St. *Ilk* —4A **28**
Charlton Av. *Long E* —4H **63**
Charlton Gro. *Bees* —1F **65**
Charnock Av. *Nott* —5D **44**
Charnwood Av. *Bees* —5D **54**
Charnwood Av. *Keyw* —5G **79**
Charnwood Av. *Long E* —3D **72**
Charnwood Av. *Sand* —1C **62**
Charnwood Gdns. *Nott* —6F **33**
Charnwood Gro. *Bing* —5D **50**
Charnwood Gro. *Huck* —4D **6**
Charnwood Gro. *W Bri* —4A **58**
Charnwood La. *Arn* —1C **34**
Charnwood Way. *Wdbgh* —1C **24**
Charter Pk. *Ilk* —2A **40**
Chartwell Av. *Rud* —6F **67**
Chartwell Gro. *Nott* —2E **35**
Chase Pk. *Nott* —6C **46**
Chatham Ct. *Nott* —1A **32**
Chatham St. *Nott* —3G **45**
Chatsworth Av. *Bees* —3C **64**
Chatsworth Av. *Cltn* —1G **47**
Chatsworth Av. *Long E* —1A **74**
Chatsworth Av. *Nott* —5D **32**
Chatsworth Av. *Rad T* —5G **49**
Chatsworth Clo. *Sand* —1D **62**
Chatsworth Ct. *Huck* —5G **7**
Chatsworth Ct. *W Hal* —1B **38**
Chatsworth Dri. *Huck* —5G **7**
Chatsworth Pl. *Ilk* —4F **39**
Chatsworth Rd. *W Bri* —3D **58**
Chaucer St. *Ilk* —6B **28**
Chaucer St. *Nott* —4F **45** (2B **4**)
Chaworth Av. *Watn* —4A **18**
Chaworth Rd. *Bing* —5D **50**
Chaworth Rd. *Colw* —3H **47**
Chaworth Rd. *W Bri* —5A **58**
Cheadle Clo. *Bilb* —1D **42**
Cheadle Clo. *Map* —5D **34**
Cheapside. *Nott* —5G **45** (4E **5**)
Cheddar Rd. *Nott* —5C **66**
Chedington Av. *Nott* —1F **35**
Chediston Va. *Nott* —5F **21**
Chedworth Clo. *Nott* —4B **46**
Chelmsford Rd. *Nott* —5D **32**
Chelmsford Ter. *Nott* —5D **32**
(off Chelmsford Rd.)
Chelsbury Ct. *Arn* —6A **22**
Chelsea Clo. *Nut* —4E **31**
Chelsea St. *Nott* —6D **32**
Cheltenham Clo. *Bees* —3H **63**
Cheltenham St. *Nott* —3C **32**
Chennel Nook. *Cotg* —3G **71**
Chepstow Rd. *Nott* —5C **66**
Cherhill Clo. *Nott* —6B **66**
Cheriton Dri. *Ilk* —4G **27**
Cherry Av. *Huck* —6H **7**
Cherry Clo. *Arn* —5A **22**
Cherry Clo. *Breas* —5A **62**
Cherry Hill. *Keyw* —4H **79**
Cherry Orchard. *Cotg* —2E **71**
Cherry Orchard Mt. *Nott* —1F **33**
Cherry St. *Bing* —5F **51**
Cherry Tree Clo. *Ilk* —3H **39**
Cherry Tree Clo. *Rad T* —1F **61**
Cherry Tree Clo. *Ris* —1B **62**
Cherry Tree La. *Edw* —2D **68**
Cherry Wood Dri. *Nott* —2H **43**
Cherrywood Gdns. *Nott* —1C **46**
Chertsey Ct. *Nott* —6B **34**
Chertsey St. *W Hal* —1B **38**
Cherwell Ct. *Nott* —1F **31**
Chesham Clo. *Nut* —4D **30**
Chesham Dri. *Bees* —6B **42**
Chesham Dri. *Nott* —5F **33**
Cheshire Ct. *W Bri* —6H **57**
Chesil Av. *Nott* —4B **44**
Chesil Cotts. *Nott* —4B **44**
Cheslyn Dri. *Nott* —1A **44**
Chesnuts, The. *Ged* —6B **36**
Chesterfield Av. *Bing* —5E **51**
Chesterfield Av. *Ged* —4F **35**
Chesterfield Av. *Long E* —6H **63**
Chesterfield Ct. *Ged* —4F **35**
Chesterfield Dri. *Bur J* —2G **37**

Chesterfield St. *Cltn* —2F **47**
Chester Grn. *Bees* —3G **63**
Chesterman Dri. *Aws* —3D **28**
Chester Rd. *Nott* —4E **47**
Chestnut Av. *Bees* —5F **55**
Chestnut Av. *Bing* —5E **51**
Chestnut Av. *Nott* —5D **34**
Chestnut Bank. *Hean* —4B **14**
Chestnut Dri. *Nut* —6B **18**
Chestnut Gro. *Arn* —4C **22**
Chestnut Gro. *Bur J* —3F **37**
Chestnut Gro. *Ged* —6H **35**
Chestnut Gro. *Huck* —1H **19**
Chestnut Gro. *Nott* —2G **45**
Chestnut Gro. *Rad T* —5F **49**
Chestnut Gro. *Sand* —4C **52**
Chestnut Gro. *W Bri* —4H **57**
Chestnut La. *Bar F* —1E **75**
Chestnut Rd. *Lan M* —2E **15**
Chestnuts, The. *Long E* —5C **62**
Chestnuts, The. *Nott* —6B **34**
Chestnut, The. *Rad T* —6E **49**
Chettles Ind. Est. *Nott* —4B **44**
Chetwin Rd. *Nott* —4C **42**
Chetwynd Rd. *Bees* —2B **64**
(Highfield Rd.)
Chetwynd Rd. *Bees* —3A **64**
(High Rd.)
Cheverton Ct. *Nott* —2G **45**
Chevin Gdns. *Nott* —5E **21**
Cheviot Clo. *Arn* —3F **21**
Cheviot Ct. *Bees* —2C **64**
Cheviot Dri. *Nott* —5F **19**
Cheviot Rd. *Long E* —4C **62**
Chewton Av. *Eastw* —4C **16**
Chewton St. *Eastw* —4B **16**
Cheyny Clo. *Nott* —2G **57**
Chichester Clo. *Ilk* —1C **40**
Chichester Clo. *Nott* —6C **20**
Chichester Dri. *Cotg* —1E **71**
Chidlow Rd. *Nott* —2D **42**
Chigwell Clo. *Nut* —5D **30**
Chillon Way. *Huck* —5D **6**
Chiltern Clo. *Arn* —3F **21**
Chiltern Dri. *W Hal* —1C **38**
Chiltern Gdns. *Long E* —4C **62**
Chiltern Way. *Nott* —1F **33**
Chilton Dri. *Watn* —6A **18**
Chilvers Clo. *Nott* —6E **21**
Chilwell Ct. *Nott* —6B **20**
Chilwell La. *Bees* —4B **54**
Chilwell Manor Golf Course.
—1E **65**
Chilwell Meadows Nature
Reserve. —1D **64**
Chilwell Retail Pk. *Bees* —4B **64**
(in two parts)
Chilwell Rd. *Bees* —6F **55**
(in two parts)
Chilwell St. *Nott* —6D **44**
Chine Gdns. *W Bri* —6G **57**
Chingford Rd. *Nott* —1E **43**
Chippendale St. *Nott* —6D **44**
Chippenham Rd. *Nott* —1F **33**
Chisbury Grn. *Nott* —6B **66**
Chisholm Way. *Nott* —1E **33**
Chiswick Ct. *Nott* —4G **33**
Christchurch Rd. *Huck* —1D **18**
Christina Av. *Nott* —3A **32**
Christina Cres. *Nott* —3A **32**
Christine Clo. *Huck* —2A **8**
Christine Ct. *Nott* —2C **46**
Christopher Clo. *Nott* —4G **43**
Chrysalis Way. *Eastw* —2G **15**
Church Av. *Day* —6A **22**
Church Av. *Long E* —3C **72**
Church Av. *Nott* —6D **44**
Church Clo. *Day* —6A **22**
Church Clo. *Nott* —3G **45** (1E **5**)
Church Clo. *Trow* —5E **41**
Church Ct. *Cotg* —6E **49**
Church Cres. *Bees* —1A **64**
Church Cres. *Day* —6H **21**
Church Cft. *W Bri* —3B **58**
Churchdale Av. *S'fd* —2G **53**
Church Dri. *Day* —6H **21**
Church Dri. *Huck* —4G **7**
Church Dri. *Ilk* —2H **27**
Church Dri. *Keyw* —4G **79**

Church Dri. *Nott* —6F **33**
Church Dri. *Sand* —4D **52**
Church Dri. *W Bri* —4B **58**
Church Dri. E. *Day* —6A **22**
Churchfield Ct. *Nott* —4E **21**
Churchfield La. *Nott* —2C **44**
Churchfield Ter. *Nott* —5C **32**
Churchfield Way. *Nott* —4E **21**
Church Ga. *Cols B* —5C **70**
Church Gro. *Nott* —6C **44**
Church Hill. *Kimb* —1H **29**
Church Hill. *Plum* —1G **79**
Churchill Av. *Ilk* —1D **40**
Churchill Clo. *Arn* —1B **34**
Churchill Dri. *Rud* —6F **67**
Churchill Dri. *S'fd* —3G **53**
Church Pk. *Colw* —4H **47**
Church La. *Arn* —4A **22**
Church La. *Bar F* —1E **75**
Church La. *Bees* —4D **64**
Church La. *Bing* —5F **51**
Church La. *Bulw* —6A **20**
Church La. *Coss* —5E **29**
Church La. *Cotg* —2E **71**
Church La. *Epp* —5G **13**
Church La. *L'by & Huck* —1G **7**
Church La. *Plum* —6G **69**
Church La. *S'fd* —4F **53**
Church La. *Thrum* —4B **74**
Church Mdw. *C'tn* —5H **11**
Church M. *Nott* —2H **57**
Churchmoor Ct. *Arn* —4A **22**
Churchmoor La. *Arn* —4A **22**
Church Rd. *B Vil* —1C **20**
Church Rd. *Bur J* —3F **37**
Church Rd. *Greas* —3G **17**
Church Rd. *Newt* —1F **17**
Church Rd. *Nott* —2H **45**
Churchside Gdns. *Nott* —1C **44**
Church Sq. *Hean* —4D **14**
Church Sq. *Nott* —6D **44**
Church St. *Arn* —5B **22**
Church St. *Bees* —3B **54**
(Derby Rd.)
Church St. *Bees* —5F **55**
(Middle St.)
Church St. *Bing* —5F **51**
Church St. *Cltn* —2G **47**
Church St. *Eastw* —4A **16**
Church St. *Got* —6H **75**
Church St. *Hean* —4D **14**
Church St. *Ilk* —3H **27**
Church St. *Lamb* —5C **24**
Church St. *Lent* —6C **44**
(in two parts)
Church St. *Old B* —5C **32**
Church St. *Rud* —6G **67**
Church St. *Sand* —4D **52**
Church St. *Shelf* —6H **37**
Church St. *S'fd* —4F **53**
Church Vw. *Breas* —6A **62**
Church Vw. *Ged* —6H **35**
Church Vw. *Ilk* —2A **40**
Church Vw. *Los* —1A **14**
Church Vw. Clo. *Arn* —4F **21**
Church Wlk. *Cltn* —2G **47**
Church Wlk. *Eastw* —3B **16**
Church Wlk. *S'fd* —4F **53**
Church Wlk. *Wdbgh* —1C **24**
Church Way. *Ilk* —3H **27**
Church Wilne Water Sports Club.
—2A **72**
Churnet Clo. *Nott* —1C **66**
Churston Ct. *Bees* —5G **55**
Cinderhill Footway. *Nott* —3B **32**
Cinderhill Gro. *Ged* —5G **35**
Cinderhill Rd. *Nott* —3H **31**
Cinderhill Wlk. *Nott* —1H **31**
Citadel St. *Nott* —4C **44**
City Link. *Nott* —6H **45** (6G **5**)
City Rd. *Bees* —4G **55**
City Rd. *Nott* —2B **56**
City, The. *Bees* —5G **55**
(in two parts)
Clandon Dri. *Nott* —6D **32**
Clanfield Rd. *Nott* —2E **43**
Clapham St. *Nott* —4C **44**
Clara Mt. Rd. *Hean* —4E **15**
Clarborough Dri. *Arn* —1C **34**
Clare Clo. *Nott* —3C **32**

Clarehaven. *S'fd* —6G **53**
Claremont Av. *Bees* —3C **54**
Claremont Av. *Huck* —6G **7**
Claremont Dri. *W Bri* —2G **67**
Claremont Gdns. *Nott* —6F **33**
Claremont Rd. *Nott* —6F **33**
Claremont Ter. *Nott* —3E **45** (1A **4**)
Clarence Ct. *Nott* —4A **46** (3H **5**)
Clarence Rd. *Bees* —3D **64**
Clarence Rd. *Long E* —1E **73**
Clarence St. *Nott* —4A **46** (2H **5**)
Clarendon Chambers. *Nott*
—4F **45** (2C **4**)
Clarendon Ct. *Nott* —1F **45**
Clarendon Pk. *Nott* —1F **45**
Clarendon St. *Nott* —4F **45** (2B **4**)
Clare St. *Nott* —4G **45** (3E **5**)
Clare Valley. *Nott* —5B **45** (5B **4**)
Clarewood Gro. *Nott* —6C **66**
Clarges St. *Nott* —1A **32**
Clarke Av. *Arn* —5B **22**
Clarke Av. *Los* —3A **14**
Clarke Dri. *Long E* —3C **72**
Clarke Rd. *Nott* —1A **58**
Clarke's La. *Bees* —1D **64**
Clarkson Dri. *Bees* —5H **55**
Claude St. *Nott* —2C **56**
Claxton St. *Hean* —3B **14**
Claxton Ter. *Hean* —3B **14**
Clay Av. *Nott* —4C **34**
Claye St. *Long E* —6G **63**
Clayfield Clo. *Nott* —1G **31**
Claygate. *Nott* —2C **46**
Clay La. *Hean* —3D **14**
Claypole Rd. *Nott* —2D **44**
Clayton Ct. *Bees* —6G **55**
Clayton Ct. *Nott* —4D **44**
Clayton Gro. *Los* —1A **14**
Claytons Dri. *Nott* —1C **56**
Claytons Wharf. *Nott* —1C **56**
Clether Rd. *Nott* —3D **42**
Cleve Av. *Bees* —2G **63**
Cleveland Av. *Long E* —4H **63**
Cleveland Clo. *Nott* —4C **44**
Cleveley's Rd. *Bees* —2G **63**
Clevely Way. *Nott* —2C **66**
Cliff Boulevd. *Kimb* —6H **17**
(in two parts)
Cliff Cres. *Rad T* —5F **49**
Cliff Dri. *Rad T* —4G **49**
Cliffe Hill Av. *S'fd* —4F **53**
Cliffgrove Av. *Bees* —5D **54**
Cliffmere Wlk. *Nott* —4B **66**
(in two parts)
Clifford Av. *Bees* —3E **55**
Clifford Clo. *Keyw* —3H **79**
Clifford Clo. *Long E* —3C **72**
Clifford Ct. *Nott* —4D **44**
Clifford St. *Long E* —6G **63**
Clifford St. *Nott* —3D **44**
Cliff Rd. *Cltn* —3F **47**
Cliff Rd. *Nott* —5H **45** (5F **5**)
Cliff Rd. *Rad T* —5E **49**
Cliffs, The. *Rad T* —4G **49**
Cliff, The. *Nott* —3H **31**
Cliff Way. *Rad T* —5F **49**
Clifton Av. *Long E* —6A **64**
Clifton Av. *Rud* —5G **67**
Clifton Boulevd. *Nott* —1B **56**
Clifton Cres. *Bees* —2E **65**
Clifton Grn. *Nott* —3B **66**
Clifton Gro. *Ged* —5G **35**
Clifton La. *Nott & Rud* —5E **67**
Clifton Leisure Cen. —4D **66**
Clifton M. *Nott* —5E **45** (4A **4**)
Clifton Rd. *Nott* —6E **57**
Clifton Rd. *Rud* —6F **67**
Clifton St. *Bees* —5G **55**
Clifton Ter. *Nott* —6E **45** (6A **4**)
Clinton Av. *Nott* —4G **45** (3E **5**)
Clinton Ct. *Nott* —4G **45** (2D **4**)
Clinton St. *Arn* —6A **22**
Clinton St. *Bees* —4E **55**
Clinton St. E. *Nott* —4G **45** (3E **5**)
Clinton St. W. *Nott* —4G **45** (3E **5**)
Clinton Ter. *Nott* —4E **45** (3A **4**)
Clipstone Av. *Map* —3C **34**
Clipstone Av. *Nott* —3G **45** (1C **4**)
Clipstone Clo. *Strel* —5D **30**
Clipston La. *Plum* —6H **69**

Clive Cres. *Kimb* —2A **30**
Cliveden Grn. *Nott* —4B **66**
Clock Tower. —3C **44**
(Nottingham)
Cloister Sq. *Nott* —1C **56**
Cloisters, The. *Bees* —3G **55**
Cloister St. *Nott* —1C **56**
Close Quarters. *Bees* —3C **54**
Close, The. *Bees* —1D **64**
Close, The. *Nott* —4G **33**
Cloud Av. *S'fd* —4H **53**
Clouds Hill. *Nott* —5C **66**
Cloudside Ct. *Sand* —4D **52**
Cloudside Rd. *Sand* —4C **52**
Clough Ct. *Nott* —2H **43**
Cloverdale. *Cotg* —3G **71**
Cloverfields. *C'tn* —3A **12**
Clover Grn. *Nott* —4B **32**
Cloverlands. *W Bri* —2G **67**
Cloverlands Ct. *Watn* —6A **18**
Cloverlands Dri. *Watn* —6A **18**
Clover Ri. *Newt* —4D **16**
Club Row. *Nott* —1A **40**
Clumber Av. *Bees* —6D **54**
Clumber Av. *Map* —3C **34**
Clumber Av. *N'fld* —2A **48**
Clumber Av. *Sher R* —1F **45**
Clumber Ct. *Ilk* —2B **28**
Clumber Ct. *Nott* —6E **45** (6A **4**)
Clumber Cres. N. *Nott*
—5E **45** (4A **4**)
Clumber Cres. S. *Nott*
—6E **45** (6A **4**)
Clumber Dri. *Rad T* —4G **49**
Clumber Rd. *W Bri* —4B **58**
Clumber Rd. E. *Nott* —5E **45** (5A **4**)
Clumber Rd. W. *Nott*
—5E **45** (5A **4**)
Clumber St. *Huck* —5A **8**
Clumber St. *Long E* —6F **63**
Clumber St. *Nott* —4G **45** (3E **5**)
Clyde Ter. *Nott* —3E **45** (1A **4**)
Coach Dri. *Eastw* —1B **16**
Coachmans Cft. *Nott* —4G **43**
Coachways. *M'ley* —4D **26**
Coates Av. *Huck* —2F **7**
Coatsby Rd. *Kimb* —6H **17**
Cobden Chambers. *Nott*
—5H **45** (4E **5**)
Cobden St. *Long E* —6F **63**
Cobden St. *Nott* —4C **44**
Cockayne Clo. *Sand* —2D **62**
Cocker Beck. *Lamb* —6C **24**
Cockington Rd. *Nott* —4C **42**
Cockleys. *Long E* —1E **73**
Codrington Gdns. *Nott* —5G **21**
Cogenhoe Wlk. *Arn* —3B **22**
Cogley La. *Bing* —5G **51**
Cohen Clo. *Arn* —1D **34**
Cokefield Av. *Nut* —4F **31**
Colborn St. *Nott* —2B **46**
Colchester Rd. *Nott* —6E **31**
Coleby Av. *Nott* —1C **56**
Coleby Rd. *Nott* —5F **31**
Coledale. *W Bri* —6E **58**
Coleridge Cres. *Day* —6H **21**
Coleridge St. *Nott* —3C **44**
Colesbourne Rd. *Nott* —3D **66**
Coles Wlk. *Nott* —5E **21**
Colin Broughton Ct. *Nott* —6B **20**
Colindale Gdns. *Nut* —4D **30**
Colinwood Av. *Nott* —4C **20**
College Dri. *Nott* —2B **66**
(Clifton La.)
College Dri. *Nott* —3B **66**
(Village Rd.)
College Rd. *Bees* —6E **55**
College St. *Long E* —2D **62**
College St. *Nott* —4F **45** (3B **4**)
Colley Moor Leys La. *Nott* —3D **66**
Colliers Way. *Nott* —3G **31**
Colliery Clo. *Nott* —2F **57**
Collin Av. *Sand* —1D **62**
Collin Grn. *Nott* —3H **33**
Collington St. *Bees* —5E **55**
Collington Way. *W Bri* —6H **57**
Collingwood Clo. *Nott* —1H **67**
Collingwood Rd. *Long E* —1F **73**
Collins Clo. *Nott* —2F **31**

Collins Homes. *Bees* —2E **55**
Collin St. *Bees* —5F **55**
Collin St. *Nott* —6G **45** (6E **5**)
Collison St. *Nott* —3D **44**
Collyer Rd. *C'tn* —3E **11**
Colly Ga. *Kimb* —2A **30**
Collygate Rd. *Nott* —2H **57**
Colmon Clo. *Nott* —6E **21**
Colmon Wlk. *Nott* —6E **21**
Colonsay Clo. *Trow* —6F **41**
Colston Cres. *W Bri* —1H **67**
Colston St. *Cotg* —2F **71**
Colston Rd. *Nott* —5A **20**
Coltsfoot Clo. *Bing* —6C **50**
Colville Ct. *Nott* —2F **45**
Colville St. *Nott* —2F **45**
Colville Ter. *Nott* —2F **45**
(in two parts)
Colville Vs. *Nott* —2F **45**
Colwick Bus. Pk. *Colw* —4H **47**
Colwick Country Pk. —6F **47**
Colwick Ind. Est. *Colw* —4H **47**
(in two parts)
Colwick Lodge. *Cltn* —3H **47**
Colwick Loop Rd. *Colw* —4G **47**
Colwick Mnr. Farm. *Colw* —4G **47**
Colwick Pk. Clo. *Colw* —4G **47**
Colwick Rd. *Nott* —6B **46**
(in two parts)
Colwick Wood Ct. *Nott* —5C **46**
Comery Av. *Nott* —3C **46**
Comet Dri. *Eastw* —3C **16**
Comfrey Clo. *Nott* —6C **20**
Commerce Sq. *Nott* —5H **45** (5F **5**)
Commercial Av. *Bees* —5F **55**
Commercial Rd. *Keyw* —5G **79**
Commercial Rd. *Nott* —6H **19**
(in two parts)
Commodore Gdns. *Nott* —5A **32**
Common Clo. *Newt* —5C **16**
Common La. *Bees* —5A **54**
Common La. *Huck* —5D **6**
Common La. *Stan & Stan C*
—4A **38**
Common La. *Watn* —6B **18**
Commons Clo. *Newt* —5C **16**
Common, The. *Huck* —5C **6**
Compton Acres. *W Bri* —5F **57**
Compton Acres Shop. Cen. *W Bri*
—6G **57**
Compton Rd. *Nott* —4F **33**
Comyn Gdns. *Nott* —3H **45** (1F **5**)
Condor Rd. *Quar H* —5B **40**
Conduit Clo. *Nott* —1G **57**
Coney Wlk. *Nott* —6C **20**
Conifer Cres. *Nott* —6C **66**
Conifer Wlk. *Nott* —2C **46**
Coningsby Gdns. E. *Wd'p* —3B **34**
Coningsby Rd. *Wd'p* —2B **34**
Coningswath Rd. *Cltn* —5E **35**
Conisborough Ter. *Nott* —2G **57**
Conisbrough Av. *Ged* —6B **36**
Coniston Av. *Nott* —5A **32**
Coniston Clo. *Gam* —4E **59**
Coniston Dri. *Ilk* —4H **39**
Coniston Rd. *Bees* —2D **54**
Coniston Rd. *Huck* —3F **7**
Coniston Rd. *Long E* —3C **62**
Connelly Clo. *Arn* —1E **35**
Connelly Ct. *Bulw* —2B **32**
Connery. *Huck* —3G **7**
Connery M. *Bees* —4B **64**
Constance St. *Nott* —6E **33**
Convent St. *Nott* —4H **45** (3F **5**)
Conway Av. *Cltn* —2A **48**
Conway Clo. *Nott* —2G **45**
Conway Cres. *Arn* —1A **34**
Conway Gdns. *Arn* —1A **34**
Conway Rd. *Cltn* —2H **47**
Conway Rd. *Huck* —2D **18**
Conway St. *Long E* —5G **63**
Conway Wlk. *Nott* —2G **45**
Cook Dri. *Ilk* —3C **40**
Cooke Clo. *Long E* —6G **63**
Cookson Av. *Ged* —5F **35**
Coombe Clo. *Nott* —6A **44**
Coombe Rd. *Newt* —1D **16**
Co-operative Av. *Huck* —3H **7**
Co-operative St. *Long E* —6G **63**

Cooper Clo. *Arn* —1E **35**
Cooper Clo. *Nott* —1F **31**
Coopers Grn. *Nott* —1E **55**
Cooper St. *N'fld* —3A **48**
Copeland Av. *S'fd* —3G **53**
Copeland Gro. *Bing* —4C **50**
Copeland Rd. *Huck* —3A **8**
Copenhagen Ct. *Nott* —6H **33**
Cope St. *Nott* —3D **44**
Coppice Av. *Ilk* —2H **27**
Coppice Clo. *Huck* —6E **7**
Coppice Dri. *Eastw* —2H **15**
Coppice Dri. *Hean* —6D **14**
Coppice Ga. *Arn* —5B **22**
Coppice Gro. *Nott* —5B **34**
Coppice Rd. *Arn* —5B **22**
Copplestone Dri. *Nott* —1E **35**
Copse Clo. *Bur J* —2F **37**
Copseside Clo. *Long E* —5C **62**
Copse, The. *Bees* —5C **54**
Copse, The. *Huck* —5A **8**
Copse, The. *Ilk* —2H **27**
Corben Gdns. *Nott* —6F **19**
Corby Rd. *Nott* —6A **34**
Corfield Av. *Hean* —6D **14**
Coriander Dri. *Nott* —4B **32**
Corinth Rd. *Nott* —3C **66**
Corn Clo. *Cotg* —3E **71**
Corncrake Av. *Nott* —4B **32**
Cornell Dri. *Arn* —5D **22**
Cornfield Rd. *Kimb* —6G **17**
Cornfields, The. *Nott* —5F **21**
Cornhill Rd. *Cltn* —1D **46**
Cornwall Av. *Bees* —1A **66**
Cornwall Rd. *Long E* —5A **64**
Cornwallis Clo. *Long E* —1F **73**
Cornwall Rd. *Arn* —6G **21**
Coronation Av. *Nott* —3F **57**
Coronation Av. *Sand* —4C **52**
Coronation Rd. *B Vil* —6C **8**
Coronation Rd. *Coss* —5D **28**
Coronation Rd. *Huck* —3F **7**
Coronation Rd. *M'ley* —4D **26**
Coronation Rd. *Nott* —4B **34**
Coronation Rd. *Nut* —2B **30**
Coronation Rd. *Stan* —3A **38**
Coronation St. *Ilk* —1B **40**
Coronation Wlk. *Ged* —6A **36**
Corporation Cotts. *Bul* —2H **37**
Corporation Oaks. *Nott* —2G **45**
Corporation Rd. *Ilk* —4C **40**
Corsham Gdns. *Nott* —2C **46**
Cosby Rd. *Nott* —6B **46**
Cossall Ind. Est. *Coss* —5D **28**
Cossall Rd. *Trow* —2E **41**
Costock Av. *Nott* —3F **33**
Cotgrave Av. *Ged* —5H **35**
Cotgrave Clo. *Strel* —5E **31**
Cotgrave La. *Toll* —2H **69**
Cotgrave Leisure and Cen., The.
—2G **71**
Cotgrave Rd. *Cotg* —5H **71**
Cotgrave Rd. *Plum* —6H **69**
Cotgrave Shop. Cen. *Cotg* —2F **71**
Cotmanhay Rd. *Ilk* —4A **28**
Coton Clo. *Nott* —2E **67**
Cotswold Clo. *Long E* —5C **62**
Cotswold Ct. *Bees* —2D **54**
Cotswold Rd. *Nott* —6D **30**
Cottage Clo. *Ilk* —4H **27**
Cottage Garden La. *Hean* —3B **14**
Cottage Mdw. *Colw* —5H **47**
Cottage Ter. *Nott* —4E **45** (3A **4**)
Cottam Dri. *Nott* —5D **20**
Cottam Gdns. *Nott* —5E **21**
Cottesmore Rd. *Nott* —5D **44**
County Bus. Pk. *Nott* —6A **46**
County Clo. *Bees* —6G **55**
County House. —5H **45** (5F **5**)
(off High Pavement)
County Rd. *Ged* —4E **35**
County Rd. *Nott* —1A **58**
Court Cres. *Nott* —5F **43**
Courtenay Gdns. *Nott* —2H **45**
Court Gdns. *W Bri* —1F **67**
Courtleet Way. *Nott* —2H **31**
Courtney Clo. *Nott* —4E **43**
Court St. *Nott* —2D **44**
Court, The. *Bees* —3A **64**

Court Vw. *Nott* —5E **45** (4A **4**)
Court Yd. *Bees* —3B **54**
Covedale Rd. *Nott* —2G **33**
Coventry Ct. *Nott* —2H **31**
Coventry La. *Bees* —2H **53**
Coventry Rd. *Bees* —4G **55**
Coventry Rd. *Nott* —6H **19**
(in two parts)
Covert Clo. *Bur J* —2E **37**
Covert Clo. *Huck* —5A **8**
Covert Clo. *Keyw* —3H **79**
Covert Cres. *Rad T* —6H **49**
Covert Rd. *W Bri* —5D **58**
Cowdrey Gdns. *Arn* —1D **34**
Cowen St. *Nott* —4H **45** (3F **5**)
Cowlairs. *Nott* —6C **20**
Cow La. *Bees* —3B **54**
Cowley St. *Old B* —4B **32**
Cowper Rd. *Newt* —5C **16**
Cowper Rd. *Wd'p* —3A **34**
Cowslip Clo. *Bing* —5C **50**
Coxmoor Clo. *Edw* —1E **69**
Coxmoor Ct. *Nott* —4E **21**
Crabtree Fld. *Colw P* —5F **47**
Crabtree Rd. *Nott* —1G **31**
Cragdale Rd. *Nott* —2G **33**
Cragmoor Rd. *Bur J* —4E **37**
Craig Moray. *Rad T* —5G **49**
Craig St. *Long E* —6G **63**
Crammond Clo. *Nott* —1F **57**
Crampton Ct. *Nott* —5E **21**
Cramworth Gro. *Nott* —4H **33**
Cranberry Clo. *W Bri* —5F **57**
Cranborne Clo. *Trow* —1F **53**
Cranbourne Gro. *Huck* —4E **7**
Cranbrook St. *Nott* —4H **45** (3F **5**)
Cranfield Wlk. *Nott* —3D **66**
Cranfleet Way. *Long E* —6C **62**
Cranford Gdns. *W Bri* —1G **67**
Cranmer Gro. *Nott* —2G **45**
Cranmer St. *Long E* —5F **63**
Cranmer St. *Nott* —2G **45**
Cranmer Wlk. *Nott* —2G **45**
Cranmore Clo. *Arn* —3C **22**
Cransley Av. *Nott* —1D **54**
Cranston Av. *Arn* —4B **22**
Cranston Rd. *Bees* —2C **54**
Cranthorne Dri. *Nott* —3E **47**
Crantock Gdns. *Keyw* —4H **79**
Cranwell Ct. *Nott* —1F **31**
Cranwell Rd. *Nott* —6D **30**
Craster Dri. *Arn* —3C **22**
Craster Dri. *Nott* —5F **19**
Craven Rd. *Nott* —2C **44**
Crawford Av. *S'fd* —3F **53**
Crawford Clo. *Nott* —4E **43**
Crawford Ri. *Arn* —5E **23**
Creeton Grn. *Nott* —5D **66**
Crescent Av. *Cltn* —6G **35**
Crescent, The. *Bees* —2C **64**
(Attenborough La. N.)
Crescent, The. *Bees* —3A **64**
(Chetwynd Rd.)
Crescent, The. *Eastw* —3C **16**
Crescent, The. *Nott* —1H **45**
Crescent, The. *Rad T* —6G **49**
Crescent, The. *Ris* —2A **62**
Crescent, The. *Stan C* —1A **38**
Crescent, The. *S'fd* —2G **53**
Crescent, The. *Wd'p* —3A **34**
Cresswell Rd. *Bees* —6B **54**
Cressy Rd. *Nott* —3D **66**
Cresta Gdns. *Nott* —5H **33**
Crest Vw. *Nott* —4F **33**
Crewe Clo. *Nott* —3D **44**
Cribb Clo. *Nott* —4F **57**
Crich Vw. *Nott* —5G **33**
Cricketers Ct. *W Bri* —2B **58**
Criftin Rd. *Bur J* —3G **37**
Cripps Hill. *Nott* —1A **56**
Critchley St. *Ilk* —6B **28**
Critch's Flat. *Kimb* —1H **29**
Crocus Pl. *Nott* —6H **45**
Crocus St. *Nott* —1G **57**
Croft Av. *Huck* —6G **7**
Croft Cres. *Aws* —2E **29**
Crofton Clo. *Bees* —2D **64**
Crofton Clo. *Nott* —3H **43**
Crofton Rd. *Bees* —3D **64**

Croft Rd. *Arn* —5B **22**
Croft Rd. *Edw* —1C **68**
Croft Rd. *Keyw* —4F **79**
Crofts, The. *Bing* —5E **51**
Cromarty Ct. *Nott* —1F **57**
Cromdale Clo. *Arn* —4E **23**
Cromer Rd. *Nott* —2A **46**
Cromford Av. *Cltn* —1F **47**
Cromford Clo. *Lan M* —1F **15**
Cromford Clo. *Long E* —2C **72**
Cromford Rd. *Lan M* —1D **14**
Cromford Rd. *W Bri* —5B **58**
Cromford Rd. Ind. Est. *Lan M*
—1F **15**
Crompton Rd. *Ilk* —1D **52**
Crompton Rd. Ind. Est. *Ilk* —6D **40**
Cromwell Av. *Ilk* —4C **40**
Cromwell Cres. *Lamb* —6B **24**
Cromwell Rd. *Bees* —4E **55**
Cromwell St. *Cltn* —2G **47**
Cromwell St. *Gilt* —5D **16**
Cromwell St. *Nott* —4E **45** (2A **4**)
Cromwell Ter. *Ilk* —4B **28**
Crookdole La. *C'tn* —4H **11**
Cropston Clo. *W Bri* —1A **68**
Cropton Cres. *Nott* —3H **43**
Cropton Gro. *Bing* —5C **50**
Cropwell Gdns. *Rad T* —1G **61**
Cropwell Grn. *Nott* —3B **46**
Cropwell Rd. *Rad T* —6F **49**
Crosby Rd. *W Bri* —2B **58**
Crossdale Dri. *Keyw* —3G **79**
Crossdale Wlk. *Nott* —5C **20**
Crossfield Ct. *Nott* —5E **21**
Crossfield Dri. *Nott* —5E **21**
Crossgate Dri. *Q Dri & Nott*
—3E **57**
Crosshill. *Cotg* —2G **71**
Crosshill Dri. *Ilk* —4G **39**
Crosslands Mdw. *Colw* —5H **47**
Cross Lea. *Dal A* —6D **38**
Crossley St. *Nott* —5F **33**
Crossman St. *Nott* —5F **33**
Cross St. *Arn* —5H **21**
Cross St. *Bees* —4F **55**
Cross St. *Cltn* —1F **47**
Cross St. *Eastw* —3C **16**
Cross St. *Long E* —5G **63**
Cross St. *N'fld* —2A **48**
Cross St. *Sand* —5E **53**
Cross, The. *Cotg* —2E **71**
Crowborough Av. *Nott* —1E **55**
Crow Ct. *Bing* —5G **51**
Crowcroft Way. *Long E* —3D **62**
Crow Hill Rd. *Cltn* —2H **47**
Crowley Clo. *Nott* —3C **42**
Crown Clo. *Long E* —6C **62**
Crown Hill Way. *Stan C* —1A **38**
Crow Pk. Dri. *Bur J* —4E **37**
Crowthorne Clo. *Nott* —4C **20**
Crowthorne Gdns. *Nott* —4C **20**
Croxall Clo. *Nott* —1C **66**
Croxley Gdns. *Nut* —4D **30**
Croydon Rd. *Nott* —4C **44**
Crummock Clo. *Bees* —3C **54**
Crusader Ct. *Nott* —4A **66**
Cuillin Clo. *Long E* —4C **62**
Cuillin Clo. *Nott* —3D **20**
Culbert Lodge. *Nott* —6D **32**
Culbert Pl. *Nott* —6D **32**
Culdrose Wlk. *Nott* —6A **34**
Cullens Ct. *Nott* —5G **33**
Cumberland Av. *Bees* —5D **54**
Cumberland Clo. *Rud* —6G **67**
Cumberland Pl. *Nott* —5F **45** (4C **4**)
Cumbria Grange. *Gam* —4E **59**
Curie Ct. *Nott* —1C **56**
Curlew Clo. *Nott* —4F **57**
Curlew Wharf. *Nott* —1E **57**
Cursley Way. *Bees* —3C **64**
Curtis St. *Huck* —5G **7**
Curzon Av. *Cltn* —2D **46**
Curzon Ct. *Nott* —3H **45** (1G **5**)
Curzon Gdns. *Nott* —3H **45** (1G **5**)
Curzon Pl. *Nott* —4H **45** (2F **5**)
Curzon St. *Got* —6H **75**
Curzon St. *Long E* —3D **62**
Curzon St. *N'fld* —2A **48**
Curzon St. *Nott* —4H **45** (2F **5**)
Cutthrough La. *Nott* —3H **55**

Cuxton Clo. *Nott* —6D **30**
Cycle Rd. *Nott* —5C **44**
Cypress Ct. *Huck* —6C **6**
Cyprus Av. *Bees* —4F **55**
Cyprus Ct. *Nott* —1G **45**
Cyprus Dri. *Bees* —4F **55**
Cyprus Rd. *Nott* —1G **45**
Cyril Av. *Bees* —4E **55**
Cyril Av. *Nott* —1B **44**
Cyril Av. *S'fd* —4F **53**
Cyril Rd. *W Bri* —3C **58**

Dabell Av. *Nott* —5E **19**
Dagmar Gro. *Bees* —5G **55**
Dagmar Gro. *Nott* —6H **33**
Daisy Clo. *Cotg* —3E **71**
Daisy Farm Rd. *Newt* —4D **16**
Daisy Rd. *Nott* —6C **34**
Dakeyne St. *Nott* —4A **46** (3H **5**)
Dalbeattie Clo. *Arn* —4D **22**
Dalby Sq. *Nott* —6A **44**
Dale Av. *Cltn* —2E **47**
Dale Av. *Long E* —4F **63**
Dale Av. *Map* —5C **34**
Dalebrook Cres. *Huck* —5C **6**
Dale Clo. *Breas* —5A **62**
Dale Clo. *Huck* —5C **6**
Dale Clo. *W Bri* —4D **58**
Dale Farm Av. *Nott* —4C **46**
Dale Gro. *Nott* —5B **46**
Dalehead Rd. *Nott* —3B **66**
Dale La. *Bees* —5E **55**
Dalemoor Gdns. *Nott* —1H **43**
Dale Rd. *Cltn* —2E **47**
Dale Rd. *Keyw* —4G **79**
Dale Rd. *Kimb* —2H **29**
Dale Rd. *Stan* —4A **38**
Dale Rd. *Stan D* —2A **52**
Daleside. *Cotg* —3E **71**
Daleside Rd. *Nott* —6B **46**
Daleside Rd. E. *Nott* —5D **46**
Dales Shop. Cen. *W Hal* —2C **38**
Dale St. *Ilk* —2B **40**
Dale St. *Nott* —5A **46**
Dale Ter. *Nott* —5B **46**
Dale Vw. *Ilk* —3A **40**
Dale Vw. Rd. *Nott* —2D **46**
Dalkeith Ter. *Nott* —2D **44**
Dallas-York Rd. *Bees* —5H **55**
Dalley Clo. *S'fd* —4G **53**
Dallimore Rd. *Ilk* —5H **39**
Dalton Clo. *S'fd* —6G **53**
Daltons Clo. *Lan M* —1E **15**
Damson Wlk. *Nott* —1D **46**
Danbury Mt. *Nott* —5H **33**
Dane Clo. *Nott* —3H **45** (1F **5**)
Dane Ct. *Nott* —3H **45** (1F **5**)
Danes Clo. *Arn* —5H **21**
Danethorpe Va. *Nott* —3G **33**
Daniels Way. *Huck* —1E **19**
Darfield Dri. *Hean* —3E **15**
Darkey La. *S'fd* —6G **53**
(in two parts)
Dark La. *Bing* —5G **51**
Dark La. *C'tn* —5G **11**
Darley Av. *Bees* —2G **63**
Darley Av. *Cltn* —6G **35**
Darley Av. *Nott* —2C **44**
Darley Dri. *Long E* —2C **72**
Darley Dri. *W Hal* —1C **38**
Darley Rd. *Nott* —2C **44**
Darley Sq. *Ilk* —2A **28**
Darlton Dri. *Arn* —6C **22**
Darnall Clo. *Nott* —6C **20**
Darnhall Cres. *Nott* —2D **42**
Daron Gdns. *Nott* —6E **21**
Dartmeet Ct. *Nott* —2B **44**
Darvel Clo. *Nott* —3H **43**
Darwin Av. *Ilk* —2A **40**
Darwin Clo. *Nott* —5C **20**
Darwin Rd. *Long E* —2D **72**
David Gro. *Bees* —2E **55**
David La. *Nott* —4B **32**
Davidson Clo. *Arn* —6E **23**
Davidson St. *Nott* —6B **46**
Davies Rd. *W Bri* —4B **58**
Davy Clo. *L'by* —1H **57**
Dawlish Clo. *Huck* —5D **6**
Dawlish Ct. *Eastw* —2H **15**

Dawlish Dri. *Nott* —2F **33**
Dawn Clo. *Huck* —2A **8**
Dawn Vw. *Trow* —1F **53**
Dawson Clo. *Newt* —4C **16**
Dawver Rd. *Kimb* —2H **29**
Daybrook Av. *Nott* —4G **33**
Daybrook Bus. Cen. *Nott* —1H **33**
Daybrook St. *Nott* —4G **33**
Deabill St. *N'fld* —3A **48**
Dead La. *Coss* —6F **29**
Deakins Pl. *Nott* —4C **44**
Deal Gdns. *Nott* —6F **19**
Dean Av. *Nott* —4D **34**
Dean Clo. *Nott* —4D **42**
Dean Rd. *Wd'p* —2A **34**
Deanscourt. *Cotg* —2G **71**
Deans Cft. *Bees* —2B **54**
Dean St. *Lan M* —2G **15**
Dean St. *Nott* —5H **45** (5G **5**)
Debdale La. *Keyw* —4F **79**
Deddington La. *Bees* —1B **54**
(in two parts)
Deepdale Av. *Ilk* —4H **39**
Deepdale Av. *S'fd* —5F **53**
Deepdale Clo. *Gam* —4D **58**
Deepdale Ct. *Hean* —4C **14**
Deepdale Rd. *Long E* —1C **72**
Deepdale Rd. *Nott* —5D **42**
Deepdene Clo. *Nott* —5G **31**
Deepdene Way. *Nott* —5G **31**
Deep Furrow Av. *Cltn* —1F **47**
Deering Ct. *Nott* —1F **57**
Deerleap Dri. *Arn* —6G **21**
Deer Pk. *Nott* —5E **43**
Deer Pk. Dri. *Arn* —5F **21**
Delia Av. *Huck* —2A **8**
Dell Way. *Nott* —3D **66**
Dellwood Clo. *Cltn* —5D **34**
Delta Ct. *Nott* —3F **45**
Delta St. *Nott* —6D **32**
Delves Ct. *Hean* —5C **14**
Delves Rd. *Hean* —5B **14**
Delville Av. *Keyw* —3G **79**
Denacre Av. *Long E* —4H **63**
Denehurst Av. *Nott* —6A **32**
Denewood Av. *Bees* —1C **54**
Denewood Cres. *Nott* —1E **43**
Denholme Rd. *Nott* —4D **42**
Denison St. *Bees* —4E **55**
Denison St. *Nott* —3D **44**
Denman St. *Nott* —4D **44**
Denman St. Central. *Nott* —4C **44**
(in three parts)
Denmark Gro. *Nott* —6H **33**
Dennett Clo. *Nott* —3A **46** (1H **5**)
Dennis Av. *Bees* —3E **55**
Dennis St. *N'fld* —2A **48**
Denstone Rd. *Nott* —4A **46**
Dentdale Dri. *Nott* —5B **42**
Denton Av. *Sand* —5C **52**
Denton Dri. *W Bri* —1H **67**
Denton Grn. *Nott* —5F **31**
Denver Ct. *S'fd* —1G **53**
(Crescent, The)
Denver Ct. *S'fd* —2G **53**
(Melbourne Rd.)
Deptford Cres. *Nott* —1A **32**
(in two parts)
Derby Gro. *Nott* —4D **44**
Derby Rd. *Bees & Nott*
—3A **54** (3A **4**)
Derby Rd. *Hean* —4B **14**
Derby Rd. *Ilk* —2G **39**
Derby Rd. *Lan M* —2G **15**
Derby Rd. *Long E* —5C **62**
Derby Rd. *Nott* —4E **45**
Derby Rd. *Ris & Sand* —1A **62**
Derby Rd. *S'fd* —6E **53**
Derby Rd. Ind. Est. *Hean* —4B **14**
Derbyshire Av. *Trow* —5F **41**
Derbyshire Av. *W Hal* —1C **38**
Derbyshire Cres. *Nott* —4G **43**
Derbyshire Dri. *Ilk* —3A **40**
Derbyshire La. *Huck* —4G **7**
Derby St. *Arn* —6B **22**
Derby St. *Bees* —4F **55**
Derby St. *Ilk* —1B **40**
Derby St. *Nott* —4F **45** (3B **4**)
Derby Ter. *Nott* —4E **45** (3A **4**)

Dereham Dri.—Elliot Durham Swimming Pool

Dereham Dri. *Arn* —1B **34**
Derry Dri. *Arn* —3B **22**
Derry Hill Rd. *Arn* —4A **22**
Derry La. *Bing* —6H **51**
Derwent Av. *Ilk* —5H **27**
Derwent Av. *W Hal* —1C **38**
Derwent Clo. *Bees* —2E **65**
Derwent Clo. *Gam* —4E **59**
Derwent Ct. *Nott* —3E **45**
Derwent Cres. *Arn* —1C **34**
Derwent Dri. *Huck* —1G **19**
Derwent St. *Long E* —1D **72**
Derwent St. Ind. Est. *Long E*
—1E **73**
Derwent Ter. *Nott* —5G **33**
Desford Clo. *Nott* —3E **33**
De Vere Gdns. *Wd'p* —2B **34**
Devitt Dri. *Huck* —2A **8**
Devon Cir. *Red* —4H **21**
Devon Clo. *Sand* —6D **52**
Devon Dri. *Nott* —5F **33**
Devon Dri. *Rud* —5H **67**
Devonshire Av. *Bees* —5E **55**
Devonshire Av. *Long E* —5A **64**
Devonshire Clo. *Ilk* —2A **28**
Devonshire Cres. *Nott* —5F **33**
Devonshire Dri. *Eastw* —3B **16**
Devonshire Dri. *S'fd* —1F **53**
Devonshire Promenade. *Nott*
—6C **44**
Devonshire Rd. *Nott* —5F **33**
Devonshire Rd. *W Bri* —5A **58**
Devon St. *Ilk* —4C **40**
Devon St. *Nott* —4B **46**
Dewberry La. *Rad T* —1H **61**
Dial, The. *Cotg* —3E **71**
Dickens Ct. *Newt* —2D **16**
Dickson Dri. *Rud* —1H **77**
Didcot Dri. *Nott* —6B **32**
Digby Av. *Nott* —4D **34**
Digby Av. *Woll* —5H **43**
Digby Ct. *Nott* —6D **44**
Digby Hall Dri. *Ged* —4E **35**
Digby St. *Ilk* —6C **28**
Digby St. *Kimb* —1F **29**
Dirac Clo. *Nott* —5A **66**
Diseworth Gro. *Nott* —2H **57**
Distillery St. *Long E* —1G **77**
Djanogly Arts Cen. & Recital Hall.
—2B **56**
Dockholm Rd. *Long E* —3E **63**
Dodford Ct. *Hean* —4E **15**
Dogwood Av. *Nott* —6F **19**
Dolphin Ct. *Nott* —5E **21**
Donbas Clo. *Bulw* —3H **31**
Doncaster Av. *Sand* —5D **52**
Doncaster Gro. *Long E* —4H **63**
Doncaster Ter. *Nott* —2G **57**
Donington Rd. *Nott* —4C **66**
Donner Cres. *Ilk* —2A **28**
Dooland Dri. *Nott* —6B **34**
Dorchester Gdns. *W Bri* —2A **68**
Dorchester Rd. *Kimb* —6H **17**
Doris Ct. *Bees* —3A **64**
Doris Rd. *Ilk* —2C **40**
Dorket Clo. *Arn* —4C **22**
Dorket Dri. *Nott* —6B **44**
*Dorket Ho. Cltn —1G **47***
(off Foxhill Rd. E.)
Dorking Rd. *Nott* —3C **44**
Dormy Clo. *Bees* —4C **54**
Dormy Clo. *Rad T* —6H **49**
Dormy Ct. *Nott* —6B **20**
Dornoch Av. *Nott* —5H **33**
Dorothy Av. *Huck* —2H **7**
Dorothy Av. *Newt* —2C **16**
Dorothy Av. *Sand* —6D **52**
Dorothy Boot Homes, The. *Nott*
—3F **57**
Dorothy Courts. *Ilk* —1A **40**
Dorothy Gro. *Nott* —3A **44**
Dorset Gdns. *W Bri* —6G **57**
Dorset St. *Nott* —4B **44**
Dorterry Cres. *Ilk* —4C **40**
Douglas Av. *Aws* —2E **29**
Douglas Av. *Cltn* —3F **47**
Douglas Av. *Hean* —3A **14**
Douglas Clo. *Rad T* —1F **61**
Douglas Cres. *Bees* —3A **64**
Douglas Cres. *Cltn* —3G **47**

Douglas Rd. *Bing* —5H **51**
Douglas Rd. *Long E* —3D **62**
Douglas Rd. *Nott* —4D **44**
Douro Dri. *Arn* —4D **22**
Dove Clo. *Bing* —6F **51**
Dovecote Dri. *Nott* —5E **43**
Dovecote La. *Bees* —5F **55**
Dovecote Rd. *Eastw & Newt*
—3D **16**
Dovecotes, The. *Bees* —6F **55**
Dovedale Av. *Long E* —1C **72**
Dovedale Circ. *Ilk* —2A **28**
Dovedale Ct. *Long E* —1D **72**
Dovedale Rd. *Nott* —3E **47**
Dovedale Rd. *W Bri* —6C **58**
Dove La. *Long E* —4E **63**
Dovenby Rd. *Nott* —2D **66**
Dover Beck Clo. *C'tn* —4A **12**
Dover Beck Dri. *Wdbgh* —1C **24**
Doveridge Av. *Cltn* —1A **48**
Doveridge Rd. *Cltn* —1H **47**
Dove St. *Nott* —6H **19**
Doveys Orchard. *C'tn* —4F **11**
Downes Clo. *Nott* —6G **19**
Downham Clo. *Arn* —1C **34**
Downing Gdns. *Nott* —5H **19**
Downing St. *Nott* —5H **19**
Downs, The. *Nott* —2E **67**
Dowson St. *Nott* —3B **46**
Doyne Ct. *Nott* —2G **57**
Drakemyre Clo. *Arn* —4D **22**
Drake Rd. *Cltn* —4B **48**
Draycott Clo. *Los* —1A **14**
Draycott Ct. *Ilk* —4B **28**
Draycott Rd. *Long E* —2B **72**
Draymans Ct. *Nott* —6D **32**
Drayton St. *Nott* —5G **33**
Drift, The. *Huck* —2H **7**
Drift, The. *Nott* —2C **66**
Dronfield Pl. *Ilk* —2A **28**
Drummond Av. *N'fld* —2B **48**
Drummond Dri. *Nut* —3E **31**
Drummond Rd. *Ilk* —6A **28**
Drury Wlk. *Nott* —5G **45** (5E **5**)
Dryden Ct. *S'fd* —2G **53**
Dryden St. *Nott* —3F **45** (1C **4**)
Drysdale Clo. *Nott* —2H **31**
Duchess Gdns. *Nott* —5H **19**
Duchess St. *Nott* —5H **19**
Dudley Ct. *Bees* —3A **54**
Duffield Clo. *Long E* —2C **72**
Duffield Ct. *Nott* —5D **20**
Duke Clo. *Nott* —2F **31**
Duke Cres. *Gilt* —4E **17**
Dukes Pl. *Ilk* —3A **28**
Dukes Pl. *Nott* —5H **45** (4G **5**)
Duke St. *Arn* —6H **21**
Duke St. *Bulw* —6H **19**
Duke St. *Huck* —4H **7**
Duke St. *Ilk* —4B **28**
Duke St. E. *Huck* —4H **7**
Duke William Mt. *Nott*
—5E **45** (5A **4**)
Dulverton Va. *Nott* —4G **31**
Dulwich Rd. *Nott* —4C **44**
Dumbles Clo. *Ilk* —3G **39**
Dumbles, The. *Lamb* —5B **24**
Dunbar Clo. *Long E* —3G **73**
Dunblane Rd. *Rud* —1G **77**
Duncombe Clo. *Nott* —2A **46**
Duncroft Av. *Ged* —6H **35**
Dundas Clo. *Nott* —3G **45** (1D **4**)
Dunelm Dri. *C'tn* —4A **12**
Dungannon Rd. *Nott* —5C **66**
Dunholme Clo. *Nott* —5H **19**
Dunkery Rd. *Nott* —5D **66**
Dunkirk Rd. *Nott* —2C **56**
Dunlin Wharf. *Nott* —1E **57**
Dunlop Av. *Nott* —5C **44**
Dunoon Clo. *Nott* —3D **20**
Dunsby Clo. *Nott* —4C **66**
Dunsford Dri. *Nott* —1E **35**
Dunsil Dri. *Q Dri* —3E **57**
Dunsil Rd. *Newt* —1D **16**
Dunsmore Clo. *Bees* —1H **65**
Dunstan St. *N'fld* —2A **48**
Dunster Rd. *Newt* —3D **16**
Dunster Rd. *W Bri* —5C **58**
Dunston Clo. *Long E* —6H **63**

Dunvegan Dri. *Nott* —3D **20**
Durham Av. *Nott* —5B **46**
Durham Chambers. *Nott*
—5G **45** (4E **5**)
Durham Clo. *Nott* —5B **46**
Durham Cres. *Nott* —1A **32**
Durham St. *Ilk* —6B **28**
Durlston Clo. *W Bri* —6F **57**
Durnford St. *Nott* —5D **32**
Dursley Clo. *Nott* —2H **31**
Dyce Clo. *Nott* —6F **19**
Dylan M. *Nott* —1E **43**
Dylan Thomas Rd. *Nott* —5F **21**

E

Eagle Clo. *Arn* —6C **22**
Eagle Clo. *Bees* —3D **54**
Eagle Ct. *Nott* —6B **20**
Eagle Rd. *Quar H* —5B **40**
Ealing Av. *Nott* —3B **32**
Eardley Rd. *Nott* —1C **32**
Earl Cres. *Ged* —4H **35**
Earl Dri. *Gilt* —4E **17**
Earls Clo. *Nott* —4C **42**
Earlsfield Dri. *Nott* —4B **20**
Earlswood Dri. *Edw* —1D **68**
Easedale Clo. *Gam* —4E **59**
*Easegill Ct. Nott —5D **20***
(off Old Farm Rd.)
East Acres. *Cotg* —2F **71**
E. Circus St. *Nott* —5F **45** (4B **4**)
Eastcliffe Av. *Ged* —4F **35**
East Clo. *Keyw* —5G **79**
Eastcote Av. *Bees* —1B **54**
East Cres. *Bees* —6H **55**
East Cft. *Nott* —6H **45**
Eastdale Rd. *Nott* —2E **47**
East Dri. *Nott* —2A **56**
Eastglade Rd. *Nott* —1D **32**
East Gro. *Bing* —5F **51**
East Gro. *Nott* —1E **45**
Eastham Clo. *Nott* —3A **46** (1H **5**)
Eastham Rd. *Arn* —1D **34**
Eastholme Cft. *Colw P* —4F **47**
Easthorpe Cotts. *Rud* —6H **67**
Easthorpe St. *Rud* —6G **67**
East Moor. *Cotg* —3G **71**
Eastmoor Dri. *Cltn* —1H **47**
E. Nelson St. *Hean* —3C **14**
East St. *Bing* —5F **51**
East St. *Got* —6H **75**
East St. *Hean* —5E **15**
East St. *Ilk* —1B **40**
East St. *Long E* —5H **63**
East St. *Nott* —4H **45** (3F **5**)
East St. *Rud* —1G **77**
East Vw. *W Bri* —5H **57**
East Vw. Ter. *Lan M* —2F **15**
Eastwell St. *Huck* —3G **7**
Eastwold. *Cotg* —3G **71**
Eastwood Clo. *Huck* —1E **19**
Eastwood Rd. *Kimb* —6F **17**
Eastwood Rd. *Rad T* —6G **49**
Eastwood St. *Nott* —2A **32**
Eaton Av. *Arn* —6C **22**
Eaton Av. *Ilk* —3H **39**
Eaton Clo. *Bees* —5H **55**
Eaton Grange Dri. *Long E*
—5C **62**
Eaton Pl. *Bing* —5E **51**
Eatons Rd. *S'fd* —5F **53**
Eaton St. *Nott* —4B **34**
Eaton Ter. *Nott* —5B **34**
Ebenezer St. *Ilk* —4B **40**
Ebenezer St. *Lan M* —2F **15**
Ebers Gro. *Nott* —1G **45**
Ebers Rd. *Nott* —6G **33**
Ebony Wlk. *Nott* —1D **46**
Ebury Rd. *Nott* —6F **33**
Eckington Clo. *W Hal* —1C **38**
Eckington Ter. *Nott* —2G **57**
Ecton Clo. *Nott* —4D **20**
Edale Clo. *Huck* —5C **6**
Edale Clo. *Long E* —1D **72**
Edale Ri. *Bees* —2G **63**
Edale Rd. *Nott* —4G **46**
Edale Sq. *Ilk* —2A **28**
Eddlestone Dri. *Nott* —4D **66**
Edenbridge Ct. *Nott* —1D **54**
Eden Clo. *Arn* —1B **34**

Edenhall Gdns. *Nott* —3D **66**
Edern Clo. *Nott* —6E **21**
Edern Gdns. *Nott* —6E **21**
Edgbaston Gdns. *Nott* —1B **44**
Edgecote Way. *Nott* —1E **33**
Edge Hill Ct. *Long E* —3G **73**
Edge Way. *Nott* —6D **30**
Edgewood Dri. *Huck* —6D **6**
Eddington Clo. *Cotg* —3G **71**
Edginton St. *Nott* —2B **46**
Edginton Ter. *Nott* —2B **46**
Edgware Rd. *Nott* —6B **20**
Edgwood Rd. *Kimb* —1H **29**
Edinbane Clo. *Nott* —3D **20**
Edinboro Row. *Kimb* —6G **17**
Edinburgh Dri. *Bing* —4D **50**
Edingale Ct. *Bees* —5B **42**
Edingley Av. *Nott* —3G **33**
Edingley Sq. *Nott* —3F **33**
Edison Village. *Nott* —2C **56**
Edith Ter. *Nott* —3C **44**
Edlington Dri. *Nott* —6C **42**
Edmond Gro. *Huck* —3A **8**
Edmonds Clo. *Arn* —3E **21**
Edmonton Ct. *W Bri* —5H **57**
Ednaston Rd. *Nott* —2B **56**
Edwald Rd. *Edw* —2D **68**
Edwalton Av. *W Bri* —4B **58**
Edwalton Clo. *Edw* —2D **68**
Edwalton Ct. *Nott* —1C **32**
Edwalton Lodge Clo. *Edw* —2C **68**
Edward Av. *Nott* —1B **44**
Edward Clo. *Huck* —1D **18**
Edward Rd. *Eastw* —3C **16**
Edward Rd. *Long E* —5F **63**
Edward Rd. *Nut* —2C **30**
Edward Rd. *W Bri* —2B **58**
Edwards Ct. *Nott* —2F **33**
Edwards La. *Nott* —1F **33**
(in two parts)
Edward St. *Lan M* —1F **15**
Edward St. *S'fd* —4F **53**
Edwinstowe Av. *W Bri* —4B **58**
Edwinstowe Dri. *Nott* —3G **33**
Edwin St. *Day* —1H **33**
Eelwood Rd. *Huck* —1D **18**
Egerton Dri. *S'fd* —1F **53**
Egerton Rd. *Wd'p* —3H **33**
Egerton St. *Nott* —2G **45**
Egerton Wlk. *Nott* —2G **45**
Egling Cft. *Colw* —5H **47**
Egmont Ct. *Nott* —1G **57**
Egreaves Av. *Los* —1A **14**
Egypt Rd. *Nott* —6D **32**
Eighth Av. *Lent* —6B **56**
Eisele Clo. *Nott* —1F **31**
Ekowe St. *Nott* —5D **32**
Eland St. *Nott* —6D **32**
Elder Clo. *Arn* —4D **22**
Elder Gdns. *Nott* —5E **21**
Elder Gro. *Huck* —1H **19**
Eldon Chambers. *Nott*
—5G **45** (5D **4**)
Eldon Rd. *Bees* —4C **64**
Eleanor Av. *Ilk* —4C **40**
Eleanor Cres. *S'fd* —4H **53**
Electric Av. *Nott* —4E **57**
Eley Clo. *Ilk* —5G **27**
Elford Ri. *Nott* —5B **46**
Elgar Dri. *Long E* —2D **72**
Elgar Gdns. *Nott* —3B **46**
Eliot Clo. *Long E* —2D **72**
Eliot Dri. *Ilk* —4H **39**
Eliot Wlk. *Nott* —5A **66**
Elizabeth Clo. *Huck* —6E **7**
Elizabeth Clo. *W Hal* —1B **38**
Elizabeth Ct. *Ilk* —6H **27**
Elizabeth Gro. *Ged* —5G **35**
Ella Bank Rd. *Hean* —4D **14**
Ella Rd. *W Bri* —2B **58**
Ellastone Av. *Nott* —5G **21**
Ellerby Av. *Nott* —3C **66**
Ellerslie Gro. *Sand* —6D **52**
Ellesmere Bus. Pk. *Nott* —5E **33**
Ellesmere Clo. *Arn* —6D **22**
Ellesmere Dri. *Trow* —4E **41**
Ellesmere Rd. *W Bri* —1B **68**
Ellington Rd. *Arn* —3C **22**
Elliot Durham Swimming Pool.
—6A **34**

Elliot St. Nott —4E 45 (3A 4)
Ellis Av. Huck —5H 7
Ellis Clo. Long E —1E 73
Ellis Ct. Nott —3H 45
Ellis Gro. Bees —6F 55
Ellsworth Ri. Nott —1D 32
Ellwood Cres. Nott —4A 43
Elm Av. Bees —3D 64
  (Long La.)
Elm Av. Bees —5E 55
  (Newcastle Av.)
Elm Av. Bing —5G 51
Elm Av. Cltn —2H 47
Elm Av. Huck —6E 7
Elm Av. Keyw —5H 79
Elm Av. Long E —4E 63
Elm Av. Nott —2G 45
Elm Av. Nut —1B 30
Elm Av. Sand —4D 52
Elm Bank. Nott —1G 45
Elm Bank Dri. Nott —1G 45
Elmbridge. Nott —6F 21
Elm Clo. Keyw —5H 79
Elm Clo. Nott —2G 45
Elmdale Gdns. Nott —1H 43
Elm Dri. Cltn —2H 47
Elm Gro. Arn —4C 22
Elmhurst Av. Nott —5E 35
Elmore Ct. Nott —3E 45
Elms Clo. Rud —1H 77
Elmsdale Gdns. Bur J —3F 37
Elmsfield Av. Hean —3E 15
Elms Gdns. Rud —1G 77
Elmsham Av. Nott —4C 20
Elms Pk. Rud —1H 77
Elms, The. Colw —3H 47
Elms, The. Watn —6H 17
Elmsthorpe Av. Nott —5C 44
Elmswood Gdns. Nott —4H 33
Elm Tree Av. W Bri —4H 57
Elmtree Rd. C'tn —4F 11
Elm Vw. Nott —3D 44
Elnor St. Lan —3G 15
Elson St. Nott —1D 44
Elston Gdns. Nott —1C 66
Elston M. Nott —2D 46
Elstree Dri. Nott —3G 43
Elswick Clo. Nott —5F 21
Elswick Dri. Bees —1H 65
Elterwater Dri. Gam —4E 59
Eltham Clo. Nott —4F 31
Eltham Dri. Nott —4F 31
Eltham Rd. W Bri —4B 58
Elton Clo. S'fd —3G 53
Elton M. Nott —6F 33
Elton Rd. N. Nott —6F 33
Elton Ter. Nott —2D 44
Elvaston Ct. Nott —2D 32
Elvaston Dri. Long E —3B 72
Elvaston Rd. Nott —4G 43
Elveden Dri. Ilk —4G 27
Elwes Lodge. Cltn —3H 47
Emerys Rd. Ged —1B 48
  (in four parts)
Emmanuel Av. Arn —4E 21
Emmanuel Av. Nott —6C 34
Emneth Clo. Nott —1B 46
Empingham Clo. Bees —3B 64
Emsworth Clo. Ilk —4H 27
Ena Av. Nott —4B 46
Enderby Gdns. Red —4A 22
Enderby Sq. Bees —3F 55
Endsleigh Gdns. Bees —4F 55
Endsleigh Gdns. Edw —1C 68
Enfield Chambers. Nott
  —5G 45 (5E 5)
Enfield St. Bees —5E 55
Engine La. Newt —1D 16
England Cres. Hean —3E 15
Ennerdale Clo. Gam —4E 59
Ennerdale Rd. Long E —3D 62
Ennerdale Rd. Nott —2H 33
Ennismore Gdns. Nott —3A 44
Ennismore M. W Bri —1G 57
Enthorpe St. Nott —3H 43
Epperstone By Pass. Wdbgh
  —5E 13
Epperstone Ct. W Bri —3A 58
Epperstone Pk. —2D 12
Epperstone Rd. Epp —1B 12

Epperstone Rd. W Bri —3A 58
Epsom Rd. Bees —2G 63
Erdington Way. Bees —2G 63
Erewash Ct. Long E —4F 63
Erewash Ct. Man I —6H 27
Erewash Dri. Ilk —3C 40
Erewash Gdns. Nott —5E 21
Erewash Gro. Bees —3H 63
  (in two parts)
Erewash Mus. —1B 40
Erewash Sq. Ilk —3D 40
Erewash St. Long E —5G 63
Erewash Valley Golf Course.
  —3C 52
Eric Av. Huck —2F 7
Erith Clo. Nott —6D 30
Ernest Rd. Cltn —1D 46
Ernhale Ct. Arn —5A 22
Erskine Rd. Nott —6F 33
Esher Gro. Nott —6G 33
Eskdale Clo. Long E —2D 72
Eskdale Ct. Gam —4E 59
Eskdale Dri. Bees —6A 54
Eskdale Dri. Nott —1H 43
Esk Ho. Clo. Edw —1E 69
Essex St. Eastw —3B 16
Essex St. Ilk —6B 28
Estwic Av. Eastw —2B 16
Ethel Av. Huck —2H 7
Ethel Av. Nott —6C 34
Ethel Rd. W Bri —4B 58
Ethel Ter. Nott —6E 33
Eton Ct. W Hal —1B 38
Eton Gro. Nott —5H 43
Eton Rd. W Bri —5A 58
Eucalyptus Av. Nott —4A 66
Eugene Gdns. Nott —1H 57
Eugene St. Nott —6H 45
Europa Way. Nott —2G 67
Evans Rd. Nott —4B 32
Evedon Wlk. Nott —4F 21
Evelyn St. Bees —4H 55
Evelyn St. Nott —5A 46 (5H 5)
Eversley Wlk. Nott —5F 21
Evesham Ct. Bees —4A 64
Ewart Rd. Nott —1D 44
Ewe Lamb Clo. Bees —2H 53
Ewe Lamb La. Bees —2H 53
Ewell Rd. Nott —4E 43
Exbourne Rd. Nott —6F 31
Exbury Gdns. W Bri —1F 67
Exchange Arc. Nott —4E 5
Exchange Rd. W Bri —4B 58
Exchange Wlk. Nott —5G 45 (4E 5)
Excise Chambers. Nott —4F 5
Exeter Clo. Ged —5H 35
Exeter Rd. Nott —1E 45
Exeter Rd. W Bri —5B 58
Extension St. Ilk —1B 40
Exton Rd. Nott —4E 33
Eyam Clo. Bees —6C 42
Eyre's Gdns. Ilk —5B 28
Eyre St. Nott —5A 46 (4H 5)

Fabis Dri. Nott —1C 66
Factory La. Bees —6E 55
Factory La. Ilk —5A 28
Failsworth Clo. Nott —2C 66
Fairbank Cres. Nott —5H 33
Fairburn Clo. Bramc —4B 54
Fairburn Clo. Nott —5C 42
Faircroft Av. Sand —6D 52
Fairdale Dri. Newt —3D 16
Fairfax Clo. Nott —5D 32
Fairfield Clo. Nott —6F 57
Fairfield Cres. Long E —3C 72
Fairfield St. Bing —5E 51
Fairham Av. Got —6H 75
Fairham Brook Nature Reserve.
  —5E 67
Fairham Clo. Rud —5F 67
Fairham Ct. Nott —2E 67
Fairham Dri. Nott —5B 44
Fairham Rd. Keyw —4F 79
Fairholm Ct. Nott —3A 46 (1H 5)
Fairisle Clo. Nott —4E 67
Fairland Cres. W Bri —1H 67
Fairlawn Pl. Nott —5H 33
Fair Lea Clo. Long E —1F 73

Fairlight Way. Nott —6F 21
Fairmaid Gro. Nott —3C 66
Fairmead Clo. Nott —1C 46
Fairnley Rd. Nott —1D 42
Fairview Ct. W Bri —3H 67
Fairview Rd. Wd'p —3A 34
Fairway. Keyw —4H 79
Fairway Cres. Nwtn —1B 50
Fairway Dri. Bees —5D 54
Fairway Dri. Nott —6B 20
Fairway, The. Ged —4G 35
Falcon Clo. Lent —5C 44
Falcon Ct. Ilk —6H 27
Falconers Wlk. Arn —5G 21
Falcon Gro. Nott —6E 33
Falcon St. Nott —6E 33
Falconwood Gdns. Nott —4A 66
Fallow Clo. Nott —3C 66
Fall Rd. Hean —2H 15
Falstaff M. New B —6E 33
Falston Rd. Nott —3G 43
Faraday Building. Nott —2B 56
Faraday Ct. S'fd —2G 53
Faraday Rd. Nott —4C 44
Farfield Av. Bees —3E 55
Farfield Gro. Bees —3E 55
Farleys La. Huck —5G 7
  (in two parts)
Farley St. Nott —6H 19
Farm Av. Huck —1D 18
Farm Clo. Ilk —1C 40
Farm Clo. Long E —2G 73
Farm Clo. Nott —3C 66
Farmer St. Bradm —4A 78
Farm Rd. Bees —6C 54
Farnborough Rd. Nott —5B 66
Farndale Clo. Long E —2C 72
Farndale Dri. Nott —5B 42
Farndon Gdns. Bees —2H 63
Farndon Grn. Nott —5A 44
Farndon M. Nott —1C 46
Far New Clo. Sand —6D 52
Farnham Wlk. W Hal —1B 38
Farnsfield Av. Bur J —2G 37
Farnsworth Clo. Watn —4A 18
Far Pastures Clo. Keyw —5G 79
Farriers Cft. Ilk —4G 27
Farriers Grn. Cltn —3A 66
Farringdon Clo. Nut —4D 30
Far Rye. Nott —3F 43
Far St. Bradm —4A 78
Farthing Ct. Long E —6D 62
Farwells Clo. Nott —4A 32
Faulconbridge Clo. Nott —1H 31
Fearn Chase. Cltn —2G 47
Fearn Clo. Breas —6C 62
Fearnleigh Dri. Nott —5B 32
Featherstone Clo. Ged —4F 35
Feignies Ct. Keyw —4G 79
Felen Clo. Nott —6E 21
Fellbarrow Clo. W Bri —6E 59
Felley Clo. Huck —6E 7
Fellows Rd. Bees —4E 55
Fellows Yd. Plum —6G 69
Fell Side. Wd'p —2C 34
Fellside Clo. Gam —5E 59
Felstead Ct. Bees —2C 54
Felstead Rd. Nott —3G 43
Felton Clo. Bees —6B 54
Felton Rd. Nott —2H 57
Fenchurch Clo. Arn —4E 21
Fenroth Clo. Nott —5F 19
Fenton Ct. Nott —3D 32
Fenton Dri. Nott —3A 20
Fenton Rd. Nott —3D 32
Fenwick Clo. Nott —5F 31
Fenwick Rd. Nott —5F 31
Fergus Clo. Nott —5D 66
Ferguson Clo. Bees —3C 64
Fern Av. Nott —6F 33
Fern Clo. Bees —4B 54
Fern Cres. Eastw —2A 16
Ferndale Clo. Bees —3D 64
Ferndale Gro. Nott —3D 46
Ferndale Rd. Nott —3D 46
Ferndene Dri. Long E —6C 62
Ferngill Clo. Nott —2F 57
Fernilee Clo. W Hal —1C 38

Fern Lea Av. Cotg —3E 71
Fernleigh Av. Nott —5D 34
Fernwood Cres. Nott —5C 42
Fernwood Dri. Rad T —5F 49
Fernwood Dri. Watn —5A 18
Ferny Hollow Clo. Nott —5C 20
Ferrers Wlk. Nott —4A 46 (2H 5)
Ferriby Ter. Nott —2G 57
Ferry Lodge. Cltn —3G 47
Festival Rd. Ilk —4G 39
Festus Clo. Nott —3H 45
Festus St. N'fld —2A 48
Field Av. Huck —1D 18
Field Clo. Bees —1A 64
Field Clo. Breas —6B 62
Field Clo. Ged —5H 35
Field Ho. Clo. Nott —4D 42
Field La. Bees —1A 64
Field La. Wdbgh —1C 24
Field Rd. Ilk —2B 40
Fields Av. Rud —2G 77
Fields Farm Rd. Long E —2E 73
Field, The. Hean —2D 26
  (in two parts)
Fieldway. Nott —1F 67
Fiennes Cres. Nott —6E 45 (6A 4)
Fifth Av. Lent —5A 56
Filey St. Nott —5A 20
Finch Clo. Nott —3D 56
Finchley Clo. Nott —4A 66
Findern Grn. Nott —3C 46
Fingal Clo. Nott —4D 66
Finsbury Av. Nott —5B 46
Finsbury Pk. Clo. W Bri —6G 57
Finsbury Rd. Arn —3E 21
Finsbury Rd. Bees —6C 42
Firbank Ct. Bees —6B 54
Firbeck Rd. Arn —5C 22
Firbeck Rd. Nott —5B 42
Fir Clo. Huck —1H 19
Fir Clo. Nott —6F 19
Fircroft Av. Nott —1E 43
Fircroft Dri. Huck —6C 6
Fir Dale. Cotg —2G 71
Firecrest Way. Nott —3B 32
Firfield Av. Breas —5A 62
Firs Av. Bees —4F 55
Firsby Rd. Nott —5F 31
Firs Rd. Edw —1C 68
Firs St. Long E —3C 72
First Av. Bees —3E 55
First Av. Cltn —2E 47
First Av. Colw —4G 47
First Av. Ged —6H 35
First Av. Ilk —2B 40
First Av. Lent —5A 56
First Av. Nott —1F 45
First Av. Ris —6B 52
Firs, The. Nott —4H 33
Firth Clo. Arn —4E 23
Firth Dri. Bees —3C 64
Firth Way. Nott —5F 19
Fir Wlk. Nott —2D 46
Fisher Av. Wd'p —2B 34
Fisher Ct. Ilk —3B 40
Fisher Ga. Nott —5H 45 (5G 5)
Fisher La. Bing —5E 51
Fisher St. Nott —1D 44
Fishpond Dri. Nott —6E 45 (6A 4)
Five Acres. Nott —1E 67
Flagholme. Cotg —3F 71
Flake La. Stan D —2A 52
Flamingo Ct. Nott —1E 57
Flamstead Av. Lamb —6B 24
Flamstead Av. Los —1A 14
Flamstead Rd. Ilk —6B 28
Flamstead Rd. Nott —6D 30
Flatts La. C'tn —3G 11
Flatts, The. Bees —6B 54
Flawborough Ri. W Bri —2F 67
Flawforth Av. Rud —6H 67
Flawforth La. Rud —6H 67
Flaxendale. Cotg —3G 71
Flaxton Way. Nott —6D 20
Fleam Rd. Nott —1C 66
Fleeman Gro. W Bri —2C 58
Fleet Clo. Nott —3B 44
Fleetway Clo. Newt —4D 16
Fleetwith Clo. W Bri —6E 59
Fleming Clo. Watn —5A 18

Gleneagles Ct. *Edw* —2D **68**
Gleneagles Dri. *Arn* —4D **22**
Glenfield Av. *Kimb* —6F **17**
Glenfield Rd. *Long E* —2F **73**
Glen Helen. *Colw* —3H **47**
Glenlivet Gdns. *Nott* —4D **66**
(in two parts)
Glenloch Dri. *Nott* —5D **66**
Glenmore Rd. *W Bri* —5D **58**
Glenorchy Cres. *Nott* —5C **20**
Glenparva Av. *Red* —4A **22**
Glenridding Clo. *W Bri* —6F **59**
Glen Rd. *Bur J* —2E **37**
Glensford Gdns. *Nott* —3C **20**
Glenside. *Wd'p* —2D **34**
Glenside Rd. *Bees* —2C **54**
Glenstone Ct. *Nott* —1D **44**
Glen, The. *Nott* —4C **66**
Glentworth Rd. *Nott* —3C **44**
Glenwood Av. *Nott* —5D **42**
Glins Rd. *Nott* —5D **20**
Gloucester Av. *Bees* —6F **55**
Gloucester Av. *Nott* —5C **44**
Gloucester Av. *Nut* —4F **31**
Gloucester Av. *Sand* —1C **62**
Glover Av. *Nott* —5D **42**
Glue La. *Los* —3A **14**
Goatchurch Ct. *Nott* —4E **21**
Goathland Clo. *Nott* —5F **21**
Godber Rd. *Huck* —6E **7**
Godfrey Dri. *Ilk* —4G **39**
Godfrey St. *Hean* —4C **14**
(in two parts)
Godfrey St. *N'fld* —3A **48**
Godkin Dri. *Lan M* —1E **15**
Goldcrest Clo. *Bing* —6G **51**
Goldcrest Rd. *Nott* —3H **31**
Goldham Rd. *Nott* —1D **42**
Goldsmith Sq. *Nott* —4F **45** (2C **4**)
Goldsmith St. *Nott* —4F **45** (2C **4**)
Goldswong Ter. *Nott* —2G **45**
Golf Club Rd. *Stan D* —2C **52**
Golf Course Rd. *Keyw* —5B **80**
Golf Rd. *Rad T* —6G **49**
Gonalston La. *Epp* —6H **13**
Goodall Cres. *Huck* —5A **8**
Goodall St. *Nott* —2D **44**
Goodliffe St. *Nott* —1D **44**
Goodman Clo. *Gilt* —5E **17**
Goodwin Clo. *Sand* —5C **52**
Goodwin Dri. *Kimb* —1G **29**
Goodwin St. *Nott* —3E **45** (1A **4**)
Goodwood Av. *Arn* —5A **22**
Goodwood Cres. *Ilk* —5H **39**
Goodwood Dri. *Bees* —3H **63**
Goodwood Rd. *Nott* —5D **42**
Goole Av. *Nott* —4H **39**
Goosedale La. *B Vil* —4C **8**
Goose Fair. —2E **45**
(site of)
Goosegate. *Cotg* —2E **71**
Goose Ga. *Nott* —5H **45** (4F **5**)
Gordon Clo. *Bees* —3D **64**
Gordon Gro. *Nott* —6D **32**
Gordon Ri. *Nott* —5A **34**
Gordon Rd. *Bur J* —2G **37**
Gordon Rd. *Nott* —3A **46**
Gordon Rd. *W Bri* —4B **58**
Gordon Sq. *W Bri* —4B **58**
Gordon St. *Ilk* —6B **28**
Gordon St. *Nott* —3B **32**
Gorman Ct. *Arn* —6D **22**
Gorse Clo. *C'tn* —4F **11**
Gorse Clo. *Long E* —3D **62**
Gorse Clo. *Newt* —4D **16**
Gorse Ct. *Nott* —2C **32**
Gorse Rd. *Keyw* —4F **79**
Gorse Wlk. *Nott* —2D **46**
Gorsey Rd. *Nott* —2H **45**
Gosforth Ct. *Nott* —2H **57**
Goshawk Rd. *Quar H* —6C **40**
Gothic Clo. *Nott* —1G **32**
Goverton Sq. *Nott* —2B **32**
Gowan Clo. *Bees* —3C **64**
Goyden Clo. *Nott* —5E **21**
G.P.T. Bus. Pk. *Bees* —6G **55**
Grace Av. *Bees* —6H **55**
Grace Cres. *Hean* —3D **14**
Grace Dri. *Nott* —1B **44**
Grafton Av. *Wd'p* —2A **34**

Grafton Ct. *Nott* —4E **45** (3A **4**)
Graham St. *Ilk* —2B **40**
Graham St. *Nott* —4D **44**
Grainger Av. *W Bri* —2A **68**
Graingers Ter. *Huck* —6H **7**
Grainger St. *Nott* —1A **58**
Grampian Dri. *Arn* —3F **21**
Grampian Way. *Long E* —5C **62**
Granby Ct. *Bing* —5D **50**
Granby St. *Ilk* —5B **28**
Granby Vs. *Nott* —5B **46**
Grandfield Av. *Rad T* —5F **49**
Grandfield Cres. *Rad T* —5F **49**
Grandfield St. *Los* —1A **14**
Grange Av. *Bees* —5F **55**
Grange Av. *Breas* —5A **62**
Grange Av. *Rud* —5F **67**
Grange Clo. *Lamb* —6C **24**
Grange Clo. *Nott* —3F **57**
Grange Cres. *Ged* —4H **35**
Grange Dri. *Long E* —5H **63**
Grange Farm. *Gam* —4E **59**
Grange Farm Clo. *Bees* —4A **64**
Grangelea Gdns. *Bees* —3B **54**
Grangemoor. *Pap* —2B **8**
Grange Pk. *Long E* —5H **63**
Grange Pk. *W Bri* —6D **58**
Grange Rd. *Edw* —1C **68**
Grange Rd. *Long E* —5H **63**
Grange Rd. *Stock* —4B **32**
Grange Rd. *Wd'p* —3A **34**
Grange, The. *Smal* —5A **14**
Grange Vw. *Eastw* —2B **16**
Grange Vw. Rd. *Ged* —5H **35**
Grangewood Av. *Ilk* —2B **40**
Grangewood Ct. *Nott* —6C **42**
Grangewood Rd. *Nott* —6C **42**
Grannis Dri. *Nott* —1G **43**
Grantham Clo. *Gilt* —6E **17**
Grantham Rd. *Bing* —5F **51**
Grantham Rd. *Rad T* —1D **60**
Grantleigh Clo. *Nott* —4F **43**
(in two parts)
Granton Av. *Nott* —5D **66**
Grant St. *Nott* —4D **44**
Granville Av. *Long E* —4F **63**
Granville Ct. *Nott* —4B **46**
Granville Cres. *Rad T* —1E **61**
Granville Rd. *Nott* —4B **46**
Grasby Wlk. *Nott* —3B **66**
Grasmere Av. *Nott* —5A **32**
Grasmere Clo. *Huck* —3F **7**
Grasmere Ct. *Long E* —3D **62**
Grasmere Gdns. *Got* —5H **75**
Grasmere Rd. *Bees* —3D **54**
Grasmere Rd. *Long E* —3D **62**
Grasmere St. *Sand* —6D **52**
Grassingdale Clo. *Cltn* —5F **35**
Grassington Rd. *Nott* —3B **44**
Grassmere. *Cotg* —2G **71**
Grass St. *Ilk* —4A **28**
Grassy La. *Bees* —6G **55**
Gravelly Hollow. *C'tn* —1B **10**
Graveney Gdns. *Arn* —1D **34**
Graylands Rd. *Nott* —2D **42**
Graystones Clo. *W Bri* —6E **59**
Grazingfield. *Nott* —1E **67**
Greasley Av. *Newt* —3E **17**
Greasley Castle. —3F **17**
(remains of)
Greasley Sports &
Community Cen. —3D **16**
Greasley St. *Nott* —6H **19**
Gt. Freeman St. *Nott*
—3G **45** (1E **5**)
Gt. Hoggett Dri. *Bees* —5A **54**
Gt. Northern Clo., The. *Nott*
—6H **45** (6G **5**)
Gt. Northern Cotts. *Huck* —2H **7**
Gt. Northern Rd. *Eastw* —3H **15**
Gt. Northern Way. *N'fld* —3B **48**
Greaves Clo. *Arn* —2D **34**
Greaves Clo. *Nott* —6D **30**
Greek St. *Nott* —4E **45**
Greenacre. *Bur J* —2E **37**
Greenacre. *Edw* —1D **68**
Greenacre. *Nott* —4B **42**
Greenacre Av. *Hean* —2E **15**
Greenacres Cvn. Pk. *W Bri* —2E **59**
Greenacres Clo. *Newt* —3E **17**

Green Av. *N'fld* —2A **48**
Greenbank. *Cltn* —3F **47**
Greenbank Ct. *Nott* —5G **33**
Greenburn Clo. *Gam* —5E **59**
Green Clo. *Huck* —6A **8**
Green Clo. *Plum* —3H **79**
Greencroft. *Nott* —3D **66**
Greendale Gdns. *Nott* —1H **43**
Greendale Rd. *Arn* —1B **34**
Greendale Rd. *Nott* —3E **47**
Greenfield Gro. *Cltn* —1D **46**
Greenfields. *Lan M* —1E **15**
Greenfields Dri. *Cotg* —3F **71**
Greenfield St. *Nott* —2B **56**
Greenford Clo. *Nut* —4E **31**
Greengates Av. *Nott* —4B **34**
Greenhill Cres. *Cltn* —3G **47**
Greenhill Ri. *Cltn* —2G **47**
Greenhill Rd. *Cltn* —3G **47**
Greenhills Av. *Eastw* —2C **16**
Greenhills Rd. *Eastw* —2B **16**
Greenland Cres. *Bees* —1C **64**
Green La. *Ilk* —2C **40**
Green La. *Lamb* —4B **24**
Green La. *Nott* —3B **66**
Green Leys. *W Bri* —1G **67**
Green Platt. *Cotg* —2E **71**
Greens Ct. *Ilk* —6H **27**
Greens Farm La. *Ged* —5A **36**
Greenside Clo. *Long E* —6G **63**
Greenside Wlk. *Nott* —3E **47**
Greens La. *Kimb* —1H **29**
Green's Mill Mus. —5B **46**
Green St. *Bar F* —3E **75**
Green St. *Nott* —2H **57**
Green, The. *Bees* —1E **65**
Green, The. *Breas* —5A **62**
Green, The. *Low* —3F **25**
Green, The. *Rad T* —6E **49**
Green, The. *Rud* —1G **77**
Greenway Clo. *Rad T* —6E **49**
Greenway, The. *Sand* —5D **52**
Greenwich Av. *Nott* —3E **32**
Greenwich Pk. Clo. *W Bri* —6G **57**
Greenwood Av. *Huck* —3F **7**
Greenwood Av. *Ilk* —2C **40**
Greenwood Av. *Nott* —4F **47**
Greenwood Bonsai Studio.
—4A **10**
Greenwood Ct. *Bees* —6D **54**
Greenwood Cres. *Cltn* —3G **47**
Greenwood Gdns. *Rud* —1H **77**
Greenwood Rd. *Nott & Ct'n*
—4C **46**
Greenwood Va. *Huck* —3E **7**
Greet Ct. *Nott* —2B **44**
Greetwell Clo. *Nott* —3G **43**
Gregg Av. *Hean* —3D **14**
Gregory Av. *Lan M* —2E **15**
Gregory Av. *Lent* —6D **44**
Gregory Av. *Map* —5C **34**
Gregory Boulevd. *Nott* —2C **44**
Gregory Clo. *S'fd* —3H **53**
Gregory Ct. *Bees* —1B **64**
Gregory Ct. *Nott* —6C **44**
(Derby Rd.)
Gregory Ct. *Nott* —1D **44**
(Noel St.)
Gregory St. *Ilk* —1A **40**
Gregory St. *Nott* —6C **44**
Gregson Gdns. *Bees* —4B **64**
Grenay Ct. *Rud* —5F **67**
(in two parts)
Grenfell Ter. *Nott* —3C **32**
Grenville Dri. *Ilk* —4B **28**
Grenville Dri. *S'fd* —3G **53**
Grenville Ri. *Arn* —4B **22**
Grenville Rd. *Bees* —1H **65**
Gresham Clo. *W Bri* —4G **57**
Gresham Gdns. *W Bri* —4H **57**
Gresham Gdns. *Wd'p* —2C **34**
Gresley Dri. *Nott* —6B **46**
Gresley Rd. *Ilk* —6B **28**
Gretton Rd. *Nott* —3C **34**
Greyfriar Ga. *Nott* —6G **45** (6D **4**)
Greyhound St. *Nott* —5G **45** (3E **5**)
Greys Rd. *Wd'p* —3B **34**
Greystoke Dri. *Nott* —2C **42**
Grey St. *Newt* —4C **16**
Greythorn Dri. *W Bri* —1H **67**

Grierson Av. *Nott* —5F **21**
Griffon Rd. *Quar H* —5B **40**
Griffs Hollow. *Cltn* —2G **47**
Grimesmoor Rd. *C'tn* —3A **12**
Grimsby Ter. *Nott* —3G **45** (1E **5**)
Grimston Rd. *Nott* —3C **44**
Grindon Cres. *Nott* —3A **20**
Grindslow Av. *W Hal* —1C **38**
Grinsbrook. *Lent* —5C **44**
Gripps Comn. *Cotg* —3F **71**
Gripps, The. *Cotg* —3F **71**
Grisedale Ct. *Bees* —1A **64**
Gritley M. *Nott* —1F **57**
Grizedale Gro. *Bing* —5B **50**
Groome Av. *Los* —1A **14**
Grosvenor Av. *Breas* —5B **62**
Grosvenor Av. *Long E* —3C **72**
Grosvenor Av. *Nott* —6G **33**
Grosvenor Ct. Nott —1G **45**
(off Elm Bank Dri.)
Grosvenor Rd. *Eastw* —2B **16**
Grouville Dri. *Wd'p* —2C **34**
Grove Av. *Bees* —5E **55**
Grove Av. *Nott* —3E **45**
Grove Clo. *Bur J* —2F **37**
Grove Ct. *Bees* —5D **54**
Grove M. *Eastw* —4A **16**
Grover Av. *Nott* —4C **34**
Grove Rd. *Bing* —4F **51**
Grove Rd. *Nott* —6D **44**
Groveside Cres. *Nott* —2A **66**
Grove St. *Bees* —6G **55**
Grove, The. *Breas* —5B **62**
Grove, The. *C'tn* —4A **12**
Grove, The. *Nott* —5F **33**
(Haydn Av.)
Grove, The. *Nott* —3D **44**
(Southey St.)
Grundy St. *Nott* —2C **44**
Guardian Ct. *Nott* —1A **44**
Guinea Clo. *Long E* —5C **62**
Gunn Clo. *Nott* —6G **19**
Gunnersbury Way. *Nut* —4D **30**
Gunthorpe Clo. *Nott* —4F **33**
Gunthorpe Dri. *Nott* —4F **33**
Gunthorpe Rd. *Ged* —4E **35**
Gutersloh Ct. *S'fd* —3H **53**
Guy Clo. *S'fd* —5G **53**
Gwenbrook Av. *Bees* —6E **55**
Gwenbrook Rd. *Bees* —6E **55**
Gwndy Gdns. *Nott* —6E **21**
GX Superbowl. —2C **56**
Gypsum La. *Got* —6G **75**

H

Hackworth Clo. *Newt* —2D **16**
Hadbury Rd. *Nott* —4D **32**
Hadden Ct. *Nott* —4D **42**
Haddon Clo. *Cltn* —5F **35**
Haddon Clo. *Huck* —5G **7**
Haddon Clo. *W Hal* —1C **38**
Haddon Cres. *Bees* —2C **64**
Haddon Nurseries. *Ilk* —4A **28**
Haddon Rd. *W Bri* —5B **58**
Haddon St. *Ilk* —4A **28**
Haddon St. *Nott* —5F **33**
Haddon Way. *Long E* —3B **72**
Haddon Way. *Rad T* —5G **49**
Hadleigh Clo. *Bees* —3G **63**
Hadley St. *Ilk* —4C **40**
Hadrian Gdns. *Nott* —3E **21**
Hadstock Clo. *Sand* —1D **62**
Hagg La. *Dal A* —4B **38**
(in two parts)
Hagg La. *Epp* —6H **13**
(in two parts)
Hagley Clo. *Nott* —3C **46**
Haileybury Cres. *W Bri* —6B **58**
Haileybury Rd. *W Bri* —6B **58**
Haise Ct. *Nott* —2F **31**
Halberton Dri. *W Bri* —1H **67**
Hales Clo. *Cotg* —2E **71**
Haley Clo. *Kimb* —1F **29**
Halifax Ct. *Nott* —6D **30**
Halifax Pl. *Nott* —5H **45** (5F **5**)
Halina Ct. *Bees* —4F **55**
Hallam Ct. *Ilk* —4A **28**
Hallam Fields Rd. *Ilk* —5C **40**
Hallam Rd. *Bees* —5F **55**
Hallam Rd. *Nott* —5C **34**

Hallam's La. *Arn* —6B **22**
Hallams La. *Bees* —1C **64**
Hallam Way. *W Hal* —1B **38**
Hall Clo. *Rad T* —6E **49**
Hall Ct. *W Hal* —2C **38**
Hall Cft. *Bees* —6F **55**
Hallcroft Rd. *Ilk* —1B **40**
Hall Dri. *Bees* —6C **54**
Hall Dri. *Got* —6G **75**
Hall Dri. *Nott* —6E **43**
Hall Dri. *Sand* —5D **52**
Hall Farm Clo. *Toll* —4F **69**
Hallfields. *Edw* —2D **68**
Hall Gdns. *Bees* —4B **54**
Hallington Dri. *Hean* —4B **14**
Hallowell Dri. *Nott* —3F **43**
Hall Pk. Dri. *Eastw* —2A **16**
Hall Rd. *Lan M* —1G **15**
Halls La. *Newt* —5C **16**
Halls Rd. *S'fd* —5F **53**
Hall St. *Nott* —4H **33**
Hall Vw. Dri. *Nott* —3D **42**
Halstead Clo. *Bees* —1C **64**
Halstead Clo. *Nott* —4H **31**
Haltham Wlk. *Nott* —5B **66**
Hambledon Dri. *Nott* —4H **43**
Hambleton Clo. *Long E* —4C **62**
Hambling Clo. *Nott* —6G **19**
Hamilton Clo. *Arn* —4E **23**
Hamilton Clo. *Bees* —3H **63**
Hamilton Ct. *Nott* —2D **66**
(Farnborough Rd.)
Hamilton Ct. *Nott* —6F **45** (6B **4**)
(Hamilton Dri.)
Hamilton Dri. *Nott* —6F **45** (6B **4**)
Hamilton Dri. *Rad T* —5F **49**
Hamilton Gdns. Nott —6F **33**
(off Alexandra St.)
Hamilton Pl. *Nott* —5B **46**
Hamilton Rd. *Long E* —4F **63**
Hamilton Rd. *Nott* —1F **45**
Hamilton, The. *Nott* —1C **56**
Hamlet, The. *Hean* —2C **14**
Hammersmith Clo. *Nut* —3E **31**
Hampden Gro. *Bees* —5E **55**
Hampden St. *Gilt* —5D **16**
Hampden St. *Lan M* —2F **15**
Hampden St. *Nott* —3F **45** (1C **4**)
Hampshire Dri. *Sand* —6D **52**
Hampstead Ct. Nott —4G **33**
(off St Albans St.)
Hampstead Rd. *Nott* —6A **34**
Hampton Clo. *Bees* —2F **63**
Hampton Clo. *W Hal* —1B **38**
Hampton Ct. *Hean* —3B **14**
Hampton Rd. *W Bri* —5A **58**
Handel St. *Nott* —4A **46** (3H **5**)
Hand's Rd. *Hean* —4D **14**
Hankin St. *Huck* —5A **8**
Hanley Av. *Bees* —3B **54**
Hanley St. *Nott* —4F **45** (3C **4**)
Hannah Cres. *Nott* —4F **57**
Hanover Ct. *Nott* —3D **42**
Hanslope Cres. *Nott* —3D **42**
Hanson Cres. *Huck* —4G **7**
Hanworth Gdns. *Arn* —5H **21**
Harberton Clo. *Red* —4A **22**
Harby Dri. *Nott* —5A **44**
Harcourt Cres. *Nut* —4F **31**
Harcourt Rd. *Nott* —1E **45**
Harcourt St. *Bees* —5E **55**
Harcourt Ter. *Nott* —4H **45** (2G **5**)
Harden Ct. *Nott* —5A **66**
Hardstaff Almshouses. *Ged*
—5G **35**
Hardstaff Homes, The. *Gilt* —5E **17**
Hardstaff Rd. *Nott* —4C **46**
Hardwick Av. *W Hal* —1C **38**
Hardwick Ct. *Long E* —3B **72**
Hardwicke Rd. *Bees* —2C **64**
Hardwick Gro. *Bing* —5D **50**
Hardwick Gro. *Nott* —5E **45**
Hardwick Gro. *W Bri* —2B **58**
Hardwick Pl. *Ilk* —4G **39**
Hardwick Rd. *Park T*
—6E **45** (6A **4**)
Hardwick Rd. *Sher* —4G **33**
Hardwood Clo. *Nott* —6G **19**
Hardy Barn. *Ship* —5E **15**
Hardy Clo. *Kimb* —6H **17**

Hardy Clo. *Long E* —1F **73**
Hardy's Dri. *Ged* —6H **35**
Hardy St. *Kimb* —6H **17**
Hardy St. *Nott* —3E **45**
Harebell Gdns. *Bing* —5C **50**
Harewood Av. *Nott* —2B **32**
Harewood Clo. *Rad T* —6G **49**
Harewood Clo. *Sand* —1C **62**
Harkstead Rd. *Nott* —4F **21**
Harlaxton Dri. *Long E* —4A **64**
Harlaxton Dri. *Nott* —5D **44**
Harlaxton Wlk. *Nott* —3G **45** (1E **5**)
Harlech Clo. *Ilk* —4G **27**
Harlech Ri. *Bees* —1B **64**
Harlequin Clo. *Rad T* —6H **49**
Harlequin Ct. *Eastw* —2H **15**
Harley St. *Nott* —6D **44**
Harlow St. *W Hal* —2B **38**
Harlow Gro. *Ged* —5G **35**
Harmston Ri. *Nott* —3D **32**
(in two parts)
Harnett Clo. *Nott* —5H **45** (5F **5**)
Harold Av. *Lan M* —1F **15**
Harold Ct. *Nott* —5A **46** (4H **5**)
Harold St. *Nott* —5A **46** (4H **5**)
Harpenden Sq. *Nott* —4G **31**
Harpole Wlk. *Arn* —3B **22**
Harrier Gro. *Huck* —1E **19**
Harriett St. *S'fd* —4F **53**
Harrimans Dri. *Bees* —5B **62**
Harrimans La. *Lent L* —4B **56**
Harrington Clo. *Ged* —6B **36**
Harrington Dri. *Nott* —5D **44**
Harrington St. *Long E* —2D **72**
Harris Clo. *Nott* —4F **43**
Harrison Ct. *Bing* —5C **50**
Harrison Rd. *S'fd* —3F **53**
**Harrison's Plantation Nature
Reserve. —4G 43**
Harris Rd. *Bees* —5D **54**
Harrogate Rd. *Nott* —4E **47**
Harrogate St. *N'fld* —2H **47**
Harrowby Rd. *Nott* —5D **44**
Harrow Dri. *Ilk* —5C **40**
Harrow Gdns. *Nott* —5A **44**
Harrow Rd. *Huck* —6D **6**
Harrow Rd. *Nott* —5G **43**
Harrow Rd. *W Bri* —5A **58**
Harry Peel Ct. *Bees* —5G **55**
Harston Gdns. *W Bri* —2F **67**
Hart Av. *Sand* —5C **52**
Hartcroft Rd. *Nott* —1E **33**
Hartford Clo. *Nott* —1H **57**
Hartington Av. *Cltn* —6F **35**
Hartington Av. *Huck* —5C **6**
Hartington Clo. *W Hal* —1C **38**
Hartington Pl. *Ilk* —2A **28**
Hartington Rd. *Nott* —4G **33**
Hart Lea. *Sand* —5D **52**
Hartley Ct. *Nott* —3D **44**
Hartley Dri. *Bees* —5H **55**
Hartley Rd. *Nott* —3C **44**
Hartness Rd. *Nott* —4A **66**
Hartside Clo. *Gam* —4E **59**
Hartside Gdns. *Long E* —4C **62**
Hart St. *Lent* —6D **44**
Hartwell St. *Nott* —3H **45**
Hartwood Dri. *S'fd* —2F **53**
Harvest Clo. *Bing* —5D **50**
Harvest Clo. *Nott* —5D **20**
Harvey Clo. *Rud* —2H **77**
Harvey Ct. *Nott* —1C **56**
Harvey Cft. *Trow* —5E **41**
Harvey Rd. *Nott* —1F **43**
Harwich Clo. *Nott* —5G **19**
Harwill Cres. *Nott* —5H **31**
Harwood Clo. *Arn* —5D **22**
Haslam St. *Nott* —6F **45** (6C **4**)
Haslemere Rd. *Long E* —5D **62**
Haslemere Rd. *Nott* —1B **44**
Hassock La. N. *Ship* —6F **15**
Hassock La. S. *Ship* —1G **27**
Hassocks La. *Bees* —4H **55**
Hassocks, The. *Bees* —4H **55**
Hastings St. *Cltn* —2E **47**
Haswell Rd. *Nott* —2A **44**
Hatchard Wlk. *Hean* —3F **15**
Hatfield Av. *Sand* —1D **62**
Hatfield Dri. *W Bri* —1G **67**

Hatfield Rd. *Nott* —6G **33**
Hatherleigh Clo. *Nott* —1E **35**
Hathern Clo. *Long E* —2F **73**
Hathern Grn. *Bees* —3G **55**
Hatley Clo. *Nott* —2F **57**
Hatton Clo. *Arn* —3E **21**
Hatton Crofts. *Long E* —1E **73**
Hatton Gdns. *Nut* —4D **30**
Havelock St. *Ilk* —2B **40**
Haven Clo. *W Bri* —6H **57**
Havenwood Ri. *Nott* —5B **66**
Haverhill Cres. *Nott* —3B **20**
Haversham Clo. *Nott* —5B **32**
Hawarden Ter. *Nott* —2D **44**
Hawkhurst Dri. *Nott* —1D **54**
Hawkins Ct. *Ilk* —3B **28**
Hawkridge Gdns. *Nott*
—4A **46** (2H **5**)
Hawkridge St. *Nott* —4H **45** (2H **5**)
Hawkshead Clo. *W Bri* —6F **59**
Hawksley Gdns. *Nott* —3A **66**
Hawksley Rd. *Nott* —2D **44**
Hawks Wood Clo. *Bees* —1B **64**
Hawksworth Av. *Nott* —3H **33**
Hawksworth Rd. *W Bri* —2B **58**
Hawksworth St. *Nott*
—4A **46** (3H **5**)
Hawley Mt. *Nott* —4B **34**
Haworth Ct. *Nott* —4A **66**
Hawthorn Av. *Breas* —5B **62**
Hawthorn Av. *Cotg* —3F **71**
Hawthorn Av. *Huck* —4F **7**
Hawthorn Clo. *Edw* —1D **68**
Hawthorn Clo. *Keyw* —5G **79**
Hawthorn Clo. *Nott* —2F **57**
Hawthorn Clo. *Wdbgh* —1C **24**
Hawthorn Cres. *Arn* —4C **22**
Hawthorne Av. *Long E* —1E **73**
Hawthorne Av. *S'fd* —5F **53**
Hawthorne Gro. *Bees* —5H **55**
Hawthorne Ri. *Aws* —3D **28**
Hawthorn Vw. *Nott* —1F **57**
(in two parts)
Hawthorn Wlk. *Nott* —2D **46**
Hawton Cres. *Nott* —5A **44**
Hawton Spinney. *Nott* —5A **44**
Hayden La. *Huck* —1H **7**
Haydn Av. *Nott* —5F **33**
Haydn Rd. *Nott* —5E **33**
Haydock Clo. *Kimb* —6H **17**
Hayes Clo. *W Hal* —1C **38**
Hayes Rd. *Keyw* —4F **79**
Hayles Clo. *Nott* —1F **33**
Hayling Clo. *Ilk* —4G **27**
Hayling Dri. *Nott* —6B **32**
Haynes Av. *Trow* —4E **41**
Haynes Clo. *Nott* —2D **66**
Hay's Clo. *Ilk* —5H **27**
Haywood Ct. *Nott* —5A **46** (4H **5**)
Haywood Rd. *Nott* —5B **34**
Haywood St. *Nott* —5A **46** (4H **5**)
Hayworth Rd. *Sand* —6D **52**
Hazelbank Av. *Nott* —6B **34**
Hazel Clo. *Bing* —5G **51**
Hazel Clo. *Hean* —4B **14**
Hazel Dri. *Nut* —1B **30**
Hazel Gro. *Huck* —6G **7**
Hazel Gro. *Map* —3C **34**
Hazel Hill Cres. *Nott* —5F **21**
Hazelhurst Gdns. *Nott* —6H **19**
Hazel Meadows. *Huck* —6G **7**
Hazelmere Gro. *Lent* —5C **44**
Hazel St. *Nott* —5H **19**
(in two parts)
Hazel Way. *L'by* —1H **7**
Hazelwood. *Cotg* —2G **71**
Hazelwood Clo. *Newt* —3D **16**
Hazelwood Rd. *Nott* —2C **44**
Hazelwood Dri. *Huck* —5C **6**
Headingley Gdns. *Nott* —1B **44**
Healey Clo. *Nott* —1G **57**
**Heanor & District Heritage Cen.
—5D 14**
Heanor Ga. Ind. Est. *Hean* —4B **14**
(in two parts)
Heanor Ga. Rd. *Hean* —4A **14**
Heanor Leisure Cen. —4D 14
Heanor Rd. *Ilk* —2H **27**
Heanor Rd. *Los* —1A **14**

Heard Cres. *Bees* —3F **55**
Hearn La. *Arn* —5D **22**
Heathcoat Building. *Nott* —2B **56**
Heathcoat St. *Nott* —5H **45** (4F **5**)
Heather Clo. *Newt* —4D **16**
Heather Clo. *Nott* —2H **45**
(Hungerhill Rd.)
Heather Clo. *Nott* —6H **19**
(Thames St.)
Heather Ct. *Hean* —4F **15**
Heather Cres. *Breas* —5B **62**
Heather Cft. *W Bri* —1G **67**
Heatherington Gdns. *Nott* —4E **21**
Heatherley Dri. *Nott* —3D **32**
Heather Ri. *Bees* —2E **55**
Heather Rd. *Cltn* —6F **35**
Heather Va. *W Bri* —5F **57**
Heathervale. *W Bri* —1C **40**
Heathfield Gro. *Bees* —2C **64**
Heathfield Rd. *Nott* —3D **32**
Heath Gdns. *Breas* —5C **62**
Heath, The. *Gilt* —5D **16**
Heaton Clo. *Nott* —6B **34**
Heckington Dri. *Nott* —4H **43**
Hedderley Wlk. *Nott* —3H **45** (1F **5**)
Heddington Gdns. *Arn* —5G **21**
Hedges Dri. *Ilk* —5B **40**
Hedley St. *Nott* —1E **45**
Hedley Vs. *Nott* —6E **33**
Heighington Gro. *Nott* —3C **32**
Helen Clo. *Bees* —5D **54**
Hellebore Clo. *Nott* —6C **20**
Helm Clo. *Nott* —6F **19**
Helmesdale. *Arn* —4D **22**
Helmsdale Gdns. *Nott* —4D **20**
Helmsley Dri. *Eastw* —2H **15**
Helston Dri. *Nott* —1G **57**
Helvellyn Clo. *Nott* —1G **57**
Helvellyn Way. *Long E* —3D **62**
Hemingway Clo. *Cltn* —2E **47**
Hemingway Clo. *Newt* —4E **17**
Hemlock Av. *Long E* —4F **63**
Hemlock Av. *S'fd* —3G **53**
Hemlock Gdns. *Nott* —1F **31**
Hemlock La. *Ilk* —4H **39**
Hempshill La. *Nott* —1F **31**
(Low Wood Rd.)
Hempshill La. *Nott* —1H **31**
(Sellers Wood Dri.)
Hemsby Gdns. *Nott* —5H **19**
(in two parts)
Hemscott Clo. *Nott* —5F **19**
Hemswell Clo. *Nott* —4C **46**
Hendon Ri. *Nott* —1B **46**
Hendre Gdns. *Nott* —6E **21**
Henley Clo. *N'fld* —3A **48**
Henley Gdns. *S'fd* —2G **53**
Henley Ri. *Nott* —4E **33**
Henley Way. *W Hal* —1B **38**
Henning Gdns. *Nott* —5E **21**
Henrietta St. *Nott* —1A **32**
Henry Ct. *Nott* —1G **57**
Henry Rd. *Bees* —5G **55**
Henry Rd. *Nott* —6D **44**
Henry Rd. *W Bri* —3A **58**
Henry St. *Huck* —5H **7**
Henry St. *Red* —3A **22**
Henry St. *Snei* —5A **46** (4H **5**)
Henshaw Av. *Ilk* —4H **39**
Henshaw Pl. *Ilk* —3A **28**
Henson Sq. *Bees* —3B **54**
Hensons Row. *Nott* —5B **32**
Hepple Dri. *Nott* —6F **19**
Herald Clo. *Bees* —4H **55**
Herbert Buzzard Ct. *Huck* —5A **8**
(off Hankin St.)
Herbert Rd. *Nott* —6F **33**
Hereford Rd. *Ged* —4H **35**
Hereford Rd. *Nott* —4D **46**
Hereford Rd. *Wd'p* —2A **34**
Hermitage Sq. *Nott* —5B **46**
Hermitage Wlk. *Ilk* —4B **40**
Hermitage Wlk. *Nott*
—6E **45** (6A **4**)
Hermon St. *Nott* —4E **45**
Heron Dri. *Lent* —5C **44**
Herons Ct. *W Bri* —1E **69**
Heron Wharf. *Nott* —1D **56**
Herrywell La. *Cotg* —6H **71**
Hervey Grn. *Nott* —3C **66**

Heskey Clo. *Nott* —3G **45**
Heskey Wlk. *Nott* —3G **45** (1E **5**)
Heslington Av. *Nott* —1C **44**
Hethbeth Ct. *Nott* —1G **57**
Hethersett Gdns. *Nott* —5H **19**
Hetley Rd. *Bees* —3F **55**
Hexham Av. *Ilk* —5C **40**
Hexham Clo. *W Bri* —5C **58**
Hexham Gdns. *Nott* —3E **21**
Heyford Ct. *Hean* —4E **15**
Hey St. *Long E* —3D **72**
Hickings La. *S'fd* —3G **53**
Hickling Rd. *Nott* —5C **34**
Hickling Way. *Cotg* —4G **71**
Hickton Dri. *Bees* —4B **64**
Highbank Dri. *Nott* —5C **66**
Highbury Av. *Nott* —2A **32**
Highbury Clo. *Nut* —4D **30**
Highbury Rd. *Keyw* —3G **79**
Highbury Rd. *Nott* —6A **20**
Highbury Wlk. *Nott* —1A **32**
High Chu. St. *Nott* —6D **32**
(in two parts)
Highclere Dri. *Cltn* —1H **47**
Highcliffe Rd. *Nott* —4C **46**
Highcroft. *Nott* —3B **34**
High Cft. Clo. *Long E* —2G **73**
Highcroft Dri. *Nott* —4B **42**
Highcross Ct. *Nott* —3D **44**
High Cross Leys. *Nott*
—3G **45** (1E **5**)
Highcross St. *Nott* —4H **45** (3F **5**)
Highfield Ct. *Bees* —5F **55**
Highfield Dri. *Cltn* —2D **46**
Highfield Dri. *Ilk* —4F **39**
Highfield Dri. *Nut* —3F **31**
Highfield Gro. *W Bri* —4B **58**
Highfield Rd. *Bees* —1A **64**
Highfield Rd. *Keyw* —3G **79**
Highfield Rd. *Nott* —2B **56**
Highfield Rd. *Nut* —3E **31**
Highfield Rd. *W Bri* —4B **58**
Highfields Science Pk. *Nott*
—2B **56**
Highfield St. *Long E* —3E **63**
Highgate Clo. *Cltn* —5E **35**
Highgate Dri. *Ilk* —4G **27**
Highgrove Av. *Bees* —5D **54**
Highgrove Clo. *Hean* —4A **14**
Highgrove Gdns. *Edw* —1C **68**
High Hazels Ct. *Newt* —1D **16**
High Hazels Rd. *Cotg* —1G **71**
High Hazles Clo. *Ged* —4G **35**
High Holborn. *Ilk* —4A **28**
High Hurst. *C'tn* —4G **11**
High La. Central. *W Hal* —6D **26**
High La. E. *W Hal* —6E **27**
High La. W. *W Hal* —1A **38**
High Leys Rd. *Huck* —6F **7**
High Mdw. *Toll* —4F **69**
High Pavement. *Nott*
—5H **45** (5F **5**)
High Rd. *Bees* —5F **55**
(Acacia Wlk.)
High Rd. *Bees* —6E **55**
(Hall Dri.)
High Rd. *Bees* —3A **64**
(Rutland Av.)
High Spannia. *Kimb* —6H **17**
High St. *Arn* —6B **22**
High St. *Hean* —3C **14**
High St. *Huck* —4G **7**
High St. *Ilk* —1B **40**
High St. *Kimb* —1H **29**
High St. *Long E* —5G **63**
High St. *Los* —1A **14**
High St. *Nott* —5G **45** (4E **5**)
High St. *Rud* —6G **67**
High St. *S'fd* —4G **53**
High St. Av. *Arn* —6A **22**
High St. Pl. *Nott* —5G **45** (4E **5**)
Highurst Ct. *Nott* —4E **45**
Highurst St. *Nott* —4E **45**
High Vw. Av. *Keyw* —4H **79**
High Vw. Ct. *Nott* —1H **45**
Highwood Av. *Nott* —1F **43**
Highway Gro. *Nott* —4B **66**
Hilary Clo. *Nott* —6D **42**
Hilcot Dri. *Nott* —6H **31**
Hillary Pl. *Ilk* —4F **39**

Hillbeck Cres. *Nott* —5C **42**
Hill Clo. *Newt* —4E **17**
Hill Clo. *W Bri* —5D **58**
Hillcrest Clo. *Watn* —6A **18**
Hillcrest Dri. *Huck* —5D **6**
Hillcrest Gdns. *Bur J* —2E **37**
Hill Crest Gro. *Nott* —4F **33**
Hill Crest Pk. Ind. Est. *C'tn*
—2H **11**
Hillcrest Rd. *Keyw* —3G **79**
Hillcrest Vw. *Cltn* —6D **34**
Hill Dri. *Bing* —4D **50**
Hill Farm Ct. *Edw* —3C **68**
Hillfield Gdns. *Nott* —3C **20**
Hillfield Rd. *S'fd* —3H **53**
Hillgrove Gdns. *Nott* —5E **21**
Hilliers Ct. *Nott* —5D **20**
Hillingdon Av. *Nut* —4D **30**
Hillington Ri. *Nott* —6G **21**
Hill Ri. *Trow* —5E **41**
Hill Rd. *Bees* —2B **64**
Hill Rd. *B Vil* —1C **20**
Hill Rd. *Hean* —4B **14**
Hillsford Clo. *Nott* —4G **43**
Hillside. *Lan M* —2E **15**
Hill Side. *Nott* —6B **44**
Hillside Av. *Nott* —3C **34**
Hillside Cres. *Bees* —3E **55**
Hillside Dri. *Bur J* —2F **37**
Hillside Dri. *Long E* —5D **62**
Hillside Gro. *Sand* —5C **52**
Hillside Rd. *Bees* —2A **64**
(Highfield Rd.)
Hillside Rd. *Bees* —2C **54**
(Ullswater Cres.)
Hillside Rd. *Rad T* —6G **49**
Hills Rd. *Wd'p* —3A **34**
Hill Syke. *Low* —3G **25**
Hillview Av. *Nott* —5H **33**
Hillview Rd. *Bees* —3A **64**
Hill Vw. Rd. *Cltn* —6C **34**
Hilton Clo. *Long E* —3B **72**
Hilton Ct. *W Bri* —6D **58**
Hilton Cres. *W Bri* —6D **58**
Hilton Rd. *Nott* —5B **34**
Hinchin Brook. *Lent* —5C **44**
Hinshelwood Ct. *Nott* —5A **66**
Hinsley Clo. *Arn* —5D **22**
Hinsley Ct. *Nott* —4C **42**
Hirst Ct. *Nott* —4E **45** (2A **4**)
Hirst Cres. *Nott* —5F **43**
Hoare Rd. *Bees* —3B **64**
Hobart Clo. *Nott* —2G **57**
Hobart Dri. *S'fd* —2H **53**
Hobson Dri. *Ilk* —3A **40**
Hockerwood. *Nott* —1C **66**
Hockley. *Nott* —5H **45** (4G **5**)
Hodgkin Clo. *Nott* —4A **66**
Hodgkinson St. *N'fld* —3A **48**
Hodson Ho. *Nott* —5G **33**
Hoefield Cres. *Nott* —1G **31**
Hoe Hill Vw. *Toll* —4F **69**
Hoewood Rd. *Nott* —6G **19**
Hogan Gdns. *Nott* —4E **21**
Hogarth Clo. *S'fd* —5G **53**
Hogarth St. *Nott* —3B **46**
Hoggbarn La. *Los* —1B **14**
Hoggetts Clo. *Bees* —5B **54**
Hogg La. *Rad T* —6E **49**
(in two parts)
Hoggs Fld. *Eastw* —3B **16**
Holbeck Rd. *Huck* —2H **7**
Holbeck Rd. *Nott* —3B **44**
Holborn Av. *Nott* —4B **46**
Holborn Clo. *Nut* —4D **30**
Holborn Pl. *Bulw* —6A **20**
Holbrook Ct. *Nott* —5C **66**
Holbrook St. *Hean* —3E **15**
Holby Clo. *Nott* —5D **20**
Holcombe Clo. *Nott* —5H **31**
Holdale Rd. *Nott* —3D **46**
Holden Ct. *Nott* —4E **45** (2A **4**)
Holden Cres. *Nut* —1C **30**
Holden Gdns. *S'fd* —5G **53**
Holden Rd. *Bees* —4E **55**
Holden St. *Nott* —4E **45** (2A **4**)
Holgate. *Nott* —3A **66**
Holgate Rd. *Nott* —2G **57**
Holgate Wlk. *Huck* —5E **7**
Holkham Av. *Bees* —6C **54**

Holkham Clo. *Arn* —1C **34**
Holkham Clo. *Ilk* —4G **27**
Holland Clo. *Got* —6H **75**
Holland Mdw. *Long E* —2F **73**
Holland St. *Nott* —2D **44**
Holles Cres. *Nott* —6E **45** (6A **4**)
Hollies, The. *Edw* —1C **68**
Hollies, The. *Eastw* —3B **16**
Hollies, The. *Sand* —6C **52**
Hollington Rd. *Nott* —3G **43**
Hollingworth Av. *Sand* —2D **62**
Hollins, The. *C'tn* —3A **12**
Hollinwell Av. *Nott* —4H **43**
Hollinwell Ct. *Edw* —2D **68**
Hollinwood La. *C'tn* —4D **10**
(in two parts)
Hollis St. *Nott* —6E **33**
Hollows, The. *Long E* —5A **64**
Hollows, The. *Nott* —1E **67**
Hollowstone. *Nott* —5H **45** (5G **5**)
(in two parts)
Holly Av. *Breas* —4B **62**
Holly Av. *Cltn* —2F **47**
Holly Av. *Nott* —3F **57**
Holly Av. *Nott* —2C **46**
Hollybrook Gro. *Watn* —6B **18**
Holly Clo. *Bing* —5G **51**
Holly Clo. *Huck* —6H **7**
Holly Copse Nature Reserve.
—5H **29**
Holly Ct. *Bees* —3C **54**
Holly Ct. *Nott* —2B **56**
Hollycroft. *W Bri* —1C **68**
Hollydale Rd. *Nott* —3D **46**
Hollydene Clo. *Huck* —6C **6**
Hollydene Cres. *Nott* —3H **31**
Hollyfarm Ct. *Newt* —4E **17**
Holly Gdns. *Nott* —2B **46**
Hollygate Ind. Pk. *Cotg* —1G **71**
Hollygate La. *Cotg* —2F **71**
Holly La. *Bees* —6E **55**
Holly Rd. *Watn* —6H **17**
Hollythorpe Pl. *Huck* —6D **6**
Holme Clo. *Ilk* —5H **27**
Holme Clo. *Wdbgh* —1D **24**
Holme Cft. *W Hal* —2C **38**
Holmefield Cres. *Ilk* —1C **40**
Holme Gro. *W Bri* —1D **58**
Holme La. *Hol P & Rad T* —6B **48**
Holme Lea. *Sand* —5D **52**
Holme Lodge. *Cltn* —3G **47**
Holme Pierrepont Country Pk.
—6A **48**
Holme Pierrepont Hall. —6B **48**
Holme Pierrepont National
Watersports Cen. —1G **59**
Holme Rd. *Bing* —5F **51**
Holme Rd. *W Bri* —2B **58**
Holmes Clo. *Lan M* —2E **15**
Holmesfield Dri. *Hean* —5D **14**
Holmes Rd. *Breas* —5A **62**
Holmes St. *Hean* —3B **14**
Holme St. *Nott* —1A **58**
Holmewood Cres. *Nott* —1E **33**
Holmewood Dri. *Gilt* —5D **16**
Holmfield Rd. *Bees* —2C **64**
Holmsfield. *Keyw* —5G **79**
Holroyd Av. *Nott* —5B **46**
Holt Gro. *C'tn* —3H **11**
Holwood Ct. *Nott* —1G **31**
Holyoake Dri. *Long E* —6H **63**
Holyoake Rd. *Nott* —4E **35**
Holyrood Ct. *Bees* —2C **54**
Holywell Rd. *Ilk* —4G **27**
Home Clo. *Arn* —5H **21**
Home Cft., The. *Bees* —4B **54**
Home Farm Clo. *Got* —6G **75**
Homefield Av. *Arn* —3C **22**
Homefield Rd. *Nott* —2B **44**
Homestead. *Lan M* —1E **15**
Homewell Wlk. *Nott* —2D **66**
Honeysuckle Clo. *Nott* —6E **31**
Honeysuckle Gro. *Bing* —6D **50**
Honeysuckle Gro. *Nott* —3H **31**
Honeywood Ct. *Nott* —2C **46**
Honeywood Dri. *Nott* —2C **46**
Honingham Clo. *Arn* —2B **34**
Honingham Rd. *Ilk* —4G **27**
Honister Clo. *Gam* —4E **59**
Honister Clo. *Nott* —6B **66**

Honiton Clo. *Bees* —3A **64**
Honiton Rd. *Nott* —6E **31**
Hood Cotts. *Nott* —5H **33**
Hood St. *Nott* —5H **33**
Hooley Clo. *Long E* —1D **72**
Hooley Pl. *Nott* —4H **33**
Hoopers Wlk. *Nott* —1G **57**
Hooton Rd. *Cltn* —2E **47**
Hooton St. *Nott* —4B **46**
Hope Clo. *Nott* —1F **57**
Hopedale Clo. *Nott* —4C **44**
Hope Dri. *Nott* —6F **45** (6B **4**)
Hope St. *Bees* —4E **55**
Hope St. *Ilk* —2B **40**
Hopewell Clo. *Rad T* —4G **49**
Hopewell Wlk. *Ilk* —2B **28**
Hopkins Ct. *Eastw* —2B **16**
Horace Av. *S'fd* —4E **53**
Hornbeam Clo. *Ilk* —2D **40**
Hornbeam Gdns. *Nott* —6F **19**
Hornbuckle Ct. *Nott* —4D **44**
Hornchurch Rd. *Nott* —1D **42**
Hornsby Wlk. *Nott* —5C **20**
Horridge St. *Ilk* —3B **28**
Horsecroft Clo. *Ilk* —5G **27**
Horsendale Av. *Nott* —3E **31**
Horsham Dri. *Nott* —5D **20**
Horsley Cres. *Lan M* —2E **15**
Hoselett Fld. Rd. *Long E* —2G **73**
Hoten Rd. *Nott* —6B **46**
Hotspur Clo. *Nott* —2C **32**
Hotspur Rd. *Colw* —3G **47**
Houghton Clo. *Nott* —3E **31**
Houldsworth Ri. *Arn* —3A **22**
Hound Rd. *W Bri* —3A **58**
Hounds Ga. *Nott* —5G **45** (5C **4**)
(in two parts)
Houseman Gdns. *Nott* —1G **57**
Houston Clo. *Nott* —4C **20**
Hovenden Gdns. *Nott* —2C **44**
Hove Rd. *Nott* —2C **32**
Howard Clo. *Long E* —4G **63**
Howard St. *Nott* —4G **45** (2E **5**)
Howarth Clo. *Long E* —6C **62**
Howbeck Rd. *Arn* —5D **22**
Howden Rd. *Nott* —3A **20**
Howell Jones Rd. *Bees* —2B **64**
Howells Clo. *Nott* —5G **21**
Howick Dri. *Nott* —6F **19**
Howitt St. *Hean* —3D **14**
Howitt St. *Long E* —6G **63**
Hoylake Cres. *Nott* —2D **42**
Hoylake Wlk. *Nott* —5E **21**
Hoyland Av. *Nott* —1C **56**
Hoyle Rd. *C'tn* —2H **11**
Hubert Ct. *Nott* —3D **44**
Hubert St. *Nott* —3D **44**
Huckerby Rd. *Ilk* —5G **27**
Hucknall Aerodrome. —3E **19**
Hucknall By-Pass. *Huck* —4E **7**
Hucknall Clo. *Strel* —5D **30**
Hucknall Cres. *Ged* —5G **35**
Hucknall Ind. Pk. *Huck* —1F **19**
Hucknall La. *Nott* —5A **20**
Hucknall Leisure Cen. —3H **7**
Hucknall Rd. *Nott & Nott* —4B **20**
Hudson St. *Nott* —3B **46**
Hufton's Ct. *Hean* —6E **15**
Hufton's Dri. *Hean* —6D **14**
Hugessen Av. *Huck* —3A **8**
Huggett Gdns. *Nott* —4E **21**
Humber Clo. *Nott* —1G **57**
Humber Lodge. *Bees* —4G **55**
Humber Rd. *Bees* —4G **55**
Humber Rd. *Long E* —4E **63**
Humber Rd. S. *Bees* —5H **55**
Humberston Rd. *Nott* —6C **42**
Hungerhill La. *Wdbgh* —3H **23**
Hungerhill Rd. *Nott* —2H **45**
Hunger Hill Yd. *Ilk* —3C **40**
Hungerton St. *Nott* —6D **44**
Hunston Clo. *Nott* —2G **43**
Hunt Av. *Hean* —3C **14**
Hunter Rd. *Arn* —1E **35**
Hunters Clo. *Nott* —5E **57**
Huntingdon Dri. *Nott*
—5F **45** (5B **4**)
Huntingdon St. *Nott*
—3G **45** (1D **4**)
Huntingdon Wlk. *Sand* —6D **52**

Huntingdon Way. *Bees* —3H **63**
Huntley Clo. *Nott* —4E **67**
Hurcomb St. *Nott* —2B **46**
Hurley Ct. *W Hal* —1C **38**
Hurst Dri. *Stan* —3A **38**
Hurts Cft. *Bees* —1D **64**
Hurt's Yd. *Nott* —4G **45** (3D **4**)
Huss's La. *Long E* —6H **63**
Hutchinson Grn. *Nott*
　　　　　　—3H **45** (1F **5**)
Hutton Clo. *Bees* —2D **54**
Hutton St. *Nott* —6B **46**
Huxley Clo. *Nott* —2D **42**
Hyde Clo. *Nott* —1D **66**
Hyde Pk. Clo. *W Bri* —6G **57**
Hyson Clo. *Nott* —1D **44**
Hyson St. *Nott* —2D **44**

Ian Gro. *Cltn* —1H **47**
Ikea Way. *Gilt* —6E **17**
Ilam Sq. *Ilk* —2A **28**
Ilford Clo. *Nott* —4H **27**
Ilkeston Rd. *Hean* —4D **14**
Ilkeston Rd. *Ilk* —6B **40**
Ilkeston Rd. *Nott* —4B **44** (3A **4**)
　(in two parts)
Ilkeston Rd. *Sand & Sand* —2E **53**
Ilkeston Rd. *S'fd & Bees*
　　　　　　—1G **53**
Ilkeston Rd. *Trow* —4D **40**
Imperial Av. *Bees* —5E **55**
Imperial Av. *Ged* —6G **35**
Imperial Rd. *Bees* —5E **55**
Imperial Rd. *Nott* —1B **32**
Inchwood Clo. *Bees* —3H **63**
Incinerator Rd. *Nott* —1A **58**
Independent St. *Nott* —3D **44**
Indoor Athletics Arena. —2F **43**
Indoor Bowls Hall. —5A **64**
Info. Cen. —5G **45** (4E **5**)
　(off Smithy Row, Wilford)
Ingham Gro. *Nott* —6C **44**
Ingham Rd. *Long E* —3E **63**
Ingleborough Gdns. *Long E*
　　　　　　—5C **62**
Ingleby Clo. *Cotg* —3F **71**
Ingleby Clo. *Nott* —5B **42**
Ingleby Rd. *Long E* —3B **72**
Inglefield Rd. *Ilk* —3B **40**
Inglewood Rd. *Nott* —4C **66**
Ingram Rd. *Nott* —1A **32**
Ingram Ter. *Nott* —1A **32**
Inham Cir. *Bees* —5C **54**
Inham Clo. *Bees* —6A **54**
Inham Rd. *Bees* —6A **54**
Innes Clo. *Cltn* —2E **47**
Instow Ri. *Nott* —3H **45** (1G **5**)
Intake Rd. *Keyw* —4F **79**
International Model Cen. —4E **9**
Iona Dri. *Trow* —4E **40**
Iona Gdns. *Nott* —4E **21**
Ipswich Cir. *Nott* —4C **46**
Ireland Av. *Bees* —6G **55**
Ireland Clo. *Bees* —6G **55**
Iremonger Rd. *Nott* —1H **57**
Irene Ter. *Nott* —5D **32**
Ireton Gro. *Bees* —3D **64**
Ireton St. *Bees* —5E **55**
Ireton St. *Nott* —4E **45** (2A **4**)
Irwin Dri. *Nott* —2F **31**
Isaac Newton Cen. *Nott* —2B **56**
Isaacs La. *S'fd* —4H **53**
Isabella St. *Nott* —6G **45** (6D **4**)
Isandula Rd. *Nott* —5D **32**
Island, The. *Eastw* —4B **16**
Islay Clo. *Arn* —4B **22**
Islay Clo. *Trow* —6F **41**
Ivatt Dri. *Nott* —6B **46**
Ives Clo. *W Bri* —1G **67**
Ivy Clo. *Watn* —4H **17**
Ivy Gro. *Cltn* —2F **47**
Ivy Gro. *Nott* —1E **45**
Ivy La. *Eastw* —3A **16**

Jacklin Gdns. *Nott* —4E **21**
Jackson Av. *Ilk* —6A **28**
Jackson Av. *Sand* —5C **52**
James St. *Arn* —5A **22**

James St. *Kimb* —1H **29**
Japonica Dri. *Nott* —3H **31**
Jardines, The. *Bramc* —2C **54**
Jarrow Gdns. *Nott* —3D **20**
Jarvis Av. *Nott* —3D **46**
Jasmine Clo. *Bees* —2D **54**
Jasmine Clo. *Clif* —4A **66**
Jasmine Clo. *Strel* —6E **31**
Jasmine Ct. *Hean* —4G **15**
Jasmine Rd. *Nott* —4C **32**
Jasper Clo. *Rad T* —1E **61**
Jayne Clo. *Ged* —5A **36**
Jayne Clo. *Nott* —3E **43**
J.B's Bingo & Entertainment Cen.
　　　　　　—4C **66**
Jebb's La. *Bing* —5F **51**
Jedburgh Clo. *Kimb* —6G **17**
Jedburgh Clo. *Nott* —3H **45** (1G **5**)
Jedburgh Wlk. *Nott* —3H **45** (1G **5**)
Jenned Rd. *Arn* —3C **22**
Jenner St. *Nott* —6F **33**
Jenness Av. *Nott* —4C **20**
Jennison St. *Nott* —6A **20**
Jenny Burton Way. *Huck* —6A **8**
Jermyn Dri. *Arn* —4E **21**
Jersey Gdns. *Nott* —3A **46** (1H **5**)
Jervis Ct. *Ilk* —4B **28**
Jesmond Rd. *Nott* —1B **32**
Jessamine Ct. *Bees* —5G **55**
Jessops La. *Ged* —4H **35**
Joan Av. *Hean* —3C **14**
John Carroll Ct. *Nott* —3B **46**
John Carrol Leisure Cen. —4D **44**
John Quinn Ct. *Nott* —6D **32**
Johnson Av. *Huck* —6H **7**
Johnson Dri. *Hean* —3D **14**
Johnson Rd. *Nott* —5C **44**
John's Pl. *Hean* —4B **14**
Johns Rd. *Rad T* —6G **49**
John St. *Hean* —3B **14**
John St. *Ilk* —6B **28**
John St. *New B* —6D **32**
Joseph Ct. *Ilk* —4A **28**
Joyce Av. *Bees* —2H **63**
Joyce Av. *Nott* —3H **33**
Joyce Clo. *Nott* —3H **33**
Jubilee Ct. *Nott* —6D **30**
Jubilee Rd. *Day* —1A **34**
Jubilee St. *Kimb* —6G **17**
Jubilee St. *Nott* —5B **46**
Judson Av. *S'fd* —5H **53**
Julian Clo. *Ilk* —3D **40**
Julian Rd. *W Bri* —3D **58**
Julie Av. *Hean* —4E **15**
Jumelles Dri. *C'tn* —4F **11**
Junction Rd. *Long E* —1A **74**
Juniper Clo. *Nott* —4A **66**
Juniper Ct. *Gilt* —5E **17**
Juniper Ct. *Nott* —3E **45**
　(off Waterloo Promenade)
Juniper Gdns. *Bing* —5G **51**

Kappler Clo. *N'fld* —2A **48**
Karen Ri. *Arn* —4C **22**
Katherine Dri. *Bees* —2H **63**
Kayes Ct. *S'fd* —4F **53**
Kayes Wlk. *Nott* —5H **45** (5F **5**)
Keats Clo. *Day* —6H **21**
Keats Clo. *Long E* —2D **72**
Keats Clo. *Nut* —1B **30**
Keats Dri. *Huck* —5D **6**
Kedleston Clo. *Bees* —6C **54**
Kedleston Clo. *Long E* —2C **72**
Kedleston Dri. *Ilk* —4H **27**
Kedleston Dri. *S. Ilk* —4A **28**
Keeling Clo. *Newt* —4D **16**
Keepers Clo. *B Vil* —1C **20**
Kegworth Rd. *Got* —6F **75**
Keighton Dri. *Nott* —2A **56**
Keilder Dri. *Bing* —5C **50**
Kelfield Clo. *Nott* —2C **32**
Kelham Grn. *Nott* —3B **46**
Kelham M. *Nott* —1D **46**
Kelham Way. *Eastw* —2A **16**
Kelling Clo. *Nott* —1E **33**
Kelly Wlk. *Nott* —4F **57**
Kelsey Clo. *Bees* —2E **65**
Kelso Gdns. *Nott* —1F **57**
Kelstern Clo. *Nott* —4H **31**

Kelvedon Gdns. *Nott*
　　　　　　—3A **46** (1H **5**)
Kelvin Clo. *S'fd* —6E **53**
Kelvin Rd. *Nott* —2C **46**
Kemmel Rd. *Nott* —2B **32**
Kempsey Clo. *Nott* —5C **20**
Kempson St. *Rud* —6G **67**
Kempton Clo. *Kimb* —6G **17**
Kempton Dri. *Arn* —4C **22**
Kendal Clo. *Huck* —3F **7**
Kendal Ct. *W Bri* —3D **58**
Kendal Dri. *Bees* —3D **54**
Kendale Ct. *Nott* —6B **34**
Kendleston Wlk. *Nott* —5E **21**
Kendrew Ct. *Nott* —4A **66**
Kenia Clo. *Cltn* —1F **47**
Kenilworth Ct. *Bees* —3G **55**
Kenilworth Ct. *Nott* —6F **45** (6B **4**)
Kenilworth Dri. *Ilk* —4G **39**
Kenilworth Rd. *Bees* —3G **55**
Kenilworth Rd. *Nott* —6F **45** (6B **4**)
Ken Martin Pool & Lido. —4A **20**
Kenmore Gdns. *Nott*
　　　　　　—3H **45** (1G **5**)
Kennedy Av. *Long E* —2E **73**
Kennedy Clo. *Day* —6H **21**
Kennedy Dri. *S'fd* —2G **53**
Kennel La. *Ann* —2A **6**
Kenneth Rd. *Arn* —3B **22**
Kennington Rd. *Nott* —4B **44**
Kenrick Rd. *Nott* —6C **34**
　(in two parts)
Kenrick St. *N'fld* —2A **48**
Kensal Ct. *W Bri* —3A **58**
Kensington Av. *Hean* —4A **14**
Kensington Clo. *Bees* —4A **64**
Kensington St. Nott —4G **33**
　(off St Albans St.)
Kensington Gdns. *Cltn* —2G **47**
Kensington Gdns. *Ilk* —2C **40**
Kensington Pk. Clo. *W Bri* —6G **57**
Kensington Rd. *Sand* —1C **62**
Kensington St. *Ilk* —3B **40**
Kenslow Av. *Nott* —2C **44**
Kent Av. *Bees* —1F **65**
Kentmere Clo. *Gam* —4E **59**
Kenton Av. *Nut* —4D **30**
Kenton Ct. *Nott* —2H **57**
Kent Rd. *Ged* —4E **17**
Kent Rd. *Nott* —5B **34**
Kent Rd. *S'fd* —2F **53**
Kent St. *Nott* —4H **45** (3F **5**)
Kentwood Rd. *Nott* —5B **46**
Kenyon Rd. *Nott* —6B **44**
Keppel Ct. *Ilk* —4B **28**
Kersall Ct. *Nott* —2B **32**
Kersall Dri. *Nott* —2B **32**
Kersall Gdns. *Huck* —4H **7**
Kersall Gdns. Cres. *Huck* —4H **7**
Kestrel Clo. *Cltn* —6D **34**
Kestrel Clo. *Quar H* —5B **40**
Kestrel Dri. *Bing* —6F **51**
Keswick Clo. *Bees* —3D **54**
Keswick Clo. *Gam* —4E **59**
Keswick Clo. *Ilk* —4H **39**
Keswick Ct. *Long E* —3D **62**
Keswick Ct. *Nott* —5A **46** (4H **5**)
Keswick St. *Nott* —5A **46** (4H **5**)
Kett St. *Nott* —6H **19**
Keverne Clo. *Nott* —5A **32**
Kevin Rd. *Nott* —1D **54**
Kew Clo. *W Bri* —2G **67**
Kew Cres. *Hean* —4F **15**
Kew Gdns. *Nut* —4E **31**
Keys Clo. *Nott* —6G **19**
Key St. *Nott* —4B **46**
Keyworth La. *Bun* —6B **78**
Keyworth Rd. *Ged* —4E **35**
Kibworth Clo. *Nott* —3D **32**
　(in two parts)
Kiddier Av. *Arn* —6D **22**
Kilbourne Rd. *Arn* —4D **22**
Kilbourn St. *Nott* —3G **45**
Kilburn Clo. *Bees* —1B **54**
Kilburn Dri. *Ilk* —4H **27**
Kilby Av. *Nott* —3C **46**
Kilby Ho. *Long E* —6F **63**
Kildare Rd. *Nott* —1B **46**
Kildonan Clo. *Nott* —5D **30**
Killerton Grn. *Nott* —6D **66**

Killerton Pk. Dri. *W Bri* —1F **67**
Killisick Ct. *Arn* —5D **22**
Killisick La. *Arn* —3D **22**
Killisick Rd. *Arn* —5C **22**
Kilnbrook Av. *Arn* —4D **22**
Kiln Clo. *W Hal* —6C **26**
Kilnwood Clo. *Nott* —2C **46**
Kilsby Rd. *Nott* —3D **66**
Kilverston Rd. *Sand* —5C **52**
Kilverton Clo. *Nott* —5A **44**
Kilvington Rd. *Arn* —6D **22**
Kimber Clo. *Nott* —3D **42**
Kimberley Clo. *Kimb* —2H **29**
Kimberley Eastwood By-Pass.
　　　　　　Eastw —3H **15**
Kimberley Recreation Cen.
　　　　　　—1A **30**
Kimberley Rd. *Nut* —2B **30**
Kimberley St. *Nott* —5C **46**
Kimbolton Av. *Nott* —4D **44**
Kindlewood Dri. *Bees* —4B **64**
King Charles St. *Nott*
　　　　　　—5F **45** (5C **4**)
King Edward Ct. *Nott*
　　　　　　—4H **45** (3F **5**)
King Edward Gdns. *Sand* —5D **52**
King Edward St. *Huck* —5G **7**
King Edward St. *Nott*
　　　　　　—4H **45** (3F **5**)
King Edward St. *Sand* —5D **52**
Kingfisher Clo. *Bees* —6H **55**
Kingfisher Clo. *Nott* —3B **32**
Kingfishers Ct. *W Bri* —1E **69**
Kingfisher Wharf. *Nott* —1E **57**
King George Av. *Ilk* —1A **40**
King John's Arc. *Nott* —4E **5**
King John's Chambers. *Nott* —4E **5**
Kinglake Pl. *Nott* —1G **57**
Kingrove Av. *Bees* —5D **54**
Kings Av. *Ged* —5G **35**
Kingsbridge Av. *Nott* —1E **35**
Kingsbridge Way. *Bees* —5C **54**
Kingsbury Dri. *Nott* —1G **43**
Kings Clo. *Hean* —4A **14**
Kingsdale Clo. *Long E* —2C **72**
Kingsdown Mt. *Nott* —1E **55**
Kingsford Av. *Nott* —3C **44**
Kingsley Cres. *Long E* —3D **72**
Kingsley Dri. *N'fld* —3A **48**
Kingsley Rd. *Nott* —5C **46**
Kingsmead Av. *Trow* —1F **53**
King's Mdw. Rd. *Nott* —1E **57**
Kingsmoor Clo. *Nott* —6C **20**
King's Pl. *Nott* —5H **45** (4F **5**)
Kings Rd. *Sand* —5D **52**
Kingsthorpe Clo. *Nott* —6B **34**
Kingston Av. *Ilk* —5C **40**
Kingston Ct. *Nott* —5A **46** (4H **5**)
Kingston Ct. *W Hal* —1B **38**
Kingston Dri. *Cotg* —4F **71**
Kingston Rd. *W Bri* —5A **58**
King St. *Bees* —5G **55**
King St. *Eastw* —3B **16**
King St. *Ilk* —6B **28**
King St. *Long E* —5F **63**
King St. *Nott* —5G **45** (5D **4**)
Kings Wlk. *Nott* —4G **45** (3D **4**)
Kingsway. *Hean* —3B **14**
Kingsway. *Ilk* —4B **40**
Kingsway. *Rad T* —1E **61**
Kingsway Gdns. *Huck* —1E **19**
Kingsway Rd. *Huck* —1E **19**
Kingswell Rd. *Arn* —6B **22**
Kingswood Clo. *W Bri* —6H **57**
Kingswood Rd. *Nott* —4H **43**
Kingswood Rd. *W Bri* —6H **57**
Kinlet Rd. *Nott* —1E **33**
Kinoulton La. *Nott* —6H **81**
Kinross Cres. *Nott* —3G **43**
Kinsale Wlk. *Nott* —3C **66**
Kipling Clo. *Nott* —5A **66**
Kippis St. *Nott* —4H **45** (3F **5**)
Kirby Clo. *Nott* —2C **6**
Kirby Rd. *Newt* —2C **16**
Kirkbride Ct. *Bees* —5A **64**
Kirk Bldgs. *Cltn* —2F **47**
Kirkby Av. *Ilk* —3B **40**
Kirkby Gdns. *Nott* —1H **57**
Kirk Clo. *Bees* —1D **64**
Kirk Cotts. *Nott* —3C **32**

Kirkdale Clo.—Lillie Ter.

Kirkdale Clo. *Nott* —5B **42**
Kirkdale Gdns. *Long E* —1D **72**
Kirkdale Rd. *Long E* —2D **72**
Kirkdale Rd. *Nott* —3D **46**
Kirkewhite Ct. *Nott* —1H **57**
Kirkewhite St. W. *Nott* —1G **57**
Kirkewhite Wlk. *Nott* —1G **57**
Kirkfell Clo. *W Bri* —6E **59**
Kirkfield Dri. *Breas* —5A **62**
Kirkham Clo. *Hean* —4B **14**
Kirkham Dri. *Bees* —3H **63**
Kirkhill. *Bing* —4E **51**
Kirkland Dri. *Bees* —3C **64**
Kirk La. *Rud* —6G **67**
Kirkley Gdns. *Arn* —5C **22**
Kirkman Rd. *Los* —1A **14**
Kirk Rd. *Nott* —5C **34**
Kirkstead Gdns. *Nott* —2D **44**
Kirkstead St. *Nott* —2D **44**
Kirkstone Ct. *Long E* —3D **62**
Kirkstone Dri. *Gam* —4E **59**
Kirkwhite Av. *Long E* —6F **63**
Kirtle Clo. *Nott* —1H **43**
Kirtley Dri. *Nott* —1E **57**
Kirton Av. *Long E* —6F **63**
Kittiwake M. *Lent* —5C **44**
Kiwi Clo. *Huck* —6D **6**
Knapp Av. *Eastw* —4B **16**
Kneesall Gro. *Huck* —4H **7**
Kneeton Clo. *Ged* —3F **35**
Kneeton Rd. *Nott* —3G **33**
Kneeton Va. *Nott* —3G **33**
Knighton Av. *Nott* —3C **44**
Knighton Rd. *Wd'p* —2H **33**
Knightsbridge Ct. *Nott* —*4G 33*
 (off Newstead St.)
Knightsbridge Dri. *Nut* —4E **31**
Knightsbridge Dri. *W Bri* —1G **67**
Knightsbridge Gdns. *Huck* —1F **7**
Knightsbridge Way. *Huck* —2E **7**
Knights Clo. *Bees* —3H **63**
Knights Clo. *Nott* —5D **20**
Knight's Clo. *W Bri* —2G **67**
Knight St. *N'fld* —2A **48**
Knightwood Dri. *B Vil* —6F **9**
Kniveton Pk. *Ilk* —2H **39**
Knole Rd. *Nott* —5D **30**
Knole Street Baths. —1D **44**
Knoll Av. *Huck* —6G **7**
Knowle Hill. *Kimb* —2A **30**
 (in two parts)
Knowle La. *Kimb* —3A **30**
Knowle Pk. *Kimb* —2A **30**
Knowles Wlk. *Arn* —5G **21**
Kozi Kots. *N'fld* —2H **47**
Krebs Clo. *Nott* —4E **21**
Kyle Vw. *Nott* —4E **21**
Kyme St. *Nott* —4D **44**
Kynance Gdns. *Nott* —6F **57**

Labray Rd. *C'tn* —3G **11**
Laburnum Av. *Keyw* —5A **80**
Laburnum Clo. *Sand* —4D **52**
Laburnum Gdns. *Nott* —2C **32**
Laburnum Gro. *Bees* —6H **55**
Laburnum Gro. *Huck* —6H **7**
Laburnum St. *Nott* —2H **45**
Lace Cen. & Costume Mus.
 (off Castle Ga.) —5G **45 (5D 4)**
Lace Hall Mus. —5H **45 (5F 5)**
 (off High Pavement)
Lace Market. —5H **45 (4F 5)**
 (off Broadway)
Lace Market Theatre.
 (off Halifax Pl.) —5H **45 (5F 5)**
Lace Rd. *Bees* —4F **55**
Lace St. *Nott* —2B **56**
Lacey Av. *Huck* —6G **7**
Lacey Clo. *Ilk* —4G **27**
Lacey Fields Rd. *Hean* —4E **15**
Ladbrooke Cres. *Nott* —4A **32**
Ladybank Ri. *Arn* —5E **23**
Lady Bay Av. *W Bri* —2B **58**
Lady Bay Bri. *Nott & W Bri* —1A **58**
Lady Bay Ct. *W Bri* —2C **58**
Lady Bay Rd. *W Bri* —2C **58**
Ladybridge Clo. *Bees* —2E **65**
Ladycroft Av. *Huck* —4G **7**
Ladylea Rd. *Long E* —3C **72**

Ladysmith St. *Nott* —5C **46**
Ladysmock Gdns. *Nott* —1H **57**
Ladywood Rd. *Ilk* —5E **39**
Lake Av. *Los* —1A **14**
Lakehead Ho. *Nott* —4C **66**
Lakeland Av. *Huck* —6A **8**
Lakeside Av. *Long E* —3E **73**
Lakeside Bus. Cen. *Ship* —1E **27**
Lakeside Cres. *Long E* —2E **73**
Lake St. *Nott* —3D **44**
Lamartine St. *Nott* —4H **45 (2G 5)**
Lamb Clo. Dri. *Newt* —1C **16**
Lambert Cotts. *Nott* —4F **45 (3B 4)**
Lambert Gdns. *Nott* —1A **44**
Lambert St. *Nott* —2C **44**
Lambeth Ct. *Bees* —4H **55**
Lambeth Rd. *Arn* —3E **21**
Lambie Clo. *Nott* —4A **44**
Lambley Almshouses. *Nott* —1H **45**
Lambley Av. *Nott* —4D **34**
Lambley Bridle Rd. *Bur J* —1D **36**
Lambley Ct. *Nott* —4B **34**
Lambley La. *Bur J* —2D **36**
Lambley Rd. *Low* —5G **25**
Lambley St. *Nott* —6H **19**
Lambourne Dri. *Nott* —4F **43**
Lambourne Gdns. *Wd'p* —2C **34**
Lambton Clo. *Ilk* —4A **28**
Lamcote Gdns. *Rad T* —6E **49**
Lamcote Gro. *Nott* —2H **57**
Lamcote M. *Rad T* —6E **49**
Lamcote St. *Nott* —2H **57**
Laming Gap La. *Cotg* —3C **80**
Lamins La. *B Vil* —6F **9**
Lammas Gdns. *Nott* —1H **57**
Lamorna Gro. *Nott* —5F **57**
Lamplands. *Cotg* —2E **71**
Lamp Wood Clo. *C'tn* —4G **11**
Lanark Clo. *Nott* —6A **44**
Lancaster Av. *Sand* —1C **62**
Lancaster Av. *S'fd* —5G **53**
Lancaster Ct. *Nott* —2D **46**
Lancaster Rd. *B Vil* —1C **20**
Lancaster Rd. *Huck* —1D **18**
Lancaster Rd. *Nott* —2D **46**
Lancaster Way. *Nott* —5D **30**
Lancelot Dri. *Watn* —4H **17**
Lancelyn Gdns. *W Bri* —1A **68**
Landcroft Cres. *Nott* —1E **33**
Landmere Clo. *Ilk* —4G **27**
Landmere Gdns. *Nott* —6B **34**
Landmere La. *Rud & Edw* —3H **67**
 (in two parts)
Landmere La. *W Bri* —2F **67**
Landsdown Gro. *Long E* —4H **63**
Landseer Clo. *Nott* —3C **44**
Laneham Av. *Arn* —6C **22**
Laneside Av. *Bees* —3G **63**
Lane, The. *Aws* —3E **29**
Laneward Clo. *Ilk* —3H **27**
Langar Clo. *Nott* —3G **33**
Langar Rd. *Bing* —6E **51**
Langbank Av. *Nott* —4C **20**
Langdale Dri. *Long E* —1C **72**
Langdale Gro. *Bing* —5B **50**
Langdale Rd. *Nott* —4D **46**
Langden Ct. *Long E* —1G **73**
Langdon Clo. *Long E* —4C **62**
Langdown Clo. *Nott* —5G **19**
Langford Rd. *Arn* —6D **22**
Langham Av. *Nott* —3C **46**
Langham Dri. *Bur J* —2F **37**
Langley Av. *Arn* —1B **34**
Langley Av. *Ilk* —2H **27**
Langley Mill By-Pass. *Brins*
 —1E **15**
Langstrath Dri. *W Bri* —1E **69**
Langstrath Rd. *Nott* —4C **66**
Langton Clo. *Colw* —3G **47**
Langtree Gdns. *Bing* —4F **51**
Langtry Gro. *Nott* —6E **33**
Lansdown Clo. *Bees* —1B **64**
Lansdowne Dri. *Long E* —1H **67**
Lansdowne Rd. *Nott* —3C **32**
Lansing Clo. *Nott* —5D **66**
Lanthwaite Clo. *Nott* —4D **66**
Lanthwaite Rd. *Nott* —4D **66**
Lapford Clo. *Nott* —1F **35**
Larch Clo. *Arn* —5G **21**

Larch Clo. *Bing* —5G **51**
Larch Clo. *Huck* —6H **7**
Larch Cres. *Bees* —4E **55**
Larch Cres. *Eastw* —3A **16**
Larchdene Av. *Nott* —6D **42**
Larch Dri. *Sand* —3D **52**
Larch Gdns. *Nott* —6G **19**
Larch Way. *Keyw* —5A **80**
Largs Clo. *Nott* —3C **20**
Lark Clo. *Bees* —6A **54**
Larkdale St. *Nott* —3E **45 (1A 4)**
Larkfield Rd. *Nott* —2B **30**
Larkland's Av. *Ilk* —2C **40**
Larkspur Av. *Red* —3A **22**
Larwood Gro. *Nott* —3G **33**
Lascelles Av. *Ged* —5F **35**
Latham St. *Nott* —6H **19**
Lathkill Av. *Ilk* —2A **28**
Lathkill Clo. *Nott* —6H **19**
Lathkill Dri. *Nott* —4E **45 (2A 4)**
Lathkilldale Cres. *Long E* —2C **72**
Latimer Clo. *Nott* —1A **32**
Latimer Dri. *Bees* —6B **42**
Laughton Av. *W Bri* —1G **67**
Laughton Cres. *Huck* —1E **19**
Launceston Cres. *Nott* —1E **67**
Launder St. *Nott* —1G **57**
Laurel Av. *Keyw* —5H **79**
Laurel Cres. *Long E* —1E **73**
Laurel Cres. *Nut* —6B **18**
Laurel Rd. *Cltn* —1F **47**
Laurie Av. *Nott* —1E **45**
Laurie Clo. *Nott* —1E **45**
Lauriston Dri. *Nott* —3B **32**
Lavender Clo. *Nott* —6E **31**
Lavender Cres. *Cltn* —6F **35**
Lavender Gdns. *Hean* —4F **15**
Lavender Gro. *Bees* —6H **55**
Lavender Wlk. *Nott* —2H **45**
Laver Clo. *Arn* —6D **22**
Lawdon Rd. *Arn* —4C **22**
Lawley Av. *Bees* —2G **55**
Lawn Clo. *Hean* —3D **14**
Lawn Mill Rd. *Kimb* —6G **17**
Lawn Ter. *Ilk* —1A **40**
Lawrence Av. *Aws* —2E **29**
Lawrence Av. *Breas* —5A **62**
Lawrence Av. *Colw* —4G **47**
Lawrence Av. *Eastw* —3B **16**
Lawrence Clo. *Cotg* —2F **71**
Lawrence St. *Long E* —5F **63**
Lawrence St. *Sand* —4D **52**
Lawrence St. *S'fd* —5F **53**
Lawrence Way. *Nott* —1E **57**
Lawson Av. *Long E* —6G **63**
Lawson St. *Nott* —3E **45 (1A 4)**
Lawton Dri. *Nott* —4A **20**
Laxton Av. *Nott* —2B **32**
Laxton Dri. *Huck* —5E **7**
Leabrook Clo. *Nott* —2A **66**
Leabrook Gdns. *Huck* —3A **8**
Leacroft Rd. *Nott* —2B **44**
Leadale Av. *Huck* —3A **8**
Leaf Clo. *Huck* —2H **7**
Leafe Clo. *Bees* —3C **64**
Leafield Grn. *Nott* —3C **66**
Leafy La. *Hean* —4D **14**
Leahurst Gdns. *W Bri* —6D **58**
Leahurst Rd. *W Bri* —6C **58**
Leahy Gdns. *Nott* —1D **32**
Leake Rd. *Got* —6H **75**
Leamington Dri. *Bees* —1C **64**
Leander Clo. *Nott* —5F **57**
Leas, The. *Bul* —2H **37**
Lechlade Clo. *W Hal* —1B **38**
Lechlade Rd. *Nott* —1E **33**
Ledbury Va. *Nott* —1H **43**
Leech Ct. *Gilt* —6D **16**
Lee Cres. *Ilk* —1D **40**
Lee La. *Hean* —4F **15**
Leen Clo. *B Vil* —1D **20**
Leen Clo. *Huck* —3A **8**
Leen Ct. *Nott* —1C **56**
Leen Dri. *Bulw* —2H **7**
Leen Dri. *Huck* —2H **7**
Leen Ga. *Nott* —1B **56**
Leen Mills La. *Huck* —2H **7**
Leen Pl. *Nott* —4C **44**
Leen Valley Golf Course. —4B **8**
Leen Valley Way. *Huck* —6A **8**

Leen Vw. Ct. *Nott* —1G **31**
Lee Rd. *Bur J* —2G **37**
Lee Rd. *C'tn* —3F **11**
Lees Barn Rd. *Rad T* —1D **60**
Lees Hill Footpath. *Nott* —6A **46**
Lees Hill St. *Nott* —5A **46**
Lees Rd. *Nott* —6C **34**
Leicester Ho. *S'fd* —3H **53**
Leicester St. *Long E* —1G **73**
Leigh Clo. *W Bri* —5G **57**
Leigh Rd. *Bees* —2H **63**
Leighton St. *Nott* —3B **46**
Leiston Gdns. *Nott* —5E **21**
Leisure Cen. —5B **22**
 (Rushcliffe Comp. Sch.
)**Leisure Cen.** —4C **66**
 (Nottingham)
Leivers Av. *Arn* —5B **22**
Lema Clo. *Nott* —5B **20**
Lendal Ct. *Nott* —4E **45 (2A 4)**
Lendrum Ct. *Bur J* —3F **37**
Leniscar Av. *Los* —1A **14**
Len Maynard Ct. *Nott* —2C **46**
Lennox St. *Nott* —4H **45 (3G 5)**
Lenton Av. *Nott* —5E **45**
Lenton Av. *Toll* —4E **69**
Lenton Baths. —6D **44**
Lenton Boulevd. *Nott* —4D **44**
Lenton Cir. *Toll* —4E **69**
Lenton Ct. *Nott* —6E **45 (6A 4)**
 (Lenton Av.)
Lenton Ct. *Nott* —5D **44**
 (Lombard Clo.)
Lenton Hall Dri. *Nott* —1A **56**
Lenton La. *Nott* —1D **56**
 (in two parts)
Lenton Mnr. *Nott* —6C **44**
Lenton Rd. *Nott* —6E **45 (6A 4)**
Lenton St. *Sand* —5E **53**
Leonard Av. *Nott* —5F **33**
Leonard Cheshire Clo. *Hean*
 —4F **15**
Leonard St. *Bulw* —2H **31**
Leopold St. *Long E* —5F **63**
Le Page Ct. *Nott* —2G **43**
Leroy Wallace Av. *Nott* —3D **44**
Lerwick Clo. *Nott* —4E **67**
Leslie Av. *Bees* —6F **55**
Leslie Av. *Kimb* —2H **29**
Leslie Av. *Nott* —1E **45**
Leslie Gro. *C'tn* —4H **11**
Leslie Rd. *Nott* —1E **45**
Letchworth Cres. *Bees* —1C **64**
Letcombe Rd. *Nott* —2C **66**
Levens Clo. *W Bri* —6E **59**
Leverton Ct. *W Bri* —6B **58**
Leverton Grn. *Nott* —3C **66**
Leverton Wlk. *Arn* —5C **22**
Levick Ct. *Nott* —1G **57**
Lewcote La. *W Hal* —6E **27**
Lewindon Ct. *Wd'p* —3A **34**
Lewis Clo. *Nott* —3H **45 (1F 5)**
Lexington Gdns. *Nott* —3H **33**
Leybourne Dri. *Nott* —1C **32**
Leyland Clo. *Bees* —3H **63**
Leys Ct. *Rud* —1G **77**
Leys, The. *Keyw* —6H **69**
Leys, The. *Nott* —4A **66**
Ley St. *N'fld* —2A **48**
Leyton Cres. *Bees* —6H **55**
Library Rd. *Nott* —2A **56**
Lichfield Clo. *Bees* —2G **63**
Lichfield Clo. *Long E* —6H **63**
Lichfield Rd. *Nott* —5C **46**
Liddell Gro. *Nott* —4F **43**
Liddington St. *Nott* —6D **32**
Lido. —6G **33**
Lilac Av. *Cltn* —1E **47**
Lilac Clo. *Keyw* —5A **80**
Lilac Clo. *Nott* —6E **31**
Lilac Cres. *Bees* —6H **55**
Lilac Gro. *Bees* —6H **55**
Lilac M. *Ilk* —4H **27**
Lilac Rd. *Huck* —6H **7**
Lilacs, The. *Bees* —5G **55**
Lilian Hind Ct. *Nott* —5F **19**
Lilleker Ri. *Arn* —4A **22**
Lillie Ter. *Nott* —5B **46**

Lillington Rd. *Nott* —6H **19**
Lily Av. *N'fld* —2A **48**
Lily Gro. *Bees* —6H **55**
Lime Av. *Lan M* —3G **15**
Lime Clo. *Nut* —1A **30**
Lime Clo. *Rad T* —6F **49**
Limefield Ct. *W Bri* —2C **58**
Lime Gro. *Long E* —5F **63**
Lime Gro. *Sand* —5D **52**
Lime Gro. *S'fd* —6F **53**
Lime Gro. Av. *Bees* —6E **55**
Limekiln Ct. *Nott* —5G **19**
Lime La. *Arn* —6A **10**
Limes, The. *Bar F* —1E **75**
Limes, The. *M'ley* —4C **26**
Lime St. *Ilk* —2B **40**
Lime St. *Nott* —6H **19**
Lime Ter. *Long E* —5F **63**
Lime Tree Av. *Nott* —4H **31**
  (Broxtowe La.)
Lime Tree Av. *Nott* —6H **43**
  (Digby Av.)
Limetree Clo. *Keyw* —5H **79**
Lime Tree Ct. *Bees* —2G **55**
Limetree Ct. *Ilk* —3G **39**
Limetree Ri. *Ilk* —3G **39**
Lime Tree Rd. *Huck* —1H **5**
Limmen Gdns. *Nott*
  —3A **46** (1H **5**)
Limpenny St. *Nott* —3E **45**
Linby Av. *Huck* —4H **7**
Linby Clo. *Ged* —5G **35**
Linby Clo. *Nott* —2H **33**
Linby Dri. *Strel* —5D **30**
Linby Gro. *Huck* —3H **7**
Linby La. *L'by & Pap* —1A **8**
Linby Rd. *Huck* —3H **7**
Linby St. *Nott* —5A **20**
Linby Wlk. *Huck* —3G **7**
Lincoln Av. *Sand* —1C **62**
Lincoln Cir. *Nott* —5B **45** (5A **4**)
Lincoln Clo. *S'fd* —2G **53**
Lincoln Ct. *Nott* —2E **43**
Lincoln Gro. *Rad T* —6F **49**
Lincoln St. *Nott* —4G **45** (3E **5**)
Lincoln St. *Old B* —4C **32**
Lindale Clo. *Gam* —5E **59**
Lindbridge Rd. *Nott* —5F **31**
Linden Av. *Nott* —4A **66**
Linden Ct. *Bees* —6G **55**
Linden Gro. *Bees* —6G **55**
Linden Gro. *Ged* —6B **36**
Linden Gro. *Sand* —4C **52**
Linden Gro. *S'fd* —5G **53**
Linden St. *Nott* —2H **45**
Lindfield Clo. *Nott* —5G **31**
Lindfield Rd. *Nott* —5F **31**
Lindisfarne Gdns. *Nott* —4E **21**
Lindley St. *Newt* —1D **16**
Lindley Ter. *Nott* —2C **44**
Lindrick Clo. *Edw* —1E **69**
Lindsay St. *Nott* —2D **44**
Lindum Gro. *Nott* —6B **46**
Lindum Rd. *Nott* —4B **32**
Linette Clo. *Nott* —5E **33**
Linford St. *Bees* —5B **42**
Ling Cres. *Rud* —5G **67**
Lingfield Ct. *Nott* —6D **42**
Lingford. *Cotg* —2G **71**
Lingford St. *Huck* —5H **7**
Lingmell Clo. *W Bri* —5E **59**
Lingwood La. *Wdbgh* —3B **24**
Linkin Rd. *Bees* —5E **54**
Linkmel Clo. *Nott* —2E **57**
Linkmel Rd. *Eastw* —2G **15**
Linksfield Ct. *W Bri* —3G **67**
Linnell St. *Nott* —3B **46**
Linsdale Clo. *Nott* —4B **42**
Linsdale Gdns. *Ged* —3F **35**
Linton Ri. *Nott* —3C **46**
Linwood Cres. *Eastw* —4B **16**
Lion Clo. *Nott* —5A **32**
Lismore Clo. *Nott* —4C **44**
Lissett Av. *Ilk* —2A **40**
Lister Clo. *Nott* —1C **56**
Listergate. *Nott* —5G **45** (5E **5**)
Listergate Sq. *Nott* —5G **45** (5E **5**)
Listowel Cres. *Nott* —5C **66**
Litchen Clo. *Ilk* —5B **28**
Litchfield Ri. *Arn* —3A **22**

Littlebounds. *W Bri* —4H **57**
Littlegreen Rd. *Wd'p* —2B **34**
Lit. Hallam Hill. *Ilk* —4A **40**
Lit. Hallam La. *Ilk* —3B **40**
Lit. Hayes. *W Bri* —1G **67**
Lit. John Wlk. *Nott* —2H **45**
Little La. *C'tn* —4F **11**
Little La. *Kimb* —2H **29**
Little La. *Toll* —2G **69**
Lit. Lime La. *Arn* —6A **10**
  (in two parts)
Lit. Lunnon. *Bar F* —1E **75**
Lit. Meadow. *Cotg* —3G **71**
Littlemore La. *Bradm* —4A **78**
Lit. Oakwood Dri. *Nott* —3B **20**
Lit. Ox. *Colw* —5H **47**
Lit. Tennis St. *Nott* —6C **46**
Lit. Tennis St. S. *Nott* —1C **58**
Littlewell La. *Stan D* —1B **52**
Lit. Wood Ct. *Huck* —6E **7**
Littlewood Gdns. *Nott* —4C **42**
Litton Clo. *Ilk* —3A **28**
Litton Clo. *Wd'p* —3A **34**
Liverpool St. *Nott* —4A **46** (3H **5**)
Llanberis Gro. *Nott* —5A **32**
Lloyd St. *Nott* —5G **33**
Loach Ct. *Nott* —4A **44**
Lobelia Clo. *Nott* —2H **45**
Lock Clo. *Bees* —2G **65**
Lock Clo. *Ilk* —3G **39**
Lockerbie St. *Cltn* —3H **47**
Lock La. *Long E* —3D **72**
Lock La. *Sand* —6D **52**
Locksley La. *Nott* —1C **66**
Lockton Av. *Hean* —5C **14**
Lockwood Clo. *Bees* —1A **66**
Lockwood Clo. *Nott* —4E **21**
Lodge Clo. *Nott* —1B **44**
Lodge Clo. *Red* —3A **22**
Lodge Farm La. *Arn* —4A **22**
Lodge Rd. *Long E* —2F **73**
Lodge Rd. *M'ley* —4C **26**
Lodge Rd. *Newt* —5C **16**
Lodge Row. *M'ley* —4C **26**
Lodgewood Clo. *Nott* —1G **31**
Lodore Clo. *W Bri* —5E **59**
Logan Sq. *Nott* —3C **32**
Logan St. *Nott* —1A **32**
Lois Av. *Nott* —6D **44**
Lombard Clo. *Nott* —6D **44**
Lombardy Lodge. *Bees* —4A **64**
London Rd. *Nott* —5H **45** (6G **5**)
  (in two parts)
Long Acre. *Bing* —5E **51**
Long Acre. *Huck* —4D **6**
Longacre. *Wd'p* —3B **34**
Long Acre E. *Bing* —5F **51**
Longbeck Av. *Nott* —1H **33**
Longbridge La. *Hean* —2B **14**
Longclose Ct. *Nott* —1G **31**
Longdale Rd. *Nott* —1H **33**
Longden Clo. *Bees* —1H **53**
Longden St. *Nott* —4A **46** (3H **5**)
Long Eaton Stadium. —5H 63
Longfellows Clo. *Nott* —5F **21**
Longfield Cres. *Ilk* —4B **40**
Longfield La. *Ilk* —4B **40**
Longford Cres. *Nott* —3A **20**
Long Hill Ri. *Huck* —5F **7**
Longlands Clo. *Bees* —1H **65**
Longlands Dri. *W Bri* —6F **59**
Longlands Rd. *Bees* —1H **65**
Long La. *Bees* —3D **64**
Long La. *Ship* —1H **27**
Long La. *Watn* —4A **18**
Longleat Cres. *Bees* —6C **54**
Longmead Clo. *Nott* —1G **33**
Longmead Dri. *Nott* —1G **33**
Long Mdw. Hill. *Low* —3F **25**
Longmoor Gdns. *Long E* —3C **62**
Longmoor La. *Breas* —4A **62**
Longmoor La. *Sand* —3C **62**
Longmoor Rd. *Long E* —3C **62**
Longore Sq. *Nott* —5B **44**
Longridge Rd. *Wd'p* —3B **34**
Long Row. *Nott* —5G **45** (4D **4**)
Long Row E. *Nott* —5G **45** (4E **5**)
Long Row W. *Nott* —5G **45** (4D **4**)
Long Stairs. *Nott* —5H **45** (5G **5**)
Longthorpe Ct. *Arn* —6B **22**

Longue Dri. *C'tn* —4F **11**
  (in two parts)
Longwall Av. *Q Dri & Nott* —2E **57**
Long W. Cft. *C'tn* —3E **11**
Longwood Ct. *Nott* —5D **20**
Lonscale Clo. *W Bri* —6E **59**
Lonsdale Dri. *Bees* —3G **63**
Lonsdale Rd. *Nott* —3C **44**
Lord Haddon Rd. *Ilk* —6A **28**
Lord Nelson St. *Nott* —5B **46**
Lord St. *Nott* —5B **46**
Lorimer Av. *Ged* —4H **35**
Lorna Ct. *Nott* —6H **33**
Lorne Clo. *Nott* —2G **45**
Lorne Gro. *Rad T* —6F **49**
Lorne Wlk. *Nott* —2G **45**
Lortas Rd. *Nott* —5D **32**
Loscoe-Denby La. *Den V & Los* —1A **14**
Loscoe Gdns. *Nott* —6F **33**
Loscoe Grange. *Los* —2A **14**
Loscoe Mt. Rd. *Nott* —5G **33**
Loscoe Rd. *Hean* —2B **14**
Loscoe Rd. *Nott* —6G **33**
Lothian Rd. *Toll* —4E **69**
Lothmore Ct. *Nott* —1F **57**
Lotus Clo. *Nott* —2A **46**
Loughborough Av. *Nott* —5B **46**
Loughborough Rd. *Bradm* —2H **77**
Loughborough Rd. *W Bri & Rud* —5A **58**
Loughrigg Clo. *Nott* —2F **57**
Louis Av. *Bees* —4E **55**
Louise Av. *N'fld* —1A **48**
Lovell Clo. *Nott* —2F **31**
Lowater St. *Cltn* —2D **46**
Lowcroft. *Wd'p* —3B **34**
Lowdham La. *Wdbgh* —1D **24**
Lowdham Rd. *Epp* —1G **25**
Lowdham Rd. *Ged* —4E **35**
Lowdham St. *Nott* —4A **46** (3H **5**)
Lwr. Beauvale. *Newt* —2C **16**
Lwr. Bloomsgrove Rd. *Ilk* —5B **28**
Lwr. Brook St. *Long E* —6G **63**
Lwr. Canaan. *Rud* —5H **67**
Lwr. Chapel St. *Ilk* —6B **28**
Lwr. Clara Mt. Rd. *Hean* —4E **15**
Lower Ct. *Bees* —4G **55**
Lwr. Dunstead Rd. *Lan M* —2E **15**
Lwr. Eldon St. *Nott* —5A **46** (5H **5**)
Lwr. Gladstone St. *Hean* —3C **14**
Lwr. Granby St. *Ilk* —5B **28**
Lwr. Maples. *Ship* —6H **15**
Lwr. Middleton St. *Ilk* —6C **28**
Lwr. Nelson St. *Hean* —3B **14**
Lwr. Orchard St. *S'fd* —4F **53**
Lwr. Park St. *S'fd* —5E **53**
Lwr. Parliament St. *Nott* —4H **45** (3E **5**)
Lwr. Regent St. *Bees* —5G **55**
Lower Rd. *Bees* —4H **55**
Lwr. Stanton Rd. *Ilk* —3B **40**
Lwr. Whitworth Rd. *Ilk* —3B **40**
Loweswater Ct. *Gam* —4E **59**
Lowlands Dri. *Keyw* —3H **79**
Lowlands Lea. *Hean* —3D **14**
Low Pavement. *Nott* —5G **45** (5E **5**)
Lows La. *Stan D* —1B **52**
  (in two parts)
Low Wood Rd. *Nott* —2E **31**
Loxley St. *Nott* —1H **43**
Lucerne Clo. *Nott* —5F **57**
Lucknow Av. *Nott* —1H **45**
Lucknow Ct. *Nott* —1H **45**
Lucknow Dri. *Nott* —1H **45**
Lucknow Rd. *Nott* —1H **45**
Ludford Rd. *Nott* —5A **20**
Ludgate Clo. *Arn* —3E **21**
Ludham Av. *Nott* —5H **19**
Ludlam Av. *Gilt* —6C **16**
Ludlow Av. *W Bri* —4B **58**
Ludlow Clo. *Bees* —2D **54**
Ludlow Hill Rd. *W Bri* —6B **58**
Lulworth Clo. *W Bri* —6G **57**
Lulworth Ct. *Kimb* —6H **17**
Lune Clo. *Bees* —2E **65**
Lupin Clo. *Nott* —2H **45**
Luther Clo. *Nott* —2A **46**
Luton Clo. *Nott* —6B **32**

Lutterell Ct. *W Bri* —6H **57**
Lutterell Way. *W Bri* —6D **58**
Lybster M. *Nott* —1F **57**
Lychgate Ct. *Wat* —5H **17**
Lydia Gdns. *Eastw* —4A **16**
Lydney Pk. *W Bri* —5F **57**
Lyle Clo. *Kimb* —6G **17**
Lyme Pk. *W Bri* —6F **57**
Lymington Gdns. *Nott* —3B **46**
Lymn Av. *Ged* —5H **35**
Lynam Ct. *Nott* —6H **19**
Lyncombe Gdns. *Keyw* —3H **79**
Lyndale Rd. *Bees* —3A **54**
Lynden Av. *Long E* —1F **73**
Lyndhurst Gdns. *W Bri* —1H **67**
Lyndhurst Gro. *Long E* —4F **63**
Lyndhurst Rd. *Nott* —5B **46**
Lynmouth Cres. *Nott* —2C **44**
Lynmouth Dri. *Ilk* —4H **27**
Lynncroft. *Eastw* —2C **16**
Lynstead Dri. *Huck* —6C **6**
Lynton Ct. *Nott* —2B **46**
Lynton Gdns. *Arn* —5C **22**
Lynton Rd. *Bees* —5C **54**
Lyons Clo. *Rud* —5F **67**
Lytham Dri. *Edw* —2E **69**
Lytham Gdns. *Nott* —4E **21**
Lythe Clo. *Nott* —6E **57**
Lytton Clo. *Nott* —4A **46** (2H **5**)

M

Mabel Gro. *W Bri* —3C **58**
Mabel St. *Nott* —1H **57**
Macauley Gro. *Nut* —1B **30**
Macdonald Sq. *Ilk* —4G **39**
Machins La. *Edw* —2C **68**
Mackinley Av. *S'fd* —2G **53**
Maclaren Gdns. *Rud* —1H **77**
Maclean Rd. *Cltn* —2E **47**
Macmillan Clo. *Nott* —5B **34**
Madford Bus. Pk. *Day* —1H **33**
Madryn Wlk. *Nott* —6E **21**
Mafeking St. *Nott* —5C **46**
Magdala Rd. *Nott* —1G **45**
Magdalene Way. *Huck* —3G **7**
Magnolia Clo. *Nott* —6E **31**
Magnolia Ct. *Bees* —2D **54**
Magnolia Gro. *Huck* —1H **19**
Magnus Ct. *Bees* —5G **55**
Magnus Rd. *Nott* —4G **33**
Magson Clo. *Nott* —4A **46**
Maiden La. *Nott* —5H **45** (4G **5**)
Maidens Dale. *Arn* —5H **21**
Maid Marian Way. *Nott* —5F **45** (4C **4**)
Maidstone Dri. *Nott* —1D **54**
Main Rd. *Cotg* —4D **60**
Main Rd. *Ged* —6H **35**
Main Rd. *Lent* —5A **56**
Main Rd. *Plum* —5G **69**
Main Rd. *Rad T* —6E **49**
Main Rd. *Shelf* —1H **49**
Main Rd. *Watn* —4H **17**
Main Rd. *Wilf* —5F **57**
Main St. *Aws* —2E **29**
Main St. *Bradm* —4A **78**
Main St. *Breas* —5A **62**
Main St. *Bulw* —1H **31**
  (in two parts)
Main St. *Bur J* —3F **37**
Main St. *C'tn* —3D **10**
Main St. *Eastw* —4B **16**
Main St. *Epp* —5E **13**
Main St. *Gam* —4E **59**
Main St. *Keyw* —6G **79**
Main St. *Kimb* —1H **29**
Main St. *Lamb* —6B **24**
Main St. *L'by* —1G **7**
Main St. *Long E* —6G **63**
Main St. *M'ley* —3C **26**
Main St. *Newt* —3E **17**
Main St. *Oxt* —1B **12**
Main St. *Pap* —1B **8**
Main St. *Stan D* —3B **52**
Main St. *Strel* —5B **30**
Main St. *Wdbgh* —1B **24**
Main St. Bulwell. *Bulw* —6H **19**
Maitland Av. *Wd'p* —3B **34**
Maitland Rd. *Wd'p* —3B **34**
Major St. *Nott* —4G **45** (2D **4**)

Malbon Clo.—Middle Furlong M.

Okehampton Cres. *Nott* —1E **35**
Old Acres. *Wdbgh* —1D **24**
Old Bank Ct. *Nott* —5B **32**
Old Brickyard. *Nott* —2C **46**
Oldbury Clo. *Nott* —6B **66**
Old Chu. St. *Nott* —1C **56**
Old Coach Rd. *Nott* —3E **43**
(in three parts)
Old Coppice Side. *Hean* —5C **14**
(in two parts)
Old Derby Rd. *Eastw* —2H **15**
Old Dri. *Bees* —3D **54**
Old Epperstone Rd. *Low* —1G **25**
Old Farm Ct. *Bar F* —1E **75**
Old Farm Rd. *Nott* —5D **20**
Old Hall Clo. *C'tn* —4G **11**
Old Hall Dri. *Nott* —6H **33**
Oldham Ct. *Nott* —1C **64**
Oldknow St. *Nott* —3D **44**
Old Lenton St. *Nott*
　　　　　　—4H **45** (3F **5**)
Old Lodge Dri. *Nott* —3H **33**
Old Main Rd. *Bul* —2G **37**
(in two parts)
Old Mnr. Clo. *Wdbgh* —1D **24**
Old Market Square.
　(off S. Parade)—5G **45** (4D **4**)
Old Mkt. Sq. *Nott* —4D **4**
Old Melton Rd. *Keyw* —6G **69**
Old Mill Clo. *Bees* —3A **64**
Old Mill Clo. *B Vil* —2B **20**
Old Mill Clo. *Nott* —4D **44**
Old Mill Ct. *Bing* —4E **51**
Oldmoor Wood Nature Reserve.
　　　　　　—1H **41**
Old Oak Rd. *Nott* —3E **67**
Old Pk., The. *Cotg* —1F **71**
Old Pond, The. *Hean* —5E **15**
Old Rd. *Rud* —4H **67**
Old School Clo. *Nott* —5C **66**
Old St. *Nott* —4G **45** (2E **5**)
Old Tollerton Rd. *Gam* —4E **59**
Olga Rd. *Nott* —3B **46**
Olive Av. *Long E* —1B **72**
Olive Gro. *Bur J* —2F **37**
Oliver Clo. *Hean* —3F **15**
Oliver Clo. *Nott* —3E **45** (1A **4**)
Oliver Rd. *Ilk* —4G **39**
Oliver St. *Nott* —3E **45** (1A **4**)
Ollerton Rd. *Arn* —1A **22**
Olton Av. *Bees* —2F **55**
Olympus St. *Huck* —2D **18**
Onchan Av. *Cltn* —3G **47**
Onchan Dri. *Cltn* —3G **47**
Orange Gdns. *Nott* —1H **57**
Orby Clo. *Nott* —3B **46**
Orby Wlk. *Nott* —4B **46**
Orchard Av. *Bing* —5D **50**
Orchard Av. *Cltn* —2G **47**
Orchard Bus. Pk. *Ilk* —6H **27**
Orchard Clo. *Breas* —5B **62**
Orchard Clo. *Bur J* —2F **37**
Orchard Clo. *Nott* —3A **66**
Orchard Clo. *Rad T* —6E **49**
Orchard Clo. *Toll* —5F **69**
Orchard Clo. *W Hal* —2C **38**
Orchard Ct. *Cltn* —2G **47**
Orchard Ct. *Ged* —5F **35**
Orchard Ct. *Huck* —5G **7**
Orchard Ct. *Lan M* —2F **15**
Orchard Ct. *Nott* —1C **44**
Orchard Cres. *Bees* —6C **54**
Orchard Dri. *C'tn* —4A **12**
Orchard Gro. *Arn* —1G **33**
Orchard Pk. Ind. Est. *Sand*
　　　　　　—5E **53**
Orchard Ri. *Hean* —3D **14**
Orchard Ri. *Lamb* —6C **24**
Orchards, The. *Ged* —6A **36**
Orchard St. *Got* —6H **75**
Orchard St. *Huck* —5G **7**
Orchard St. *Ilk* —2B **40**
Orchard St. *Kimb* —1H **29**
Orchard St. *Lan M* —2F **15**
Orchard St. *Long E* —6G **63**
Orchard St. *Newt* —4C **16**
Orchard, The. *Stan D* —3B **52**
Orchard Way. *Sand* —2C **62**
Orchid Clo. *W Bri* —1G **67**
Ordnance Ct. *Bees* —2C **64**

Orford Av. *Nott* —1D **66**
Orford Av. *Rad T* —1E **61**
Orion Clo. *Nott* —2E **43**
Orion Dri. *Nott* —2E **43**
Orlando Dri. *Cltn* —1H **47**
Orlock Wlk. *Nott* —2F **33**
Ormonde St. *Lan M* —1F **15**
Ormonde Ter. *Lan M* —1F **15**
Ormonde Ter. *Nott* —5G **33**
Ornsay Clo. *Nott* —4C **20**
Orpean Way. *Bees* —3G **63**
Orston Av. *Arn* —6C **22**
Orston Dri. *Nott* —5A **44**
Orston Grn. *Nott* —6B **44**
Orston Rd. E. *W Bri* —2B **58**
Orston Rd. W. *W Bri* —2A **58**
Orton Av. *Bees* —5C **54**
Ortzen Ct. *Nott* —3D **44**
Ortzen St. *Nott* —3D **44**
Orville Rd. *Nott* —2C **32**
Osborne Av. *Nott* —4G **33**
Osborne Clo. *Sand* —1D **62**
Osborne Gro. *Nott* —4G **33**
Osborne St. *Nott* —3C **44**
Osbourne Clo. *Watn* —6B **18**
Osgood Rd. *Arn* —2E **35**
Osier Rd. *Nott* —2G **57**
Osman Clo. *Nott* —2F **57**
Osmaston Clo. *Long E* —2B **72**
Osmaston St. *Nott* —6D **44**
Osmaston St. *Sand* —6E **53**
Osprey Clo. *Bing* —6F **51**
Osprey Clo. *Nott* —4A **66**
Ossington Clo. *Nott* —3G **45** (1D **4**)
Ossington St. *Nott* —3D **44**
Osterley Gro. *Nut* —5D **30**
Oulton Clo. *Arn* —1B **34**
Oulton Lodge. *Nott* —4B **20**
Oundle Dri. *Ilk* —2D **40**
Oundle Dri. *Nott* —6A **44**
Ousebridge Cres. *Cltn* —1A **48**
Ousebridge Dri. *Cltn* —1A **48**
Oval Gdns. *Nott* —1B **44**
Overdale Clo. *Long E* —1B **72**
Overdale Rd. *Nott* —5A **32**
Overstrand Clo. *Arn* —1B **34**
Owen Av. *Long E* —1A **74**
Owers Av. *Hean* —6D **14**
Owlston Clo. *Eastw* —2B **16**
Owsthorpe Clo. *Nott* —5E **21**
Owthorpe Rd. *Nott* —5F **33**
Owthorpe Rd. *Cotg* —3F **71**
Oxborough Rd. *Arn* —6G **21**
Oxbow Clo. *Nott* —2G **57**
Oxbury Rd. *Watn* —5H **17**
Oxclose La. *Arn* —1F **33**
Oxendale Clo. *W Bri* —5E **59**
Oxengate. *Arn* —1G **33**
Oxford Rd. *W Bri* —4C **58**
Oxford Clo. *Cltn* —6G **35**
Oxford St. *Eastw* —3B **16**
Oxford St. *Ilk* —2B **40**
Oxford St. *Long E* —5F **63**
Oxford St. *Nott* —5F **45** (4B **4**)
Oxton Av. *Nott* —3G **33**
Oxton By-Pass. *Oxt* —1B **12**
Oxton Rd. *Arn & C'tn* —4B **10**
Ozier Holt. *Colw* —5G **47**
Ozier Holt. *Long E* —1E **73**

Packman Dri. *Rud* —5H **67**
Paddington M. *Nott* —3C **46**
Paddock Clo. *C'tn* —4H **11**
Paddock Clo. *Nott* —2H **31**
Paddock Clo. *Rad T* —1E **61**
Paddock Farm Cotts. *Epp* —6G **13**
Paddocks, The. *Edw* —2D **68**
Paddocks, The. *Nut* —2B **30**
Paddocks, The. *Sand* —6C **52**
Paddocks Vw. *Long E* —5D **62**
Paddock, The. *Att* —3D **54**
Paddock, The. *Bing* —5E **51**
Padge Rd. *Bees* —5H **55**
Padgham Ct. *Nott* —5E **21**
Padley Ct. *Nott* —1G **31**
Padleys La. *Bur J* —2F **37**
Padstow Rd. *Nott* —1D **32**
Paget Cres. *Rud* —5G **67**
Paignton Clo. *Nott* —5H **31**

Paisley Gro. *Bees* —4C **64**
Palais, The. —4H **45** (3F **5**)
　(off King Edward St.)
Palatine St. *Nott* —6F **45** (6B **4**)
Palin Ct. *Nott* —2D **44**
Palin Gdns. *Rad T* —6G **49**
Palin St. *Nott* —3D **44**
Palm Cotts. *Nott* —4H **33**
Palm Ct. Ind. Cen. *Nott* —6D **32**
Palmer Av. *Huck* —3G **7**
Palmer Cres. *Cltn* —2F **47**
Palmer Dri. *S'fd* —6F **53**
Palmerston Gdns. *Nott*
　(in two parts)　—3G **45** (1E **5**)
Palm St. *Nott* —3A **44**
Palmwood Ct. *Nott* —2A **32**
Papplewick La. *Huck* —4H **7**
Park Av. *Aws* —2D **88**
Park Av. *Bur J* —3F **37**
Park Av. *Cltn* —1H **47**
Park Av. *Eastw* —2A **16**
Park Av. *Huck* —4F **7**
Park Av. *Ilk* —1B **40**
Park Av. *Keyw* —4F **79**
Park Av. *Kimb* —3A **30**
Park Av. *Nott* —1G **45**
Park Av. *Plum* —3H **79**
Park Av. *Stan* —3A **38**
Park Av. *W Bri* —3B **58**
Park Av. *Wdbgh* —1B **24**
Park Av. *Wd'p* —2A **34**
Park Av. E. *Keyw* —4F **79**
Park Av. W. *Keyw* —4F **79**
Park Chase. *Nott* —2H **31**
Park Clo. *Nott* —3A **34**
Park Clo. *Stan D* —3B **52**
Park Ct. *Hean* —4D **14**
Park Ct. *Nott* —2C **56**
Park Cres. *Eastw* —1B **16**
Park Cres. *Ilk* —1C **40**
Park Cres. *Nott* —5C **42**
Parkcroft Rd. *W Bri* —5B **58**
Parkdale Rd. *Nott & Cltn* —3D **46**
Park Dri. *Huck* —6G **7**
Park Dri. *Ilk* —2B **40**
Park Dri. *Nott* —5E **45** (5A **4**)
Park Dri. *Sand* —2C **62**
Parker Clo. *Arn* —5D **22**
Parker Gdns. *S'fd* —3H **53**
Parker St. *Huck* —4H **7**
Parkgate. *Huck* —2H **7**
Park Hall. *M'ley* —4B **26**
Pk. Hall La. *W Hal* —5B **26**
Parkham Rd. *Kimb* —6H **17**
Park Heights. *Nott* —6E **45** (6A **4**)
Park Hill. *Aws* —2D **28**
Park Hill. *Nott* —4E **45**
Park Ho. Gates. *Nott* —6H **33**
Parkland Clo. *Nott* —2A **66**
Parklands Clo. *Nott* —4F **21**
Park La. *Epp* —6G **13**
Park La. *Lamb* —6C **24**
Park La. *Nott* —3C **32**
Park M. *Nott* —1G **45**
Park Ravine. *Nott* —6E **45** (6A **4**)
Park Rd. *Bees* —5E **55**
　(Bramcote Av.)
Park Rd. *Bees* —3H **53**
　(Ewe Lamb La.)
Park Rd. *B Vil* —1C **20**
Park Rd. *C'tn* —3F **11**
Park Rd. *Cltn* —2H **47**
Park Rd. *Huck* —4F **7**
Park Rd. *Ilk* —2B **40**
Park Rd. *Nott* —6D **44**
Park Rd. *Plum* —3H **79**
Park Rd. *Rad T* —5F **49**
Park Rd. *Wd'p* —2A **34**
Park Rd. E. *C'tn* —3H **11**
Park Rd. N. *Bees* —5E **55**
Park Row. *Nott* —5F **45** (5C **4**)
Parkside. *Nott* —6E **43**
Parkside. *Plum* —3H **79**
Parkside Av. *Long E* —5D **62**
Parkside Dri. *Long E* —5D **62**
Parkside Gdns. N. *Nott* —6E **43**
Parkside Gdns. S. *Nott* —1E **55**
Parkside Ri. *Nott* —1E **55**
Parkstone Clo. *W Bri* —6G **57**
Park St. *Bees* —5E **55**

Park St. *Breas* —5B **62**
Park St. *Hean* —3B **14**
　(in two parts)
Park St. *Long E* —4E **63**
Park St. *Nott* —5D **44**
Park St. *S'fd* —5E **53**
Park Ter. *Nott* —5F **45** (4B **4**)
Park Ter. *Plum* —2H **79**
Park Valley. *Nott* —5F **45** (5B **4**)
Park Vw. *Eastw* —4B **16**
Park Vw. *Hean* —4B **14**
Park Vw. *Nott* —5A **34**
Pk. View Ct. *Bees* —5D **54**
Pk. View Ct. *Nott* —4H **45** (3G **5**)
Parkview Dri. *Nott* —6E **21**
Parkway Ct. *Nott* —4D **42**
Parkwood Ct. *Nott* —2C **32**
Parkwood Cres. *Nott* —4A **34**
Parkyn Rd. *Day* —1H **33**
Parkyns St. *Rud* —6G **67**
Parliament Ter. *Nott* —4F **45** (3C **4**)
Parr Ga. *Bees* —6A **54**
Parrs, The. *Bees* —5H **55**
Parry Way. *Arn* —5D **22**
Parsons Mdw. *Colw* —5G **47**
Partridge Clo. *Bing* —6F **51**
Pasteur Ct. *Nott* —1C **56**
Pasture Clo. *Colw P* —5G **47**
Pasture La. *Long E* —1A **74**
Pasture La. *Rud* —1D **76**
Pasture Rd. *S'fd* —2F **53**
Pastures Av. *Nott* —5B **66**
Pastures, The. *C'tn* —4F **11**
Pastures, The. *Gilt* —5E **17**
Pateley Rd. *Nott* —3C **34**
Paton Rd. *Nott* —2C **32**
Patricia Dri. *Arn* —4C **22**
Patrick Rd. *W Bri* —3A **58**
Patterdale Clo. *Gam* —4E **59**
Patterdale Ct. *Bees* —6A **54**
Patterdale Rd. *Wd'p* —2B **34**
Patterson Rd. *Nott* —2D **44**
Pavilion Clo. *Nott* —2H **57**
Pavilion Rd. *Arn* —4F **21**
Pavilion Rd. *Ilk* —2A **28**
Pavilion Rd. *W Bri* —2A **58**
Paxton Gdns. *Nott* —4A **46** (2H **5**)
Payne Rd. *Bees* —2A **64**
Peache Way. *Bees* —4B **54**
Peachey St. *Nott* —4G **45** (2D **4**)
Peach St. *Hean* —4B **14**
Peacock Clo. *Rud* —1F **77**
Peacock Cres. *Nott* —3C **66**
Peacock Pl. *Ilk* —3H **27**
Peakdale Clo. *Long E* —1C **72**
Pearce Dri. *Nott* —2H **43**
Pearmain Dri. *Nott* —2B **46**
Pearson Av. *Bees* —6B **54**
Pearson Clo. *Bees* —6B **54**
Pearson Ct. *Bees* —3B **54**
Pearson Ct. *Day* —6A **22**
Pearson St. *N'fld* —3A **48**
Pearson St. *Nott* —5D **32**
Pear Tree Ct. *Nott* —3F **45**
Pear Tree Orchard. *Rud* —6G **67**
Peary Clo. *Nott* —1D **32**
Peas Hill Rd. *Nott* —3H **45** (1G **5**)
　(in two parts)
Peatburn Av. *Hean* —3A **14**
Peatfield Ct. *S'fd* —2F **53**
Peatfield Rd. *S'fd* —2F **53**
Peck La. *Nott* —5G **45** (4E **5**)
Pedestrian Way. *Nott* —5D **20**
Pedley St. *Ilk* —2B **40**
Pedmore Valley. *Nott* —6E **21**
Peel St. *Lan M* —2F **15**
Peel St. *Long E* —5G **63**
Peel St. *Nott* —3F **45** (1C **4**)
Peel Vs. *Nott* —5A **34**
Pelham Av. *Ilk* —6A **28**
Pelham Av. *Nott* —1F **45**
Pelham Cotts. *Nott* —5D **44**
　(off Pelham Cres.)
Pelham Cres. *Bees* —4H **55**
Pelham Cres. *Nott* —5D **44**
Pelham Rd. *Nott* —1F **45**
Pelham St. *Ilk* —6A **28**
Pelham St. *Nott* —5G **45** (4E **5**)
Pelham Ct. *Nott* —1F **45**

Pemberton St. *Nott* —5H **45** (5G **5**)
Pembrey Clo. *Trow* —1F **53**
Pembridge Clo. *Nott* —5B **32**
Pembroke Dri. *Nott* —6G **33**
Pembury Rd. *Nott* —4E **43**
Penarth Gdns. *Nott* —4A **34**
Penarth Ri. *Nott* —4A **34**
Pendennis Clo. *Ged* —6B **36**
Pendine Clo. *Red* —4H **21**
Pendle Cres. *Nott* —6B **34**
Pendock La. *Bradm* —5B **78**
Penhale Dri. *Huck* —6C **6**
Penhurst Clo. *Nott* —1E **67**
Penllech Clo. *Nott* —6E **21**
Penllech Wlk. *Nott* —6E **21**
Pen Moor Clo. *Long E* —1C **72**
Pennant Rd. *Nott* —5B **32**
Pennard Wlk. *Nott* —5B **66**
Penn Av. *Nott* —6C **44**
Pennhome Av. *Nott* —5G **33**
Pennie Clo. *Long E* —3F **73**
Pennine Clo. *Arn* —4F **21**
Pennine Clo. *Long E* —4C **62**
Pennyfields Boulevd. *Long E*
    —6C **62**
Pennyfoot St. *Nott* —5A **46** (5H **5**)
Penrhyn Clo. *Nott* —3H **45** (1F **5**)
Penrhyn Cres. *Bees* —1B **64**
Penrith Av. *Rad T* —5G **49**
Penrith Cres. *Nott* —5A **32**
Penshore Clo. *Nott* —4B **66**
Pentland Dri. *Arn* —3F **21**
Pentland Gdns. *Long E* —4C **62**
Pentridge Dri. *Ilk* —4G **27**
Pentwood Av. *Arn* —3B **22**
Peoples Hall Cotts. *Nott*
    (off Heathcoat St.) —4H **45** (3F **5**)
Peppercorn Gdns. *Nott* —3A **44**
Pepper La. *Stan D* —3A **52**
Pepper Rd. *C'tn* —3G **11**
Pepper St. *Nott* —5G **45** (5E **5**)
Percival Rd. *Nott* —5F **33**
Percy St. *Eastw* —3C **16**
Percy St. *Ilk* —2B **40**
Percy St. *Nott* —4B **32**
Peregrine Clo. *Lent* —5C **44**
Peri Va. Clo. *Nott* —4D **30**
Perlethorpe Av. *Ged* —5F **35**
Perlethorpe Av. *Nott* —5B **46**
Perlethorpe Clo. *Ged* —5G **35**
Perlethorpe Cres. *Ged* —5G **35**
Perlethorpe Dri. *Ged* —5F **35**
Perlethorpe Dri. *Huck* —4H **7**
Perry Gdns. *Nott* —4F **33**
Perry Gro. *Bing* —5F **51**
Perry Rd. *Nott* —5D **32**
Perth Dri. *S'fd* —2G **53**
Perth St. *Nott* —4G **45** (2E **5**)
Peters Clo. *Arn* —1E **35**
Peters Clo. *Newt* —3E **17**
Petersfield Clo. *Nott* —6D **20**
Petersgate. *Long E* —4C **62**
Petersgate Clo. *Long E* —3C **62**
Petersham M. *Nott* —6D **44**
Petersham Rd. *Long E* —3C **62**
Petworth Av. *Bees* —2H **63**
Petworth Dri. *Nott* —3D **32**
Peveril Ct. *W Bri* —4A **58**
Peveril Cres. *Long E* —2B **72**
Peveril Cres. *W Hal* —1C **38**
Peveril Dri. *Ilk* —5H **27**
Peveril Dri. *Nott* —6F **45** (6B **4**)
Peveril Dri. *W Bri* —2A **68**
Peveril M. *Nott* —5A **4**
Peveril Rd. *Bees* —3F **55**
Peveril St. *Huck* —3G **7**
Peveril St. *Nott* —3D **44**
Pewit Golf Course. —2H **39**
Philip Av. *Eastw* —4C **16**
Philip Av. *Nut* —1C **30**
Philip Gro. *Ged* —5G **35**
Phoenix Av. *Ged* —5G **35**
Phoenix Cen. *Nott* —3G **31**
Phoenix Clo. *Nott* —1F **57**
Phoenix Ct. *Eastw* —3C **16**
Phoenix Ct. *Nott* —3D **56**
Phoenix Rd. *Newt* —1D **16**
Phyllis Clo. *Huck* —2F **7**
Phyllis Gro. *Long E* —6H **63**
Piccadilly. *Nott* —1B **32**

Pickering Av. *Eastw* —3B **16**
Pieris Dri. *Nott* —4A **66**
Pierrepont Av. *Ged* —6G **35**
Pierrepont Rd. *W Bri* —3C **58**
Pilcher Ga. *Nott* —5H **45** (4E **5**)
Pilkington Rd. *Nott* —6C **34**
Pilkington St. *Nott* —6H **19**
Pimlico. *Ilk* —1A **40**
Pimlico Av. *Bees* —6B **42**
Pinder St. *Nott* —5H **45** (5G **5**)
Pine Av. *Lan M* —2E **15**
Pine Gro. *Huck* —1H **19**
Pine Hill Clo. *Nott* —4D **20**
Pinehurst Av. *Huck* —6C **6**
Pine Tree Wlk. *Eastw* —3A **16**
Pine Vw. *Nott* —3D **44**
Pinewood Av. *Arn* —4D **22**
Pinewood Gdns. *Nott* —5B **66**
Pinfold. *Bing* —5F **51**
Pinfold Clo. *Cotg* —1F **71**
Pinfold Clo. *Wdbgh* —1C **24**
Pinfold Cres. *Wdbgh* —1C **24**
Pinfold La. *Nott* —5F **33**
Pinfold La. *Shelf* —6H **37**
Pinfold La. *S'fd* —4F **53**
Pinfold Rd. *Gilt* —4E **17**
Pingle Cres. *Nott* —5D **20**
Pingle, The. *Long E* —4F **63**
Pintail Clo. *Cltn* —4B **48**
**Pioneer Meadows Local Nature
    Reserve.** —5H **39**
Piper Clo. *Huck* —2H **7**
Pippin Clo. *Nott* —2B **46**
Pitcairn Clo. *Nott* —2G **57**
Pit La. *Ship* —1F **27**
Plackett Clo. *S'fd* —3H **53**
Plains Farm Clo. *Nott* —4C **34**
Plains Gro. *Nott* —3C **34**
Plains Rd. *Nott* —4B **34**
Plane Clo. *Nott* —6F **19**
Plantagenet Ct. *Nott*
    —4H **45** (2G **5**)
Plantagenet St. *Nott*
    —4H **45** (2G **5**)
Plantation Clo. *Arn* —4F **21**
Plantation Rd. *Keyw* —4F **79**
Plantation Rd. *Nott* —5C **42**
Plantation Side. *Nott* —2C **44**
Plantations, The. *Long E* —5C **62**
Plant La. *Long E* —3C **72**
Platt La. *Long E* —3H **79**
Platts Av. *Hean* —4A **14**
Player St. *Nott* —3C **44**
Play House. —5F **45** (4C **4**)
    (off E. Circus St.)
Plaza Gdns. *Nott* —3D **32**
Pleasant Ct. *Nott* —2D **44**
Pleasant Row. *Nott* —2D **44**
Plough La. *Nott* —5A **46** (5H **5**)
Ploughman Av. *Wdbgh* —1D **24**
Plover Wharf. *Nott* —1E **57**
Plowman Ct. *S'fd* —5E **53**
Plowright Clo. *Nott* —2H **45**
Plowright St. *Nott* —2H **45**
Plumb Rd. *Huck* —4F **7**
Plumptre Almhouses. *Nott* —5G **5**
Plumptre Clo. *Eastw* —4B **16**
Plumptre Pl. *Nott* —5H **45** (5F **5**)
Plumptre Rd. *Lan M* —1F **15**
Plumptre Sq. *Nott* —5H **45** (5G **5**)
Plumptre St. *Nott* —5H **45** (5F **5**)
Plumptre Way. *Eastw* —4B **16**
Plumtree Gdns. *C'tn* —4H **11**
Plumtree Rd. *Cotg* —3D **70**
Plungar Clo. *Nott* —3H **43**
Podder La. *Nott* —1E **35**
Pointers Ct. *Nott* —2C **46**
Point, The. *Nott* —1H **45**
Polperro Way. *Huck* —6C **6**
Pond Hills La. *Arn* —5B **22**
Pool Mdw. *Colw* —4H **47**
Popham Ct. *Nott* —5H **45** (5F **5**)
Popham St. *Nott* —5H **45** (5F **5**)
Poplar Av. *Nott* —5E **33**
Poplar Av. *Sand* —4C **52**
Poplar Clo. *Bing* —5G **51**
Poplar Clo. *Cltn* —3F **47**
Poplar Cres. *Nut* —1A **30**
Poplar Rd. *Breas* —4B **62**
Poplars Av. *Bur J* —2G **37**

Poplars Clo. *Plum* —3H **79**
Poplars Rd. *Nott* —1D **56**
Poplars, The. *Bees* —4F **55**
Poplars, The. *Plum* —1G **79**
Poplars, The. *W Bri* —4B **58**
Poplar St. *Nott* —5H **45** (5G **5**)
Poplar Way. *Ilk* —4H **39**
Porchester Clo. *Huck* —4A **8**
Porchester Rd. *Bing* —5D **50**
Porchester Rd. *Nott* —4B **34**
Porlock Clo. *Long E* —4C **62**
Portage Clo. *Rad T* —1E **61**
Port Arthur Rd. *Nott* —5C **46**
Porter Clo. *Nott* —5A **66**
Porters Wlk. *Nott* —3C **46**
Portinscale Clo. *W Bri* —6E **59**
Portland Ct. *Nott* —2F **33**
Portland Cres. *S'fd* —5G **53**
Portland Gdns. *Huck* —4F **7**
Portland Grange. *Huck* —4E **7**
Portland Hill. *Nott* —2A **56**
Portland Leisure Cen. —1H **57**
Portland Pk. Clo. *Huck* —4F **7**
Portland Rd. *Bees* —4H **63**
Portland Rd. *Cltn* —5E **35**
Portland Rd. *Gilt* —5D **16**
Portland Rd. *Huck* —4H **7**
Portland Rd. *Ilk* —4B **28**
Portland Rd. *Long E* —3C **72**
Portland Rd. *Nott* —4E **45** (2A **4**)
Portland Rd. *W Bri* —5B **58**
Portland St. *Bees* —4G **55**
Portland St. *Day* —1H **33**
Portree Dri. *Nott* —4D **20**
Port Said Vs. *Nott* —6D **32**
Postern St. *Nott* —5F **45** (4C **4**)
Potomac M. *Nott* —5E **45** (5A **4**)
Potters Clo. *Nott* —6E **21**
Potters Ct. *Bees* —2D **54**
Potters Way. *Ilk* —1C **40**
Poulter Clo. *Nott* —2B **44**
Poulton Dri. *Nott* —6H **45**
Poultry. *Nott* —5G **45** (4E **5**)
Poultry Arc. *Nott* —4E **5**
Powers Rd. *Nott* —1B **46**
Powis St. *Nott* —6H **19**
Powtrell Clo. *Ilk* —4D **40**
Poynter Clo. *Hean* —4A **14**
Poynton St. *Nott* —4F **45** (3C **4**)
Poyser Clo. *New B* —6E **33**
Precinct, The. *Cotg* —2F **71**
Premier Rd. *Nott* —1E **45**
Prendwick Gdns. *Nott* —5F **21**
Prestwick Clo. *Nott* —5D **30**
Prestwood Dri. *Nott* —2H **43**
Pretoria Vs. *Nott* —5A **32**
Previn Gdns. *Nott* —3B **46**
Primrose Bank. *Bing* —5D **50**
Primrose Clo. *Nott* —1D **45**
Primrose Cres. *Cltn* —2H **47**
Primrose Hill. *Ilk* —4A **28**
Primrose Ri. *Newt* —5C **16**
Primrose St. *Cltn* —2H **47**
Primrose St. *Ilk* —4A **28**
Primula Clo. *Nott* —3A **66**
Prince Edward Cres. *Rad T*
    —1D **60**
Princess Av. *Bees* —5G **55**
Princess Clo. *Ged* —5G **35**
Princess Clo. *Hean* —3B **14**
Princess Dri. *Sand* —1D **62**
Princess St. *Long E* —5F **63**
Princes St. *Eastw* —2B **16**
Prince St. *Ilk* —3A **28**
Prince St. *Long E* —5F **63**
Prioridge. *Cotg* —3G **71**
Prior Rd. *Day* —1H **33**
Priors Clo. *Bing* —4G **51**
Priory Av. *Toll* —4E **69**
Priory Cir. *Toll* —4E **69**
Priory Clo. *Ilk* —3G **39**
Priory Ct. *Ged* —5H **35**
Priory Ct. *Nott* —6A **34**
Priory Cres. *Ged* —6H **35**
Priory M. *Nott* —1C **56**
Priory Rd. *Eastw* —4B **16**
Priory Rd. *Ged* —6H **35**
Priory Rd. *Huck* —4E **7**
Priory Rd. *W Bri* —3B **58**
Priory St. *Nott* —1C **56**

Pritchard Dri. *S'fd* —5G **53**
Private Rd. *Huck* —4E **7**
Private Rd. *Sher & Map* —5G **33**
Private Rd. *Wdbgh* —6B **12**
Private Rd. 8. *Colw I* —4H **47**
Private Rd. 5. *Colw I* —4B **48**
Private Rd. 4. *Colw I* —4B **48**
Private Rd. 1. *Colw I* —3H **47**
Private Rd. 7. *Colw I* —3H **47**
Private Rd. 3. *Colw I* —4A **48**
Private Rd. 2. *Colw I* —4H **47**
Prize Clo. *Nott* —4A **66**
Promenade. *Nott* —4H **45** (2G **5**)
Prospect Pl. *Nott* —6D **44**
Prospect Rd. *Cltn* —6C **34**
Prospect Rd. *Hean* —5E **15**
Prospect St. *Nott* —3C **44**
Prospect Ter. *Nott* —3C **44**
Providence Pl. *Ilk* —6A **28**
Prudhoe Ct. *Nott* —2H **57**
Pulborough Clo. *Nott* —3D **32**
Pullman Rd. *Nott* —5B **46**
Pumping Sta. Cotts. *Nott* —6C **46**
Purbeck Clo. *Long E* —5C **62**
Purbeck Dri. *W Bri* —6G **57**
Purchase Av. *Los* —3A **14**
Purdy Mdw. *Long E* —2B **72**
Pyatt St. *Nott* —2H **57**
Pygall Av. *Got* —6G **75**
Pym Leys. *Long E* —2B **72**
Pym St. *Nott* —3B **46**
Pym Wlk. *Nott* —3A **46** (1H **5**)

Quantock Clo. *Arn* —3F **21**
Quantock Gro. *Bing* —5C **50**
Quantock Rd. *Long E* —4C **62**
Quarry Av. *Nott* —1H **31**
Quarrydale. *Huck* —2F **7**
Quarry Hill. *Stan D* —3B **52**
Quarry Hill Ind. Est. *Ilk* —4B **40**
Quarry Hill Rd. *Ilk* —4B **40**
Quayside Clo. *Nott* —2A **58**
Queen Elizabeth Rd. *Bees* —1A **64**
Queen Elizabeth Way. *Ilk* —4G **39**
Queens Av. *Ged* —5G **35**
Queens Av. *Hean* —3B **14**
Queens Av. *Ilk* —4C **40**
Queens Av. *Stan* —3A **38**
Queensberry St. *Nott* —3C **32**
Queen's Bower Rd. *Nott* —5G **21**
Queens Bri. Rd. *Nott* —6G **45**
Queensbury Av. *W Bri* —2G **67**
Queen's Ct. *Bing* —4D **50**
Queen's Dri. *Bees* —5G **55**
Queen's Dri. *Ilk* —1A **40**
Queen's Dri. *Nott* —4E **57**
Queens Dri. *Nut* —1C **30**
Queen's Dri. *Sand* —1D **62**
Queens Rd. *Bees* —6G **55**
Queens Rd. *Nott* —6G **45**
Queen's Rd. E. *Bees* —4H **55**
Queens Rd. N. *Eastw* —3B **16**
Queens Rd. S. *Eastw* —4B **16**
Queen's Rd. W. *Bees* —1D **64**
Queen's Sq. *Eastw* —3B **16**
Queen St. *Arn* —4B **22**
Queen St. *Huck* —3F **7**
Queen St. *Ilk* —1A **40**
Queen St. *Lan M* —2G **15**
Queen St. *Long E* —6G **63**
Queen St. *Nott* —4G **45** (3D **4**)
Queens Wlk. *Nott* —2F **57**
Queen Ter. *Ilk* —1A **40**
Querneby Av. *Nott* —5A **34**
Querneby Rd. *Nott* —5A **34**
Quinton Clo. *Nott* —6F **57**
Quorn Clo. *Bees* —2E **65**
Quorndon Cres. *Long E* —2F **73**
Quorn Gro. *Nott* —4E **33**
Quorn Rd. *Nott* —4E **33**

Racecourse Rd. *Nott* —5D **34**
Radbourne Rd. *Nott* —6B **46**
Radburn Ct. *S'fd* —2G **53**
Radcliffe Gdns. *Cltn* —1F **47**
Radcliffe Lodge. *Rad T* —6E **49**
Radcliffe Mt. *W Bri* —2B **58**

Radcliffe On Trent Golf Course—Rosewall Ct.

Radcliffe on Trent Golf Course.
—1H 61
Radcliffe Rd. *Gam & Rad T* —3F 59
Radcliffe Rd. *W Bri & Gam* —2A 58
Radcliffe St. *Nott* —2H 57
Radford Boulevd. *Nott* —3C 44
Radford Bri. Rd. *Nott* —4A 44
Radford Ct. *Nott* —4D 44
Radford Ct. Ind. Est. *Nott* —4D 44
Radford Cres. *Ged* —5G 35
Radford Gro. La. *Nott* —3C 44
Radford Rd. *Nott* —5C 32
Radham Ct. *Nott* —5G 33
Radley Sq. *Nott* —2B 32
Radmarsh Rd. *Nott* —6C 44
Rad Meadows. *Long E* —1E 73
Radnor Gro. *Bing* —5C 50
Radstock Rd. *Nott* —2C 46
Radway Dri. *Nott* —6E 57
Ragdale Rd. *Nott* —5H 19
(in two parts)
Raglan Clo. *Nott* —2H 45
Raglan Ct. *Bees* —2G 55
Raglan Dri. *Ged* —6B 36
Raglan St. *Eastw* —4C 16
Raibank Gdns. *Wd'p* —2A 34
Railway Cotts. *Kimb* —1H 29
Rainham Gdns. *Rud* —1G 77
Raithby Clo. *Nott* —1E 33
Raleigh Clo. *Ilk* —4B 28
Raleigh Clo. *Nott* —4A 66
Raleigh Ct. *Nott* —3E 45 (1A 4)
Raleigh M. *Nott* —4E 45 (2A 4)
Raleigh St. *Nott* —4E 45 (2A 4)
Ralf Clo. *W Bri* —1A 68
Ramblers Clo. *Colw* —4G 47
Ramsdale Av. *C'tn* —3F 11
Ramsdale Cres. *Nott* —4H 33
Ramsdale Pk. Golf Cen. —3D 10
Ramsdale Rd. *Cltn* —6G 35
Ramsey Clo. *S'fd* —1G 53
Ramsey Ct. *Nott* —6F 33
Ranby Wlk. *Nott* —3B 46
Rancliffe Av. *Keyw* —3F 79
Randal Gdns. *Nott* —2D 44
Randal St. *Nott* —2C 44
(in two parts)
Ranelagh Gro. *Nott* —4G 43
Ranmere Rd. *Nott* —2G 43
Ranmoor Rd. *Ged* —6H 35
Ranmore Clo. *Bees* —1B 54
Rannerdale Clo. *W Bri* —5E 59
Rannoch Ri. *Arn* —4B 22
Rannock Gdns. *Keyw* —4H 79
Ranskill Gdns. *Nott* —5E 21
Ransom Dri. *Nott* —6A 34
Ransom Rd. *Nott* —6A 34
Ranson Rd. *Bees* —4C 64
Ratcliffe St. *Eastw* —3B 16
Rathgar Clo. *Nott* —5D 42
Rathmines Clo. *Nott* —6C 44
Rathvale Ct. *Bees* —1A 64
Ravena Clo. *Colw* —3G 47
Raven Av. *Nott* —3F 33
Ravenhill Clo. *Bees* —1B 64
Ravens Ct. *Nott* —2F 33
Ravensdale Av. *Long E* —3D 62
Ravensdale Dri. *Nott* —6C 42
Ravensdene Ct. *Nott* —1G 45
Ravensmore Rd. *Nott* —5F 33
Ravenswood Ri. *Arn* —6B 22
Ravensworth Rd. *Nott* —5H 19
Rawson St. *Nott* —6D 32
Raymede Clo. *Nott* —1D 32
Raymede Dri. *Nott* —1C 32
Raymond Dri. *Bing* —5G 51
Rayneham Rd. *Ilk* —4G 27
Rayner Ct. *Nott* —4D 44
Raynford Av. *Bees* —6D 54
Rays Av. *Hean* —4C 14
Ray St. *Hean* —4B 14
Read Av. *Bees* —5G 55
Read Lodge. *Bees* —4G 55
Readman Rd. *Bees* —2A 64
Rearsby Clo. *Nott* —4D 42
Recreation Rd. *Sand* —5D 52
Recreation St. *Long E* —5H 63
Recreation Ter. *S'fd* —5F 53

Rectory Av. *Nott* —5E 43
Rectory Ct. *Nott* —5F 43
Rectory Ct. *W Bri* —4B 58
Rectory Dri. *Ged* —5H 35
Rectory Gdns. *Nott* —5F 43
Rectory Pl. *Bar F* —1E 75
Rectory Rd. *Breas* —5A 62
Rectory Rd. *Colw* —4G 47
Rectory Rd. *Cotg* —2E 71
Rectory Rd. *W Bri* —4A 58
Redbourne Dri. *Nott* —3A 44
Redbridge Dri. *Nut* —4D 30
Redcar Clo. *Ged* —5G 35
Redcliffe Gdns. *Nott* —1G 45
Redcliffe Rd. *Nott* —1G 45
Redfield Rd. *Lent L* —3C 56
Redfield Way. *Nott* —2C 56
Redgates Ct. *C'tn* —3F 11
Redhill Leisure Cen. —4A 22
Redhill Lodge Dri. *Red* —4H 21
Redhill Rd. *Arn* —4A 22
Redland Av. *Cltn* —1H 47
Redland Clo. *Bees* —1C 64
Redland Clo. *Ilk* —4B 28
Redland Dri. *Bees* —2C 64
Redland Gro. *Cltn* —1G 47
Red Lion Sq. *Hean* —3C 14
Redmays Dri. *Bul* —1H 37
Redmile Rd. *Nott* —5A 32
Redoubt St. *Nott* —4C 44
Redruth Clo. *Nott* —3C 42
Redwood. *W Bri* —5F 57
Redwood Av. *Nott* —6D 42
Redwood Clo. *Huck* —3F 7
Redwood Cres. *Bees* —6G 55
Reedham Wlk. *Nott* —5F 21
Reedman Rd. *Long E* —3D 72
Rees Gdns. *Nott* —4E 21
Regatta Way. *Nott* —3E 59
Regency Ct. *Bees* —4G 55
Regents Pk. Clo. *W Bri* —6G 57
Regent St. *Bees* —4G 55
Regent St. *Ilk* —2B 40
Regent St. *Kimb* —1H 29
Regent St. *Lan M* —2F 15
Regent St. *Long E* —5F 63
Regent St. *New B* —6E 33
Regent St. *Nott* —5F 45 (4B 4)
Regent St. *Sand* —6E 53
Regina Clo. *Rad T* —1E 61
Reid Gdns. *Watn* —6B 18
Reigate Clo. *Bees* —3E 65
Reigate Dri. *Bees* —3E 65
Reigate Rd. *Nott* —5D 32
Rempstone Dri. *Nott* —2B 32
Renals Way. *C'tn* —5H 11
Renfrew Dri. *Nott* —5E 43
Renne Hogg Rd. *Nott* —3E 57
Repton Clo. *Ilk* —2D 40
Repton Rd. *Long E* —3B 72
Repton Rd. *Nott* —1B 32
Repton Rd. *W Bri* —6A 58
Retford Rd. *Nott* —4E 33
Retlaw Ct. *Bees* —6D 54
Revelstoke Av. *Nott* —4B 20
Revelstoke Way. *Nott* —4B 20
Revesby Gdns. *Nott* —2A 44
Revesby Rd. *Wd'p* —2B 34
Revill Clo. *Ilk* —5G 27
Revill Cres. *S'fd* —3H 53
Reydon Dri. *Nott* —6B 32
Reynolds Dri. *Nott* —4F 43
Rhyl Cres. *Ged* —5H 35
Ribblesdale. *Ilk* —4G 39
Ribblesdale Ct. *Bees* —1A 64
Ribblesdale Rd. *Long E* —2C 72
Ribblesdale Rd. *Nott* —2G 33
Ribble St. *Nott* —4B 46
Riber Clo. *Long E* —2F 73
Riber Clo. *W Hal* —1C 38
Riber Cres. *Nott* —2D 32
Richard Herrod Bowls Cen., The.
—1E 47
Richardson Clo. *Nott* —4A 66
Richborough Pl. *Nott* —1D 54
Richey Clo. *Arn* —6D 22
Richmond Av. *Breas* —5C 62
Richmond Av. *C'tn* —3A 12
Richmond Av. *Ilk* —3B 28
Richmond Av. *Newt* —3D 16

Richmond Av. *Nott* —2B 46
Richmond Av. *Sand* —1C 62
Richmond Clo. *W Hal* —1B 38
Richmond Ct. *Bees* —6E 55
Richmond Dri. *Nott* —6E 55
Richmond Dri. *Nott* —5H 33
Richmond Dri. *Rad T* —5F 49
Richmond Gdns. *Red* —4A 22
Richmond Rd. *W Bri* —2B 58
Richmond Ter. *Rad T* —6F 49
Ricklow Ct. *Nott* —5E 21
Rick St. *Nott* —4H 45 (3F 5)
Ridding Ter. *Nott* —3G 45 (1E 5)
Ridge La. *Rad T* —4G 49
Ridgeway. *Hean* —5D 14
Ridge Way. *Nott* —6C 20
Ridgeway Dri. *Ilk* —4F 39
Ridgeway Wlk. *Nott* —5E 21
Ridgewood Dri. *Bees* —1C 64
Ridgmont Wlk. *Nott* —5B 66
(in two parts)
Ridgway Clo. *Nott* —6E 59
Ridgway St. *Nott* —3A 46
Ridings, The. *Bul* —2G 37
Ridings, The. *Keyw* —4A 80
Ridsdale Rd. *Nott* —2G 33
Rifle St. *Nott* —4C 44
Rigg Hill Ct. *Nott* —2G 31
Rigley Av. *Ilk* —6B 28
Rigley Dri. *Nott* —6C 20
Ring Leas. *Cotg* —3F 71
Ringstead Clo. *W Bri* —6G 57
Ringstead Wlk. *Nott* —5F 21
Ringwood Cres. *Nott* —4A 44
Ringwood Rd. *Bing* —5C 50
Ripon Rd. *Nott* —4D 46
Riseborough Wlk. *Nott* —4H 19
Rise Ct. *Nott* —1F 45
Risegate. *Cotg* —2F 71
Risegate Gdns. *Cotg* —2F 71
Riseholme Av. *Nott* —6C 42
Rise Pk. Rd. *Nott* —4B 20
Rise, The. *Nott* —4H 33
Risley Ct. *Ilk* —4B 28
Risley Dri. *Nott* —1F 57
Risley La. *Breas* —2A 62
Riste's Pl. *Nott* —5H 45 (4F 5)
Ritchie Clo. *Cotg* —3G 71
Ritson Clo. *Nott* —3H 45 (1G 5)
Riverdale Rd. *Bees* —3D 64
Rivergreen. *Nott* —2C 66
Rivergreen Clo. *Bees* —1C 54
Rivergreen Cres. *Bees* —1C 54
Rivermead. *Cotg* —2F 71
Rivermead. *W Bri* —4H 57
River Rd. *Colw* —5G 47
Riverside. *Bur J* —1F 49
Riverside Clo. *Bees* —2H 65
Riverside Ind. Pk. *Nott* —3E 57
Riverside Rd. *Bees* —2G 65
Riverside Way. *Nott* —2F 57
Riverview. *Nott* —2H 57
Riverway Gdns. *Nott* —1H 57
Rivington Rd. *Bees* —3G 63
Robbie Burns Rd. *Nott* —5F 21
Robbinetts La. *Coss* —6F 29
Roberts La. *Huck* —4F 7
Roberts St. *Ilk* —3C 40
Roberts St. *Nott* —5A 46
Roberts Yd. *Bees* —4G 55
Robey Clo. *Nott* —2H 7
Robey Ter. *Nott* —2D 44
Robina Dri. *Gilt* —5E 17
Robinet Rd. *Bees* —6F 55
Robin Hood Chase. *Nott* —2H 45
Robin Hood Clo. *Eastw* —4B 16
Robin Hood Dri. *Huck* —1E 19
Robin Hood Ind. Est. *Nott*
—4A 46 (2H 5)
Robin Hood Rd. *Arn* —4G 21
Robin Hood St: *Nott*
—4A 46 (3H 5)
Robin Hood Ter. *Nott*
—4H 45 (2G 5)
Robin Hood Way. *Nott* —2F 57
Robinia Ct. *W Bri* —6C 58
Robinson Gdns. *Nott* —4A 66
Robinson Rd. *Nott* —4B 34
Robinsons Hill. *Nott* —6H 19

Robinswood Ho. *Nott* —2H 43
Robins Wood Rd. *Nott* —3H 43
Rob Roy Av. *Nott* —6D 44
Roche Clo. *Arn* —6E 23
Rochester Av. *N'fld* —2A 48
Rochester Ct. *Nott* —1F 31
Rochester Dri. *Long E* —6C 62
Rochester Wlk. *Nott* —4D 66
Rochford Ct. *Edw* —2E 69
Rock Ct. *Nott* —4B 32
Rock Dri. *Nott* —6E 45 (6A 4)
Rockford Ct. *S'fd* —2G 53
Rockford Rd. *Nott* —4D 32
Rockingham Gro. *Bing* —5C 50
Rockley Av. *Newt* —4C 16
Rockley Av. *Rad T* —5F 49
Rockley Clo. *Huck* —5C 6
Rockleys Vw. *Low* —3G 25
Rock Side. *Kimb* —1H 29
Rockside Gdns. *Huck* —4E 7
Rock St. *Nott* —5G 19
Rockwell Ct. *S'fd* —4G 53
Rockwood Cres. *Huck* —5D 6
Rockwood Wlk. *Huck* —5E 7
Rodel Ct. *Nott* —3H 45 (1F 5)
Roden St. *Nott* —4A 46 (3H 5)
Roderick St. *Nott* —3B 32
Rodney Rd. *W Bri* —5C 58
Rodney Way. *Ilk* —4B 28
Rodwell Clo. *Nott* —3A 44
Roebuck Clo. *Nott* —5F 21
Roecliffe. *W Bri* —1A 68
Roehampton Dri. *Trow* —1F 53
Roe Hill. *Wdbgh* —5C 12
(in two parts)
Roe La. *Wdbgh* —1C 24
Roes La. *C'tn* —4A 12
Roker Clo. *Nott* —6G 31
Roland Av. *Nut* —3E 31
Roland Av. *Wilf* —4F 57
Rolleston Clo. *Huck* —6D 6
Rolleston Cres. *Watn* —4H 17
Rolleston Dri. *Arn* —6C 22
Rolleston Dri. *Newt* —5C 16
Rolleston Dri. *Nott* —5D 44
Roman Dri. *Nott* —3C 32
Romans Ct. *Nott* —5C 32
Romilay Clo. *Bees* —2G 55
Romney Av. *Nott* —5D 42
Romorantin Pl. *Long E* —6G 63
Rona Ct. *Nott* —2C 32
Ronald St. *Nott* —4D 44
Rookery Gdns. *Arn* —5B 22
Rookwood Clo. *Bees* —5E 55
Roosa Clo. *Nott* —2F 31
Roosevelt Av. *Long E* —2E 73
Roper Av. *Hean* —5C 14
Ropewalk Ind. Est. *Ilk* —6C 28
Ropewalk, The. *Hean* —5D 14
Ropewalk, The. *Ilk* —6C 28
Ropewalk, The. *Nott* —4E 45 (3A 4)
Ropewalk, The. *Stan C* —6A 26
Ropsley Cres. *W Bri* —2C 58
Roscoe Av. *Red* —3A 22
Roseacre. *Bees* —6G 55
Rose Ash La. *Nott* —5F 21
Rose Av. *Ilk* —5A 28
Rosebank Dri. *Arn* —4D 22
Roseberry Gdns. *Huck* —5A 8
Roseberry St. *Nott* —3C 32
Rosebery Av. *W Bri* —2A 58
Rose Clo. *Nott* —2H 45
Rose Cotts. *Bur J* —2E 37
Rose Ct. *Long E* —4D 62
Rosecroft Dri. *Nott* —1G 33
Rosedale Clo. *Long E* —1D 72
Rosedale Dri. *Nott* —5B 42
Rosedale Rd. *Nott* —3E 47
Rosegarth Wlk. *Nott* —3B 32
Rose Gro. *Bees* —6H 55
Rose Gro. *Keyw* —3H 79
Rosegrove Av. *Arn* —4B 22
Rose Hill. *Keyw* —4G 79
Roseland Clo. *Keyw* —5G 79
Roseleigh Av. *Nott* —5D 34
Rosemary Clo. *Nott* —6E 31
Roseneath Av. *Nott* —4C 20
Rosetta Rd. *Nott* —6D 32
(in two parts)
Rosewall Ct. *Arn* —6D 22

A-Z Nottingham 105

Rosewood Cres. *Hean* —3F **15**
Rosewood Gdns. *Nott* —6F **19**
Rosewood Gdns. *W Bri* —2G **67**
Roslyn Av. *Ged* —5G **35**
Rossell Dri. *S'fd* —6F **53**
Rossendale. *Ilk* —3A **28**
Rossett Clo. *Gam* —5F **59**
Rossington Rd. *Nott* —4B **46**
Ross La. *Lamb* —6C **24**
Rosslyn Dri. *Huck* —3A **8**
Rosslyn Dri. *Nott* —5G **31**
Rosthwaite Clo. *W Bri* —6E **59**
Rothbury Av. *Trow* —1F **53**
Rothbury Gro. *Bing* —4C **50**
Rothesay Av. *Nott* —4D **44**
Rothley Av. *Nott* —4B **46**
Rothwell Clo. *Nott* —1E **67**
Roughs Woods. *Huck* —1D **18**
Roundwood Rd. *Arn* —6G **21**
Rowan Av. *S'fd* —1G **53**
Rowan Clo. *Bing* —5G **51**
Rowan Clo. *C'tn* —4F **11**
Rowan Clo. *Ilk* —4B **40**
Rowan Ct. *Nut* —1B **30**
Rowan Dri. *Keyw* —5A **80**
Rowan Dri. *Nott* —1E **67**
Rowan Gdns. *Nott* —6F **19**
Rowan Wlk. *Nott* —1C **46**
Rowe Gdns. *Nott* —1B **32**
Rowland Av. *Map* —5C **34**
Rowland M. *Nott* —2A **46**
Rowsley Av. *Long E* —2C **72**
Roxley Ct. *Bees* —4E **55**
Roxton Ct. *Kimb* —6H **17**
Royal Av. *Long E* —4F **63**
Royal Cen. *Nott* —4F **45** (3D **4**)
Royal Concert Hall.
—4G **45** (3D **4**)
(off Goldsmith St.)
Royal M. *Bees* —2C **64**
Royal Standard Ct. *Nott*
—5F **45** (5C **4**)
Roy Av. *Bees* —1H **65**
Royce Av. *Huck* —1E **19**
Royston Clo. *Nott* —2F **57**
Ruby Paddocks. *Kimb* —2H **29**
Ruddington Fields Bus. Pk. *Rud*
—2H **77**
Ruddington Framework Knitters
Mus. —1G **77**
Ruddington Grange Golf Course.
—4G **67**
Ruddington La. *Nott & Wilf* —5F **57**
Ruddington Village Mus. —6G **67**
Rudge Clo. *Nott* —4F **43**
Ruffles Av. *Arn* —2D **34**
Rufford Av. *Bees* —3A **54**
Rufford Av. *Ged* —5F **35**
Rufford Clo. *Huck* —5A **8**
Rufford Gro. *Bing* —5D **50**
Rufford Rd. *Long E* —3D **72**
Rufford Rd. *Nott* —4G **33**
Rufford Rd. *Rud* —6H **67**
Rufford Wlk. *Nott* —6H **19**
Rufford Wlk. *W Bri* —5D **58**
Ruffs Dri. *Huck* —6D **6**
Rugby Clo. *Nott* —6C **20**
Rugby Rd. *W Bri* —6G **57**
Rugby Ter. *Nott* —2D **44**
Rugeley Av. *Long E* —6H **63**
Ruislip Clo. *Kimb* —6G **17**
Runcie Clo. *Cotg* —3F **71**
Runnymede Ct. *Bees* —6G **55**
Runnymede Ct. *Nott*
—4E **45** (2A **4**)
Runswick Dri. *Arn* —5B **22**
Runswick Dri. *Nott* —4G **43**
Runton Dri. *Nott* —3D **32**
Rupert Rd. *Bing* —5D **50**
Rupert St. *Ilk* —6C **28**
Ruscombe Pl. *Nott* —3H **45**
Rushcliffe Arena. —5H **57**
Rushcliffe Av. *Cltn* —1F **47**
Rushcliffe Country Pk. —2G **77**
Rushcliffe Ct. *Nott* —1B **32**
Rushcliffe Ri. *Nott* —4H **21**
Rushcliffe Rd. *Huck* —6E **7**
Rushes, The. *Got* —6H **75**
Rushford Dri. *Nott* —5C **42**

Rush Leys. *Long E* —2F **73**
Rushmere Wlk. *Arn* —2B **34**
Rushton Gdns. *Nott* —2A **46**
Rushworth Av. *W Bri* —3A **58**
Rushworth Clo. *Nott* —2A **46**
(in two parts)
Rushworth Ct. *W Bri* —3A **58**
Rushy Clo. *Nott* —4D **42**
Rushy La. *Sand & Ris* —5A **52**
Ruskin Av. *Bees* —1D **64**
Ruskin Av. *Long E* —1C **72**
Ruskin Clo. *Day* —6H **21**
Ruskin St. *Nott* —4C **44**
Russell Av. *Nott* —4F **43**
Russell Ct. *Long E* —4F **63**
Russell Cres. *Nott* —4F **43**
Russell Dri. *Nott* —4E **43**
Russell Gdns. *Bees* —3C **64**
Russell Pl. *Nott* —4F **45** (3C **4**)
Russell Rd. *Nott* —1D **44**
Russell St. *Long E* —4F **63**
Russell St. *Nott* —3E **45** (1A **4**)
Russet Av. *Cltn* —2G **47**
Russley Rd. *Bees* —3A **54**
Ruth Dri. *Arn* —4C **22**
Rutherford Ho. *Nott* —2B **56**
Ruthwell Gdns. *Nott* —3E **21**
Rutland Av. *Bees* —3A **64**
Rutland Ct. *Man I* —6H **27**
Rutland Gro. *Sand* —6E **53**
Rutland Rd. *Bing* —5F **51**
Rutland Rd. *Ged* —4F **35**
Rutland Rd. *W Bri* —2B **58**
Rutland St. *Ilk* —6B **28**
Rutland St. *Nott* —5F **45** (5C **4**)
Rutland Ter. *Ilk* —5B **28**
Rutland Ter. *Kimb* —2A **30**
Rutland Vs. *Nott* —5B **46**
Rydal Av. *Long E* —3D **62**
Rydal Dri. *Bees* —3D **54**
Rydal Dri. *Huck* —3F **7**
Rydale Rd. *Nott* —2G **33**
Rydal Gdns. *W Bri* —6C **58**
Rydal Gro. *Nott* —4C **32**
Ryder St. *Nott* —3B **32**
Ryecroft St. *S'fd* —2G **53**
Ryehill Clo. *Nott* —1H **57**
Ryehill St. *Nott* —1H **57**
Ryeland Gdns. *Nott* —1G **57**
Ryemere Clo. *Eastw* —3A **16**
Rye St. *Nott* —6D **32**
Rylands Clo. *Bees* —1H **65**
Rylands Ct. *Bees* —6G **55**
Ryton Ct. *Nott* —2H **57**
Ryton Sq. *Nott* —6H **31**

Sabina St. *Nott* —4H **45** (1G **5**)
Saddlers Yd. *Plum* —6G **69**
Saddleworth Ct. *Nott* —3G **45**
Saffron Gdns. *Nott* —1F **57**
St Agnes Clo. *Nott* —1D **42**
St Aidans Ct. *Nott* —3C **32**
St Albans Clo. *Long E* —2G **73**
St Albans Ct. *Arn* —3F **21**
St Albans M. *Nott* —1B **32**
St Albans Rd. *Arn* —6H **21**
St Albans Rd. *B Vil* —1C **20**
St Albans Rd. *Nott* —5A **20**
St Albans St. *Sher* —4G **33**
St Andrew Clo. *Got* —6H **75**
St Andrews Clo. *Huck* —3G **7**
St Andrews Clo. *Nott* —6A **20**
St Andrews Ct. *Nott* —6B **20**
St Andrew's Dri. *Ilk* —1A **40**
St Andrew's Rd. *Nott* —2F **45**
St Ann's Gdns. *Nott* —2A **46**
St Ann's Hill. *Nott* —2G **45**
St Ann's Hill Rd. *Nott* —2G **45**
St Ann's St. *Nott* —4G **45** (2E **5**)
St Ann's Valley. *Nott* —3H **45**
St Ann's Way. *Nott* —3G **45**
(1E **5**)
St Ann's Well Rd. *Nott*
—4H **45** (2F **5**)
St Anthony Ct. *Nott* —1C **56**
St Augustines Clo. *Nott* —6E **33**
St Austell Dri. *Nott* —6F **57**
St Austins Ct. *Cltn* —1H **47**
St Austins Dri. *Cltn* —1H **47**

St Barnabas R.C. Cathedral.
(off Derby Rd.) —4F **45** (3B **4**)
St Bartholomew's Rd. *Nott* —2B **46**
St Catherines St. *Rad T* —1E **61**
St Cecilia Gdns. *Nott* —3H **45**
St Chads. *Cltn* —2H **47**
St Chad's Rd. *Nott* —4A **46**
St Christopher St. *Nott* —5B **46**
St Cuthbert's Rd. *Nott* —4A **46**
St Ervan Rd. *Nott & Wilf* —5F **57**
St Georges Ct. *Huck* —3G **7**
St Georges Dri. *Bees* —3H **63**
St Georges Dri. *Nott* —1G **57**
St Helen's Cres. *Bur J* —3F **37**
St Helens Cres. *Trow* —5E **41**
St Helen's Gro. *Bur J* —4E **37**
St Helens Rd. *W Bri* —5B **58**
St Helen's St. *Nott* —4E **45** (3A **4**)
St Helier. *Nott* —5E **45** (5A **4**)
St James Av. *Ilk* —2C **40**
St James Ct. *Huck* —3G **7**
St James Ct. *Nott* —5D **34**
St James Ct. *Sand* —2D **62**
St James's St. *Nott* —5F **45** (5C **4**)
(in two parts)
St James's Ter. *Nott* —5F **45** (5C **4**)
St James St. *S'fd* —5E **53**
St James Ter. *S'fd* —5E **53**
St John's Ct. *Cltn* —2F **47**
St John's Cres. *Huck* —6A **8**
St John's Rd. *Ilk* —2C **40**
St John's Rd. *Rud* —6G **67**
St Johns St. *Long E* —6F **63**
St Judes Av. *Nott* —5H **33**
St Laurence Ct. *Long E* —1G **73**
St Lawrence Boulevd. *Rad T*
—1D **60**
St Lawrence Clo. *Hean* —3D **14**
St Leonards Dri. *Nott* —5F **43**
St Leven Clo. *Nott* —1D **42**
St Lukes Clo. *W Bri* —6D **58**
St Luke's St. *Nott* —4A **46** (3H **5**)
St Lukes Way. *Bur J* —1F **49**
St Margaret's Av. *Nott* —1A **44**
St Mark's Av. *Nott* —4H **45** (2F **5**)
St Martins Clo. *Nott* —1E **43**
St Martin's Gdns. *Nott* —1D **42**
St Martin's Rd. *Nott* —1E **43**
St Mary's Av. *Ged* —5G **35**
St Mary's Clo. *Arn* —4B **22**
St Mary's Clo. *Bees* —4D **64**
St Mary's Cres. *Rud* —6G **67**
St Marys Ga. *Nott* —5H **45** (4F **5**)
St Mary's Pl. *Nott* —5H **45** (4F **5**)
St Marys Rd. *Bing* —4F **51**
St Mary St. *Ilk* —1A **40**
St Marys Way. *Huck* —3F **7**
St Matthias Rd. *Nott* —3A **46**
St Mawes Av. *Nott* —5F **57**
St Michael's Av. *Ged* —5G **35**
St Michael's Av. *Nott* —1D **42**
St Michaels Sq. *Bees* —3B **54**
St Michaels Vw. *Huck* —2H **7**
St Nicholas Clo. *Arn* —6A **22**
St Nicholas St. *Nott* —5G **45** (5D **4**)
St Norbert Dri. *Ilk* —4G **39**
St Patrick's Rd. *Huck* —4F **7**
St Patrick's Rd. *Ilk* —1B **30**
St Pauls Av. *Nott* —2D **44**
St Paul's St. *Nott* —4B **44**
St Pauls Ter. *Nott* —2D **44**
St Peters Chambers. *Nott* —4E **5**
St Peter's Chu. Wlk. *Nott*
—5G **45** (4E **5**)
St Peters Cres. *Rud* —6G **67**
St Peter's Ga. *Nott* —5G **45** (4E **5**)
St Peter's Sq. *Nott* —4E **5**
St Peters St. *Nott* —4C **44**
St Saviours Gdns. *Nott* —1H **57**
St Stephens Av. *Nott* —5B **46**
St Stephen's Rd. *Nott* —5A **46**
St Vincent Clo. *Long E* —1G **73**
St Wilfrid's Rd. *W Hal* —2C **38**
St Wilfrid's Sq. *C'tn* —4H **11**
Salamander Clo. *Cltn* —5F **35**
Salcey Dri. *Trow* —1F **53**
Salcombe Cir. *Red* —4H **21**
Salcombe Clo. *Newt* —4E **17**
Salcombe Cres. *Rud* —5H **67**
Salcombe Dri. *Red* —4H **21**

Salcombe Rd. *Nott* —4D **32**
Salford Gdns. *Nott* —4H **45** (2G **5**)
Salisbury Ct. *Nott* —5A **34**
Salisbury Sq. *Nott* —5C **44**
Salisbury St. *Bees* —4G **55**
Salisbury St. *Long E* —6G **63**
Salisbury St. *Nott* —5C **44**
(in two parts)
Salmon Clo. *Nott* —6F **19**
Salop St. *Day* —6H **21**
Saltburn Rd. *Nott* —3G **43**
Saltby Grn. *W Bri* —2F **67**
Salterford Av. *C'tn* —3H **11**
Salterford Rd. *Huck* —6E **7**
Saltford Clo. *Ged* —5H **35**
Salthouse Clo. *Bees* —3G **55**
Salthouse Ct. *Bees* —3G **55**
Salthouse La. *Bees* —3G **55**
Saltney Way. *Nott* —2E **67**
Samson Ct. *Rud* —5F **67**
Sandale Clo. *Gam* —5E **59**
Sandays Clo. *Nott* —2G **57**
Sandby Ct. *Bees* —6C **54**
(in two parts)
Sanders Clo. *Ilk* —5G **27**
Sandfield Ct. *Nott* —1G **31**
Sandfield Rd. *Arn* —1B **34**
Sandfield Rd. *Bees* —3G **63**
Sandfield Rd. *Nott* —5D **44**
Sandford Av. *Long E* —6G **63**
Sandford Rd. *Nott* —5B **34**
Sandgate. *Bees* —2D **54**
Sandham Wlk. *Nott* —2C **56**
Sandhurst Dri. *Bees* —3C **64**
Sandhurst Dri. *Rud* —1F **77**
Sandhurst Rd. *Nott* —4H **19**
Sandiacre Friesland Sports Cen.
—6B **52**
Sandiacre Rd. *S'fd* —5E **53**
Sandon St. *Nott* —6E **33**
Sandown Rd. *Bees* —2H **63**
Sandpiper Way. *Lent* —5C **44**
Sandringham Av. *W Bri* —3A **58**
Sandringham Cres. *Nott* —4C **42**
Sandringham Dri. *Bees* —2C **54**
Sandringham Dri. *Hean* —3A **14**
Sandringham Pl. *Huck* —3H **7**
Sandringham Pl. *Ilk* —4H **39**
Sandringham Rd. *Nott* —5B **46**
Sandringham Rd. *Sand* —2D **62**
Sands Clo. *Colw* —4G **47**
Sandside. *Cotg* —3F **71**
Sandwell Clo. *Long E* —1C **72**
Sandyford Clo. *Nott* —4A **32**
Sandy La. *Bees* —1D **54**
Sandy La. *Hol P* —1B **60**
Sandy La. *Huck* —4G **7**
Sanger Clo. *Nott* —5A **66**
Sanger Gdns. *Nott* —5A **66**
Sankey Dri. *Nott* —6G **19**
Sapele Clo. *Ged* —5A **36**
Sargent Gdns. *Nott* —3B **46**
Saskatoon Clo. *Rad T* —1E **61**
Saunby Clo. *Arn* —6D **22**
Saunten Clo. *Edw* —1E **69**
Savages Rd. *Rud* —5G **67**
Savages Row. *Rud* —5G **67**
Saville Clo. *S'fd* —3G **53**
Saville Rd. *Wd'p* —2B **34**
Savoy Workshops. *Lent* —6D **44**
Sawley Bridge Marina. —5C **72**
Sawley Rd. *Breas* —6A **62**
Sawley Rd. *Dray* —2A **73**
Sawmand Clo. *Long E* —1E **73**
Sawmills Ind. Pk. *Los* —2B **16**
Saxelby Gdns. *Nott* —5H **19**
Saxondale Dri. *Nott* —2B **32**
Saxon Grn. *Nott* —6C **44**
Saxon Way. *Cotg* —4F **71**
Saxton Av. *Hean* —3D **14**
Saxton Clo. *Bees* —4H **55**
Scafell Clo. *W Bri* —6E **59**
Scafell Way. *Nott* —6B **66**
Scalby Clo. *Eastw* —3H **15**
Scalford Dri. *Nott* —4H **43**
Scarborough Av. *Ilk* —1H **39**
Scarborough St. *Nott*
—4H **45** (2G **5**)
Scarf Wlk. *Nott* —4F **57**
Scargill Av. *Newt* —4D **16**

Taylors Cft. *Wdbgh* —1B **24**
Taylor St. *Ilk* —6B **28**
TDG Pinnacle. *W Hal* —3C **38**
Teak Clo. *Nott* —2H **45**
Tealby Clo. *Nott* —6F **19**
Teal Clo. *Cltn* —3B **48**
Teal Wharf. *Nott* —1E **57**
Teasels, The. *Bing* —6D **50**
Technology Dri. *Bees* —6G **55**
Teesbrook Dri. *Nott* —5B **42**
Teesdale Ct. *Bees* —1A **64**
Teesdale Rd. *Long E* —1C **72**
Teesdale Rd. *Nott* —5E **33**
Telford Dri. *Newt* —2D **16**
Templar Lodge. *Bees* —5H **55**
Templar Rd. *Bees* —5H **55**
Temple Cres. *Nut* —3D **30**
Temple Dri. *Nut* —3E **31**
Templeman Clo. *Rud* —5F **67**
Templeoak Dri. *Nott* —6C **42**
Tenbury Cres. *Nott* —6H **31**
Tene Clo. *Arn* —3B **22**
Tennis Ct. Ind. Est. *Nott* —6C **46**
Tennis Dri. *Nott* —5E **45** (4A **4**)
Tennis M. *Nott* —5E **45** (4A **4**)
Tennis Vw. *Nott* —5E **45** (4A **4**)
Tennyson Av. *Ged* —6H **35**
Tennyson Ct. *Huck* —5D **6**
Tennyson Ct. *Nott* —4F **33**
Tennyson Dri. *Bees* —3D **64**
Tennyson Rd. *Wd'p* —3A **34**
Tennyson St. *Ilk* —4A **28**
Tennyson St. *Nott* —3E **45** (1A **4**)
(in two parts)
Tenter Clo. *Long E* —2F **73**
Tenter Clo. *Nott* —5D **20**
Terrace St. *Nott* —2D **44**
Terrian Cres. *W Bri* —4B **58**
Terton Rd. *Nott* —5D **20**
Tetney Wlk. *Nott* —2G **43**
Tettenbury Rd. *Nott* —4D **32**
Teversal Av. *Nott* —5D **44**
Tevery Clo. *S'fd* —3G **53**
Teviot Rd. *Nott* —2D **32**
Tewkesbury Clo. *W Bri* —5C **58**
Tewkesbury Dri. *Kimb* —6G **17**
Tewkesbury Dri. *Nott* —3C **32**
Tewkesbury Rd. *Long E* —3G **73**
Thackeray's La. *Wd'p* —2H **33**
Thackeray St. *Nott* —4D **44**
Thames St. *Nott* —5B **56**
Thane Rd. *Nott* —5B **56**
Thaxted Clo. *Nott* —3D **42**
Theatre Royal. —4G **45** (3D **4**)
(off Goldsmith St.)
Theatre Sq. *Nott* —4G **45** (3D **4**)
Thelda Rd. *Keyw* —4G **79**
Thetford Clo. *Arn* —1C **34**
Third Av. *Cltn* —1D **46**
(in two parts)
Third Av. *Ged* —6H **35**
Third Av. *Ilk* —2B **40**
Third Av. *Lent* —5A **56**
Third Av. *Nott* —1F **45**
Thirlbeck. *Cotg* —3G **71**
Thirlmere. *W Bri* —6E **59**
Thirlmere Clo. *Long E* —3D **62**
Thirlmere Clo. *Nott* —2B **46**
Thirlmere Rd. *Long E* —3D **62**
Thirston Clo. *Nott* —6F **19**
Thistle Clo. *Newt* —5D **16**
Thistledown Rd. *Nott* —6C **66**
Thistle Grn. Clo. *Hean* —4F **15**
Thistle Rd. *Ilk* —5C **40**
Thomas Av. *Rad T* —5H **49**
Thomas Clo. *Nott* —3H **45** (1G **5**)
Thompson Clo. *Bees* —2C **64**
Thompson Gdns. *Nott* —5H **21**
Thompson St. *Lan M* —2F **15**
Thoresby Av. *Ged* —5F **35**
Thoresby Av. *Nott* —6B **46**
Thoresby Clo. *Rad T* —5G **49**
Thoresby Ct. *Nott* —1H **45**
Thoresby Dale. *Huck* —4H **7**
Thoresby Rd. *Bees* —2C **54**
Thoresby Rd. *Bing* —5C **50**
Thoresby Rd. *Long E* —1D **72**
Thoresby St. *Nott* —5A **46** (5H **5**)
Thor Gdns. *Nott* —4D **20**
Thornbury Way. *Nott* —6D **20**

Thorncliffe Ri. *Nott* —1G **45**
Thorncliffe Rd. *Nott* —1G **45**
Thorndale Rd. *C'tn* —4H **11**
Thorndale Rd. *Nott* —5A **32**
Thorn Dri. *Newt* —5D **16**
Thorndyke Clo. *Bees* —1H **65**
Thorner Clo. *Nott* —2C **32**
Thorney Hill. *Nott* —2C **32**
Thorneywood Mt. *Nott* —2B **46**
Thorneywood Ri. *Nott* —2B **46**
Thorneywood Rd. *Long E* —5H **63**
Thornfield Ind. Est. *Nott* —4B **46**
Thorn Gro. *Huck* —1H **19**
Thornhill Clo. *Bees* —1B **54**
Thornley St. *Nott* —2C **44**
Thornthwaite Clo. *W Bri* —5E **59**
Thornton Av. *Red* —4H **21**
Thornton Clo. *Nott* —5E **43**
Thorntons Clo. *Cotg* —2G **71**
Thornton Ter. *Nott* —2D **44**
Thorntree Clo. *Breas* —4B **62**
Thorn Tree Gdns. *Eastw* —1B **16**
Thorold Clo. *Nott* —3C **66**
Thoroton Rd. *W Bri* —2B **58**
Thoroton St. *Nott* —4E **45**
Thorpe Clo. *Nott* —5D **20**
Thorpe Clo. *S'fd* —4E **53**
Thorpe Cres. *Nott* —5D **34**
Thorpe Hill Dri. *Hean* —6C **14**
Thorpe Leys. *Long E* —2G **73**
Thorpe Rd. *Eastw* —1B **16**
Thorpe's Rd. *Hean* —4B **14**
Thorpes Rd. Ind. Est. *Hean* —5B **14**
Thorpe St. *Ilk* —4A **28**
Thrapston Av. *Arn* —3B **22**
Thraves Yd. *Rad T* —6E **49**
Three Tuns Rd. *Eastw* —3C **16**
Threlkeld Clo. *W Bri* —5E **59**
Thrumpton Av. *Long E* —6H **63**
Thrumpton Dri. *Nott* —2F **57**
Thrumpton La. *Keyw* —6B **80**
Thurlestone Dri. *Nott* —1E **35**
Thurloe Ct. *W Bri* —2G **67**
Thurman Dri. *Cotg* —2F **71**
Thurman St. *Ilk* —3C **40**
Thurman St. *Nott* —3D **44**
Thurmans Yd. *Nott* —3D **44**
Thursby Rd. *Nott* —2C **66**
Thymus Wlk. *Nott* —4A **66**
Thyra Ct. *Nott* —6A **34**
Thyra Gro. *Bees* —5G **55**
Thyra Gro. *Nott* —6H **33**
Tidworth Clo. *Nott* —3G **43**
Tilberthwaite Clo. *Gam* —5E **59**
Tilbury Ri. *Nott* —4G **31**
Tilford Gdns. *S'fd* —5G **53**
Tilstock Ct. *Watn* —5A **18**
Tilton Gro. *Ilk* —4G **39**
Tim La. *Bur J* —3F **37**
Tinker Cft. *Ilk* —2A **40**
Tinsley Rd. *Eastw* —4H **15**
Tintagel Grn. *Nott* —4C **66**
Tintern Dri. *Nott* —5B **32**
Tippett Ct. *Nott* —3B **46**
Tip Tree Clo. *Kimb* —6H **17**
Tiree Clo. *Trow* —6F **41**
Tishbite St. *Nott* —6H **19**
Tissington Clo. *Nott* —1E **45**
Tissington Rd. *Nott* —1E **45**
Titchfield St. *Huck* —5G **7**
Titchfield St. *Huck* —4H **7**
Titchfield Ter. *Huck* —4H **7**
Tithby Dri. *Nott* —3H **33**
Tithby Rd. *Bing* —6E **51**
Tithe Gdns. *Nott* —4E **21**
Tithe La. *C'tn* —4H **11**
Tiverton Clo. *Huck* —6D **6**
Tiverton Clo. *Nott* —5H **31**
Toad La. *Epp* —6G **13**
Tobias Clo. *Nott* —5D **20**
Todd Clo. *Nott* —5A **66**
Todd Ct. *Nott* —5A **66**
Toft Clo. *Cotg* —3E **71**
Toft Rd. *Bees* —2A **64**
Token Ho. Yd. *Nott* —4E **5**
Tollerton Grn. *Nott* —2B **32**

Tollerton La. *Toll* —5F **69**
Tollerton Rd. *Rad T* —5F **59**
Tollhouse Hill. *Nott* —4F **45** (3C **4**)
Tomlinson Av. *Got* —6G **75**
Tonbridge Mt. *Nott* —1D **54**
Tonnelier Rd. *Nott* —2C **56**
Top Rd. *Rud* —1G **77**
Top Row. *Bur J* —2D **48**
Top Valley Dri. *Nott* —5C **20**
Top Valley Way. *Nott* —6C **20**
Torbay Cres. *Nott* —1F **33**
Torkard Dri. *Nott* —5D **20**
Torrington Ct. *Nott* —5H **33**
Torvill Dri. *Nott* —4D **42**
Toston Dri. *Nott* —5A **44**
Totland Dri. *Bees* —5B **32**
Totland Rd. *Bees* —1C **54**
Totley Clo. *Nott* —3A **20**
Totnes Clo. *Huck* —5D **6**
Totnes Rd. *Nott* —4D **46**
Toton Clo. *Nott* —2B **32**
Toton La. *S'fd* —4F **53**
Tottle Gdns. *Nott* —3B **44**
Tottle Rd. *Nott* —3E **57**
Tourist Info. Cen. —5G **45** (4E **5**)
(off Smithy Row, Nottingham)
Tower Cres. *Kimb* —3A **30**
Towe's Mt. *Cltn* —2G **47**
Towle St. *Long E* —3C **72**
Towlson Ct. *Bees* —2D **64**
Towlsons Cft. *Nott* —4B **32**
Townsend Ct. *Nott* —4E **21**
Townside Clo. *Long E* —3D **72**
Town St. *Bees* —4A **54**
Town St. *Sand* —6D **52**
Town Vw. *Kimb* —6H **17**
Towson Av. *Lan M* —3G **15**
Towyn Ct. *Nott* —6E **21**
Tracy Clo. *Bees* —2E **55**
Trafalgar Clo. *Nott* —3D **44**
Trafalgar Rd. *Bees* —1G **65**
Trafalgar Rd. *Long E* —1F **73**
Trafalgar Sq. *Long E* —6H **63**
Trafalgar Ter. *Long E* —6H **63**
Traffic St. *Nott* —6G **45**
Trafford Gdns. *Nott* —2B **44**
Tranby Gdns. *Nott* —5F **43**
Travers Rd. *Sand* —5C **52**
Treegarth Sq. *Nott* —4F **21**
Tree Vw. Clo. *Arn* —4G **21**
Trefan Gdns. *Nott* —6E **21**
Trefoil Clo. *Bing* —6D **50**
Trelawn Clo. *Nott* —5H **33**
Tremadoc Ct. *Nott* —1F **45**
Tremayne Rd. *Nott* —3C **42**
Trenchard Clo. *Nwtn* —2B **50**
Trent Av. *Rud* —5G **67**
Trent Boulevd. *W Bri* —2B **58**
Trent Bri. *Nott* —2A **58**
Trent Bri. Bldgs. *W Bri* —2A **58**
Trent Cotts. *Long E* —3E **73**
Trent Ct. *W Bri* —2C **58**
Trent Cres. *Bees* —4G **55**
Trentdale Rd. *Cltn* —3F **47**
Trent Dri. *Huck* —2D **18**
Trent Gdns. *Bur J* —3G **37**
Trentham Dri. *Nott* —2A **44**
Trentham Gdns. *Bur J* —4D **36**
Trentham Gdns. *Nott* —2A **44**
Trent Ho. *Long E* —3C **72**
Trent La. *Bur J* —3F **37**
Trent La. *Long E* —4G **73**
Trent La. *Nott* —6B **46**
Trent Lock Golf Course. —3E **73**
Trenton Clo. *Bees* —2A **54**
Trenton Dri. *Long E* —5A **64**
Trent Rd. *Bees* —4G **55**
Trent Rd. *Ilk* —5H **39**
Trent Rd. *Nott* —5B **46**
Trentside. *Bees* —2G **65**
Trentside. *W Bri* —3A **58**
Trentside N. *W Bri* —2A **58**
Trent S. Ind. Pk. *Nott* —6C **46**
Trent St. *Long E* —5G **63**
Trent St. *Nott* —6H **45** (6F **5**)
Trent Va. Rd. *Bees* —1G **65**
Trent Valley Vw. *Nott* —6C **34**
Trentview Rd. *Nott* —1B **58**
Trent Vw. Gdns. *Rad T* —4G **49**
Tressall Clo. *Ilk* —1C **40**

Trevelyan Rd. *W Bri* —2B **58**
Trevino Gdns. *Nott* —5E **21**
Trevone Av. *S'fd* —5G **53**
Trevor Rd. *Bees* —6F **55**
Trevor Rd. *W Bri* —6C **58**
Trevose Gdns. *Nott* —4H **33**
Treyford Clo. *Nott* —1E **67**
Triangle, The. *Ilk* —3C **40**
Tricornia Dri. *Nott* —3H **31**
Trigg Ct. *Los* —1A **14**
Tring Va. *Nott* —3E **33**
Trinity Av. *Nott* —6C **44**
Trinity Clo. *Ilk* —4A **28**
Trinity Cres. *Lamb* —6C **24**
Trinity Row. *Nott* —4G **45** (3D **4**)
Trinity Sq. *Nott* —4G **45** (2E **5**)
Trinity Wlk. *Nott* —4G **45** (3E **5**)
Trinstead Way. *Nott* —6G **21**
Triumph Rd. *Nott* —4B **44**
Trivett Sq. *Nott* —5H **45** (5G **5**)
Troon Clo. *Kimb* —6G **17**
Trough La. *Watn* —5H **17**
Trough Rd. *Watn* —5H **17**
Troutbeck. *Cotg* —2G **71**
Troutbeck Cres. *Bees* —3C **54**
Trowell Av. *Ilk* —4C **40**
Trowell Av. *Nott* —4B **42**
Trowell Gdns. *Nott* —4C **42**
Trowell Gro. *Long E* —3D **62**
Trowell Gro. *Trow* —6F **41**
Trowell Pk. Dri. *Trow* —1F **53**
Trowell Rd. *Nott* —5B **42**
Trowell Rd. *S'fd* —1G **53**
Trueman Gdns. *Arn* —1D **34**
Trueman St. *Ilk* —3B **28**
Truman Clo. *Nott* —3H **45** (1F **5**)
Truman Dri. *Huck* —5G **7**
Trumans Rd. *Nott* —2H **57**
Truman St. *Kimb* —6F **17**
Truro Cres. *Nott* —2C **44**
Tudor Clo. *Colw* —4G **47**
Tudor Clo. *Long E* —4F **63**
Tudor Ct. *Huck* —6C **6**
Tudor Ct. *S'fd* —6F **53**
Tudor Falls. *Hean* —2C **14**
Tudor Gro. *Nott* —2F **45**
Tudor Pl. *Ilk* —4G **39**
Tudor Rd. *W Bri* —4B **58**
Tudor Sq. *W Bri* —4B **58**
Tudwal Clo. *Nott* —6E **21**
Tudwal Wlk. *Nott* —6E **21**
Tulip Av. *Nott* —2H **45**
Tulip Rd. *Aws* —2D **28**
Tunnel Rd. *Nott* —5E **45** (5A **4**)
Tunstall Cres. *Nott* —6G **31**
Tunstall Dri. *Nott* —3D **32**
Tunstall Rd. *Wd'p* —3B **34**
Turnberry Clo. *Bees* —5C **54**
Turnberry Clo. *Ilk* —5G **27**
Turnberry Ct. *Edw* —2E **69**
Turnberry Rd. *Nott* —1B **32**
Turner Av. *Lan M* —2E **15**
Turner Clo. *S'fd* —5G **53**
Turner Dri. *Gilt* —6D **16**
Turner Rd. *Long E* —3E **73**
Turner St. *Huck* —4G **7**
Turneys Ct. *Nott* —1A **58**
Turney St. *Nott* —2H **57**
Turnpike La. *Bees* —3G **55**
Turnstone Wharf. *Nott* —1D **56**
Turpin Av. *Ged* —4F **35**
Turrell Ct. *Bramc* —2D **54**
Turton Clo. *Lan M* —2E **15**
Tuxford Wlk. *Nott* —3B **46**
Twells Clo. *Nott* —2B **46**
Twitchell, The. *Bees* —1E **65**
Twycross Rd. *Nott* —6F **21**
Twyford Clo. *Hean* —5A **14**
Twyford Clo. *W Hal* —1B **38**
Twyford Gdns. *Nott* —1C **66**
Twyford Rd. *Long E* —3B **72**
Tyburn Clo. *Arn* —4E **21**
Tynedale Clo. *Long E* —1C **72**
Tynedale Clo. *Nott* —6B **32**
Tyne Gdns. *Huck* —2D **18**

Ulldale Ct. *Bees* —1B **64**
Ullscarf Clo. *W Bri* —6E **59**

Wintringham Cres.—Zulu Rd.

Wintringham Cres. *Wd'p* —2C **34**
Wirksworth Rd. *Ilk* —4F **39**
Wisa Ter. *Nott* —4H **33**
Wishford Av. *Nott* —6C **44**
Wisley Clo. *W Bri* —2G **67**
Wistow Clo. *Nott* —1C **44**
Withern Rd. *Nott* —6F **31**
Witney Clo. *Nott* —5C **20**
Wittering Clo. *Long E* —2G **73**
Wiverton Rd. *Bing* —5E **51**
Wiverton Rd. *Nott* —1E **45**
Woburn Clo. *Edw* —1E **69**
Woburn Cft. *Sand* —1C **62**
Woburn Ri. *Wd'p* —2D **34**
Wodehouse Av. *Got* —5H **75**
Wolds Dri. *Keyw* —5H **79**
Wolds La. *Clip* —5D **70**
Wolds La. *Keyw* —5H **79**
Wolds Ri. *Keyw* —4H **79**
Wollaton Av. *Ged* —4F **35**
Wollaton Ct. *Nott* —1C **32**
Wollaton Cres. *Bees* —3E **55**
Wollaton Hall Dri. *Nott* —6B **44**
Wollaton Hall Natural
  History Mus. —6G **43**
Wollaton Paddocks. *Nott* —5C **42**
Wollaton Pk. —6H **43**
Wollaton Ri. *Nott* —1E **55**
Wollaton Rd. *Bees* —2E **55**
Wollaton Rd. *Nott* —5E **43**
Wollaton St. *Huck* —4H **7**
Wollaton St. *Nott* —4F **45** (3B **4**)
Wollaton Va. *Nott* —5B **42**
Wolsey Av. *Nott* —4D **44**
Wood Av. *Sand* —5C **52**
Woodbank Dri. *Nott* —1D **54**
Woodborough La. *Arn & Wdbgh*
  —2D **22**
Woodborough Rd. *Nott*
  —3G **45** (1D **4**)
Woodbridge Av. *Nott* —2C **66**
Woodchurch Rd. *Arn* —4F **21**
Wood End Rd. *Hean* —3C **14**
Woodfield Rd. *Nott* —6E **31**
Woodford Clo. *Nott* —4C **20**
Woodford Rd. *Huck* —5H **7**
Woodford Rd. *Wd'p* —2C **34**
Woodgate Clo. *Cotg* —2E **71**
Woodgate Ct. *Nott* —4E **45** (3A **4**)
Woodgate La. *Cotg* —1D **70**
Wood Gro. *C'tn* —3H **11**
Woodhall Rd. *Nott* —4H **43**
Woodhedge Dri. *Nott* —1C **46**
Woodhouse St. *Nott* —4B **46**
Woodhouse Way. *Nott* —1D **42**

Woodkirk Rd. *Nott* —3D **66**
Woodland Av. *Breas* —5B **62**
Woodland Av. *Ilk* —3H **27**
Woodland Av. *Nott* —2A **32**
Woodland Clo. *Cotg* —3F **71**
Woodland Clo. *Rad T* —6H **49**
Woodland Dri. *Nott* —6H **33**
Woodland Dri. *Nut* —3F **31**
Woodland Farm Clo. *Huck* —1D **18**
Woodland Gro. *Bees* —6D **54**
Woodland Gro. *Colw* —3H **47**
Woodland Gro. *Wd'p* —3H **33**
Woodland Rd. *W Bri* —2B **58**
Woodlands. *Wat* —6A **18**
Woodlands Gro. *Huck* —1D **18**
Woodlands, The. *Rad T* —6E **49**
Woodland Way. *Eastw* —3A **16**
Wood La. *Ged* —6A **36**
Wood La. *Huck* —4E **7**
Woodlane Gdns. *Nott* —2B **46**
Woodlark Ho. *Nott* —2B **46**
Wood Leigh. *Keyw* —5G **79**
Woodleigh Gdns. *Nott* —5D **34**
Woodleys. *Nott* —2C **46**
Woodley Sq. *Nott* —3A **20**
Woodley St. *Rud* —6G **67**
Wood Link. *Nott* —6E **19**
Woodpecker Clo. *Bing* —6F **51**
Woodpecker Hill. *Dal A* —6E **39**
Woodsend Clo. *Bur J* —3F **37**
Woodsford Gro. *Nott* —3C **66**
Woodside. *Eastw* —3A **16**
Woodside Av. *Nut* —1A **30**
Woodside Clo. *Rad T* —6H **49**
Woodside Cres. *Long E* —5D **62**
Woodside Dri. *Arn* —5H **21**
Woodside Rd. *Bees* —2F **55**
  (Audley Dri.)
Woodside Rd. *Bees* —1A **64**
  (Gell Rd.)
Woodside Rd. *Bur J* —4D **36**
Woodside Rd. *Rad T* —6H **49**
Woodside Rd. *Sand* —6C **52**
Woods La. *C'tn* —4G **11**
Woodstock Av. *Nott* —3C **44**
Woodstock Cres. *Ilk* —2H **27**
Woodstock Rd. *Bees* —2G **63**
Woodstock St. *Huck* —5H **7**
Woodstock St. W. *Huck* —5H **7**
Woodston Wlk. *Arn* —3C **22**
Wood St. *Arn* —5B **22**
Wood St. *Eastw* —3B **16**
Wood St. *Ilk* —6B **28**
Wood St. *Nott* —4E **45** (3A **4**)
Woodthorpe Av. *Wd'p* —3A **34**

Woodthorpe Ct. *Nott* —4A **34**
Woodthorpe Dri. *Wd'p & Map*
  —3H **33**
Woodthorpe Gdns. *Nott* —4B **34**
Woodthorpe Grange Pk. —4A **34**
Woodthorpe Rd. *Nott* —4B **34**
Woodvale. *Nott* —5C **42**
Woodview. *Cotg* —2G **71**
Woodview Bus. Cen. *Arn* —4E **21**
Woodview St. *Nott* —4E **47**
Woodville Clo. *Bees* —5C **54**
Woodville Dri. *Nott* —4G **33**
Woodville Rd. *Nott* —5G **33**
Woodward St. *Nott* —2H **57**
Woodyard La. *Nott* —4G **43**
Woolacombe Clo. *Nott* —2F **35**
Wooliscroft Way. *Ilk* —5G **27**
Woolmer Rd. *Nott* —2G **57**
Woolpack La. *Nott* —5H **45** (4F **5**)
  (in two parts)
Wool Pk. La. *Nott* —5H **45** (4G **5**)
Woolsington Clo. *Nott* —5D **30**
Woolsthorpe Clo. *Nott* —3F **43**
Woolsthorpe Cres. *Ilk* —5H **39**
Wootton Clo. *Nott* —2D **42**
Worcester Gdns. *Wd'p* —1A **34**
Worcester Rd. *Wd'p* —2A **34**
Wordsworth Av. *Huck* —5D **6**
Wordsworth Av. *Aws* —2E **29**
Wordsworth Rd. *Day* —6H **21**
Wordsworth Rd. *Nott* —3C **44**
Wordsworth Rd. *W Bri* —5A **58**
Worksop Rd. *Nott* —4B **46**
Worrall Av. *Arn* —6B **22**
Worrall Av. *Long E* —4G **63**
Worth St. *Cltn* —1G **47**
Wortley Av. *Trow* —6F **41**
Wortley Clo. *Ilk* —1C **40**
Wortley Hall Clo. *Nott* —1A **56**
Worwood Dri. *W Bri* —1G **67**
Woulds Fld. *Cotg* —4F **71**
Wray Clo. *Nott* —4A **46** (2H **5**)
Wrenthorpe Va. *Nott* —4C **66**
Wrights Orchard. *Keyw* —5G **79**
Wright St. *N'fld* —2A **48**
Wroughton Ct. *Eastw* —3C **16**
Wroxham Dri. *Nott* —6D **42**
Wychwood Dri. *Trow* —1F **53**
Wychwood Rd. *Bing* —5C **50**
Wycliffe Gro. *Nott* —5A **34**
Wycliffe St. *Nott* —5D **32**
Wycombe Clo. *Nott* —5B **66**
Wye Gdns. *Nott* —3B **44**
Wykeham Rd. *Wd'p* —2C **34**

Wykes Av. *Ged* —5H **35**
Wymondham Clo. *Arn* —1C **34**
Wynbreck Dri. *Keyw* —4H **79**
Wyndale Dri. *Ilk* —3G **39**
Wyndham Ct. *Bees* —1B **64**
Wyndham M. *Nott* —2F **45**
Wyndings, The. *Wd'p* —3B **34**
Wynhill Ct. *Bing* —4C **50**
Wynndale Dri. *Nott* —4E **33**
Wynwood Clo. *Bees* —4B **64**
Wynwood Rd. *Bees* —4B **64**
Wynyard Clo. *Ilk* —4H **27**
Wyrale Dri. *Nott* —6E **31**
Wysall La. *Keyw* —6G **79**
Wysall Rd. *Bun* —6D **78**
Wyton Clo. *Nott* —2E **33**
Wyvern Av. *Long E* —1F **73**
Wyvern Clo. *Newt* —5C **16**
Wyville Clo. *Nott* —4C **44**

Yalding Dri. *Nott* —5C **42**
Yalding Gdns. *Nott* —5C **42**
Yarwell Clo. *Nott* —2E **47**
Yatesbury Cres. *Nott* —1E **43**
Yates Clo. *Long E* —6H **63**
Yates Gdns. *Nott* —5E **21**
Yeoman Av. *B Vil* —1D **20**
Yewbarrow Clo. *W Bri* —6E **59**
Yew Clo. *Nott* —5H **33**
Yewdale Clo. *Clif* —5B **66**
Yewdale Clo. *W Bri* —6E **59**
Yew Tree Av. *Nott* —6G **33**
Yew Tree Clo. *Rad T* —6D **48**
Yew Tree Ct. *Bees* —5F **55**
Yew Tree La. *Ged* —5A **36**
Yew Tree La. *Nott* —3A **66**
Yew Tree Rd. *Huck* —6H **7**
Yonge Clo. *Rad T* —1E **61**
York Av. *Bees* —1F **65**
York Av. *Sand* —6C **52**
York Clo. *Ged* —5H **35**
York Dri. *Nott* —5D **30**
Yorke St. *Huck* —4G **7**
York House. —2E **5**
York Rd. *Long E* —4E **63**
York St. *N'fld* —2A **48**
York St. *Nott* —3G **45** (1E **5**)
Young Clo. *Nott* —2F **31**
Yvonne Cres. *Cltn* —2H **47**

Zulla Rd. *Nott* —1G **45**
Zulu Rd. *Nott* —6D **32**